GOLDEN BOOKLET
OF THE
TRUE CHRISTIAN LIFE

by

JOHN CALVIN

*A Modern Translation
from the French and the Latin
by*
HENRY J. VAN ANDEL

BAKER BOOK HOUSE
Grand Rapids, Michigan

PREFACE

The *Golden Booklet of the True Christian Walk* was first published in 1550 in Latin and in French under the title, *De Vita Hominis Christiani*, that is *On the Life of the Christian Man*, (the present heading of Chapter Six, Book III, of the *Institutes*) and later also in English (1594) and in German (1857) under a similar name. In Dutch it appeared in 1858 with the first mentioned title. Originally the *Golden Booklet* was not a separate volume, but part of the *Institutes*. It was missing in the short first edition, but in the second, third and fourth editions it occurred as the last or twenty-first chapter, called *De Vita Christiana (On the Christian Life)*. In the fifth and sixth editions Calvin rearranged the material of the *Institutes* under four headings: The Father, the Son, the Holy Spirit, and the Church. He placed the thoroughly revised material *"On the Christian Life"* halfway Book III, and divided it into five parts, chapters six to ten inclusive. The *Institutes* were often reprinted both in Latin and in other languages, and some portions were published separately, but the *Golden Booklet* alone had the honor of being reprinted four times in Dutch, the last reprint being of 1938. The present American edition is a translation of Calvin's thoroughly revised copy, and is based on the French and Latin texts of the

"Golden Booklet" (Inst. III, Chs. 6 to 10, sixth edition).

This *Booklet* was purposely written in a simpler style than the other parts of the *Institutes*. On account of its spiritual and realistic nature it made an indelible impression on the Dutch nation which had brought forth such famous writers as John van Ruysbroec and Thomas à Kempis during the Christian Renaissance (1350–1500). But it must also have made a tremendous appeal to the Pilgrims and the Puritans and to all groups which felt the need of a balanced application of Christianity. Calvin directs himself to mind, heart and hand, for he is the first one to elaborate on the three offices of Christ. He is intellectual, mystical and practical. His basic principles satisfied many scholars, religious leaders, and statesmen. But there is, on the other hand, no other devotional book in the world like the Golden Booklet which is so profound and yet so universal. As to style, spirit, and graphic language it can vie with the great classics, like Augustine's *Confessions*, Thomas à Kempis' *Imitation of Christ*, and Bunyan's *Pilgrim's Progress*. Only it is shorter, saner, sounder, more vigorous and to the point. It should, therefore, be welcomed by all people of a genuine religious nature, but especially by those who want to carry out the values of religion in everyday life.

Although this new translation is modern, the classical text has been adhered to as closely as possible. The editor has, however, taken the liberty of giving some chapters a title more in agreement with their content; he has also given every section a heading, divided the sections into smaller units, and added a few Scriptural references in brackets.

A brief biographical note may be of interest here. John Calvin was born in 1509 in northern France, in the city of Noyon, and died in Geneva, Switzerland, in 1564. He was educated in the classics and philosophy, in law and theology in the colleges and universities of his native land. When persecution came he fled to Basel, in Switzerland, where he wrote the first edition of his *Institutes* when he was only twenty-six years of age. Then he went to visit the Duchess of Ferrara, the sister of the French King, in northern Italy because she gave shelter to a number of Reformed refugees. On his way back from Italy to Basel he was pressed into service by his friend Farel to help reform Geneva. Here Calvin founded not a new state, but a new church, the Reformed or Presbyterian church, and a new school system with a famous university. In the Academy or graduate department of this new university he became a professor of theology.

In his short life Calvin wrote 58 volumes, some in Latin, and some in French. His works are not only of a theological nature, but many contain ethical and philosophical principles which laid the foundation for a new system of thought. His *Institutes* were a textbook for dogmatics, ethics, and philosophy for two hundred years. He found thousands of ardent followers in the western countries of Europe, but also in Hungary, the Ukraine, and in Poland. His greatest influence was felt in Switzerland, the Rhine valley, the Netherlands, England and Scotland, and last, but not least, in North America. Calvin's commentaries on the Bible have become so famous that they have been newly reprinted in America. His *Institutes* have again become a textbook in many colleges and seminaries. His ideas are being studied by those who do not fully agree with his basic concepts. John Calvin was a man of a gentle nature and of colossal stature. He is now becoming the leading figure of Orthodox Protestantism in Europe and America.

HENRY J. VAN ANDEL
Calvin College, Grand Rapids, Michigan, 1952

CONTENTS

Prayer of Calvin

Almighty God and Father, grant unto us, because we have to go through much strife on this earth, the strength of thy Holy Spirit, in order that we may courageously go through the fire, and through the water, and that we may put ourselves so under thy rule that we may go to meet death in full confidence of thy assistance and without fear.

Grant us also that we may bear all hatred and enmity of mankind, until we have gained the last victory, and that we may at last come to that blessed rest which thy only begotten Son has acquired for us through his blood. Amen.

CHAPTER I

Humble Obedience, the True Imitation of Christ

I. Scripture is the Rule of Life.

1. The goal of the new life is that God's children exhibit melody and harmony in their conduct. What melody? The song of God's justice. What harmony? The harmony between God's righteousness and our obedience.

Only if we walk in the beauty of God's law do we become sure of our adoption as children of the Father.

The law of God contains in itself the dynamic of the new life by which his image is fully restored in us; but by nature we are sluggish, and, therefore, we need to be stimulated, aided in our efforts by a guiding principle.

A sincere repentance from the heart does not guarantee that we shall not wander from the straight path and sometimes become bewildered.

Let us then search Scripture to find the root principle for the reformation of our life.

2. Scripture contains a great number of exhortations, and to discuss them all would fill a large volume.

The church fathers have written big works on the virtues without prating; even a scholarly treatise cannot exhaust the profundity of one virtue.

For true devotion, however, it is not necessary to read the excellent works of the church fathers, but only to understand the one basic rule of the Bible.*

3. No one should draw the conclusion that the brevity of one treatise on Christian conduct makes the elaborate discussion of others superfluous, or that philosophy has no value.

Philosophers, however, are accustomed to speak of general principles and specific rules, but Scripture has an order all its own.

Philosophers are ambitious, and, therefore, aim at exquisite clarity and dexterous ingenuity; but Scripture has a beautiful conciseness, and a certainty which excels all philosophers.

Philosophers often make a show of affectation, but the Holy Spirit has a different method, [di-

---

* Calvin inserts here: "I am not fit to write copiously, because I love brevity. But I might try in the future; and, otherwise, I shall leave the task to others."

rect and plainspoken,] which ought not to be neglected.*

II. *Holiness is the key principle.*

1. The plan of Scripture for a Christian walk is twofold: first, that we be instructed in the law to love righteousness, because by nature we are not inclined to do so; second, that we be shown a simple rule that we may not waver in our race.

Of the many excellent recommendations, is there any better than the key principle: Be thou holy, for I am holy?

When we were dispersed like scattered sheep, and lost in the labyrinth of the world, Christ gathered us together again, that he might bring us back to himself.

2. When we hear any mention of our mystical union with Christ, we should remember that holiness is the channel to it.

Holiness is not a merit by which we can attain communion with God, but a gift of Christ, which enables us to cling to him, and to follow him.

It is God's own glory that he cannot have anything to do with iniquity and uncleanness; therefore, we must keep this in mind, if we desire to pay attention to his invitation.

---

* Calvin evidently thinks here of I Cor. 1, 2, and 3.

For why were we delivered from the quagmire of iniquity and pollution of this world, if we want to wallow in it as long as we live?

God's holiness admonishes us that we must inhabit the holy city of Jerusalem, if we wish to belong to the people of God.

Jerusalem is hallowed ground, therefore it cannot be profaned by impure inhabitants.

The Psalmist says, This one shall abide in the tabernacle of the Lord who walks uprightly and works righteousness.

The Sanctuary of the Holy One must be kept immaculate. Lev. 19:2; I Peter 1:16; Is. 35:10; Ps. 15:1 and 2, 24:3 and 4.

III. *The Imitation of Holiness means obedience to Christ.*

1. Scripture does not only show the principle of holiness, but also that Christ is the way to it.

Because the Father has reconciled us to himself in Christ, therefore he commands us to be conformed to Christ as to our pattern.

Let those who think that philosophers have the only just and orderly system of morality show us a more excellent plan than to obey and follow Christ.

The sublimest virtue according to philosophers is to live the life of nature, but Scripture points us to the perfect Christ as our example.

We should exhibit the character of Christ in our lives, for what can be more effective than this one stirring consideration? Indeed, what can be required besides?

2. The Lord has adopted us to be his children on this condition that we reveal an imitation of Christ who is the mediator of our adoption.

Unless we ardently and prayerfully devote ourselves to Christ's righteousness we do not only faithlessly revolt from our Creator, but we also abjure him as our Savior.

3. Scripture accompanies its exhortations with the promise of God's countless blessings and of our all-embracing salvation.

Therefore, since God has revealed himself as a Father, we would be guilty of the basest ingratitude if we did not behave as his children.

Since Christ has purified us through the baptism in his blood, we should not become defiled by fresh pollution.

Since Christ has united us to his body as his members, we should be anxious not to disgrace him by any blemish.

Since Christ, our Head, has ascended to heaven, we should leave our carnal desires behind, and lift our hearts upward to him.

Since the Holy Spirit has dedicated us as temples of God, we should exert ourselves not to profane his sanctuary, but to display his glory.

Since both our soul and body are destined to inherit an incorruptible and never-fading crown, we should keep them pure and undefiled till the day of our Lord.

Such are the best foundations for a proper code of conduct. Philosophers never rise above the natural dignity of man. (But Scripture points us to our only sinless Savior, Jesus Christ. Rom. 6:4ff; 8:29.)

IV. *External Christianity is not enough.*

1. Let us ask those who possess nothing but church membership, and yet want to be called Christians, how they can glory in the sacred name of Christ?

For no one has any communion with Christ, but he who has received the true knowledge of him from the word of the gospel.

The apostle denies that anyone actually knows Christ who has not learned to put off the old. man, corrupt with deceitful lusts, and to put on Christ.

External knowledge of Christ is found to be only a false and dangerous make-believe, however eloquently and freely lip servants may talk about the gospel.

2. The gospel is not a doctrine of the tongue, but of life.

It cannot be grasped by reason and memory only, but it is fully understood when it possesses the whole soul, and penetrates to the inner recesses of the heart.

Let nominal Christians cease from insulting God by boasting themselves to be what they are not, and let them show themselves disciples not unworthy of Christ, their Master.

We must assign first place to the knowledge of our religion, for that is the beginning of our salvation.

But our religion will be unprofitable, if it does not change our heart, pervade our manners, and transform us into new creatures.

3. The philosophers rightly condemn and banish with disgrace from their company those who profess to know the art of life, but who are in reality vain babblers.

With much better reason Christians ought to detest those who have the gospel on their lips, but not in their hearts.

The exhortations of the philosophers are cold and lifeless, if compared with the convictions, affections, and boundless energy of the real believers. Eph. 4:20ff.

V. *Spiritual progress is necessary.*

1. We should not insist on absolute perfection of the gospel in our fellow Christians, however much we may strive for it ourselves.

It would be unfair to demand evangelical perfection before we acknowledge anyone as a Christian.

There would be no church if we set a standard of absolute perfection, for the best of us are still far from the ideal, and we would have to reject many who have made only small progress.

2. Perfection must be the final mark at which we aim, and the goal for which we strive.

It is not lawful for you to make a compromise with God: to try to fulfill part of your duties, and to omit others at your own pleasure.

The Lord first of all wants sincerity in his service, simplicity of heart without guile and falsehood.

A double mind is in conflict with the spiritual life, for this implies an unfeigned devotion to God in the search for holiness and righteousness.

No one in this earthly prison of the body has sufficient strength of his own to press forward with a due degree of watchfulness, and the great majority [of Christians] are kept down with such great weakness that they stagger and halt, and even creep on the ground, and so make very slight advances.

3. But let everyone proceed according to his given ability and continue the journey he has begun.

There is no man so unhappy, that he will not make some progress, however small.

Let us not cease to do the utmost, that we may incessantly go forward in the way of the Lord; and let us not despair because of the smallness of our accomplishment.

Though we fall short, our labor is not lost if this day surpasses the preceeding one.

4. The one condition for spiritual progress is that we remain sincere and humble.

Let us keep our end in view, let us press forward to our goal. Let us not indulge in pride, nor give in to our sinful passions.

Let us steadily exert ourselves to reach a higher degree of holiness till we shall finally arrive at a perfection of goodness which we seek and pursue as long as we live, but which we shall attain then only, when, freed from all earthly infirmity, we shall be admitted by God into his full communion.

CHAPTER II

Self-Denial

I. *We are not our own, we are the Lord's.*

1. The Divine law contains a most fitting and well ordered plan for the regulation of our life; yet it has pleased the heavenly Teacher to direct men by a very excellent key principle.

It is the duty of believers to "present their bodies a living sacrifice, holy, acceptable unto God"; this is the only true worship.

The principle of holiness leads to the exhortation, "Be not conformed to this world; but be ye transformed by the renewing of your mind, that ye may prove what is the will of God."

It is a very important consideration that we are consecrated and dedicated to God; it means that we may think, speak, meditate, or do anything only with a view to his glory.

For that which is sacred cannot, without great injustice to God, be applied to unholy usage.

2. If we are not our own, but the Lord's, it is plain what error we must flee, and to what purpose all our deeds must be directed.

We are not our own, therefore neither our reason nor our will should guide us in our thoughts and actions.

We are not our own, therefore we should not seek what is expedient to the flesh.

We are not our own, therefore let us forget ourselves and our own interests as far as possible.

But we are God's own; to him, therefore, let us live and die.

We are God's own; therefore let his wisdom and will dominate all our actions.

We are God's own; therefore let every part of our existence be directed towards him as our only legitimate goal.

3. Oh, how greatly has the man advanced who has learned not to be his own, not to be governed by his own reason, but to surrender his mind to God!

The most effective poison to lead men to ruin is to boast in themselves, in their own wisdom and will power; the only escape to safety is simply to follow the guidance of the Lord.

Our first step should be to take leave of ourselves and to apply all our powers to the service of the Lord.

4. The service of the Lord does not only include implicit obedience, but also a willingness

to put aside our sinful desires, and to surrender completely to the leadership of the Holy Spirit.

The transformation of our lives by the Holy Spirit, which Paul calls a renewal of the mind, is the real beginning of life, but foreign to pagan philosophers.

Pagan philosophers set up reason as the sole guide of life, of wisdom and conduct; but Christian philosophy demands of us that we surrender our reason to the Holy Spirit; and this means that we no longer live for ourselves, but that Christ lives and reigns within us. Rom. 12:1; Eph. 4:23; Gal. 2:20.

II. *Seeking God's glory means self-denial.*

1. Let us therefore not seek our own but that which pleases the Lord, and is helpful to the promotion of his glory.

There is a great advantage in almost forgetting ourselves and in surely neglecting all selfish aspects; for then only can we try faithfully to devote our attention to God and his commandments.

For when Scripture tells us to discard all personal and selfish considerations, it does not only exclude from our minds the desire for wealth, the lust of power, and the favor of men, but it also banishes false ambitions, and hunger for human glory, with other more secret evils.

Indeed, a Christian ought to be disposed and prepared to keep in mind that he has to reckon with God every moment of his life.

2. A Christian will measure all his deeds by God's law, and his secret thoughts he will subject to God's will.

If a man has learned to regard God in every enterprise, he will be delivered from all vain desires.

The denial of ourselves which Christ has so diligently commanded his disciples from the beginning will at last dominate all the desires of our heart.

The denial of ourselves will leave no room for pride, haughtiness, or vainglory, nor for avarice, licentiousness, love of luxury, wantonness, or any sin born from selflove.

Without the principle of selfdenial man is either led to indulgence in the grossest vices without the least shame; or, if there is any appearance of virtue in him, it is spoiled by an evil passion for glory.

Show me a single man who does not believe in the Lord's law of selfdenial, and who yet willingly practises virtue among men.

3. All who have not been influenced by the principle of self-denial, have followed virtue merely from the love of praise.

Even those of the philosophers who have contended that virtue is desirable for its own sake, have been puffed up with so much arrogance, that it is evident they desire virtue for no other reason than to give them a chance to exercise pride.

God is so far from being pleased either with those who are ambitious of popular praise, or with hearts full of pride and presumption, that he plainly tells "they have their reward" in this world, and that (repentant) harlots and publicans are nearer to the kingdom of heaven than such persons.

4. There is no end and no limit to the obstacles of the man who wants to pursue what is right and at the same time shrinks back from selfdenial.

It is an ancient and true observation that there is a world of vices hidden in the soul of man, but Christian selfdenial is the remedy of them all.

There is deliverance in store only for the man who gives up his selfishness, and whose sole aim is to please the Lord and to do what is right in his sight.

III. *The elements of self-denial are: sobriety, righteousness and godliness.*

1. The apostle Paul gives a brief summary of a well regulated life when he says to Titus:

"The grace of God that brings salvation has appeared to all men, teaching us, that denying ungodliness and worldly lusts, we should live soberly, righteously, and godly in this present world; looking for that blessed hope, and the glorious appearing of the great God and our Savior Jesus Christ who gave himself for us, that he might redeem us from all iniquity and purify unto himself a peculiar people, zealous of good works."

Paul declares that the grace of God is necessary to stimulate us, but that for true worship two main obstacles must be removed: first, ungodliness to which we are by nature strongly inclined, and then, worldly lusts which try to overwhelm us.

Ungodliness does not only mean superstitions, but everything that hinders the sincere fear of God. And worldly lusts mean carnal affections.

Paul urges us to forsake our former desires which are in conflict with the two tables of the law, and to renounce all the dictates of our own reason and will.

2. Paul reduces all the actions of the new life to three classes: sobriety, righteousness and godliness.

Sobriety undoubtedly means chastity and temperance, as well as the pure and frugal use of temporal blessings, and patience under poverty.

Righteousness includes all the duties of justice, that every man may receive his just dues.

Godliness separates us from the pollutions of the world, and by true holiness, unites us to God.

When the virtues of sobriety, righteousness and godliness are firmly linked together, they will produce absolute perfection.

3. Nothing is more difficult than to forsake all carnal thoughts, to subdue and renounce our false appetites, and to devote ourselves to God and our brethren, and to live the life of angels in a world of corruption.

To deliver our minds from every snare Paul calls our attention to the hope of a blessed immortality, and encourages us that our hope is not in vain.

As Christ once appeared as a Redeemer, so he will at his second coming show us the bene· fits of the salvation which he obtained.

Christ dispels the charms which blind us and prevent us from longing with the right zeal for the glory of heaven.

Christ also teaches us that we must live as strangers and pilgrims in this world, that we may not lose our heavenly inheritance. Titus 2:11-14.

IV. *True humility means respect for others.*

1. Self-denial refers partly to men, but indeed, principally to God.

When Scripture commands us to conduct ourselves in such a manner towards men, as "in honor to prefer others to ourselves," and faithfully to devote our whole attention to the promotion of their advantage, it gives such commands as our heart can by no means receive without being first cured of our sinful nature.

We are all so blinded and upset by selflove that everyone imagines he has a just right to exalt himself, and to undervalue all others in comparison to self.

If God has bestowed on us any excellent gift, we imagine it to be our own achievement; and we swell and even burst with pride.

2. The vices of which we are full we carefully hide from others, and we flatter ourselves with

the notion that they are small and trivial, and we sometimes even embrace them as virtues.

If the same talents which we admire in ourselves appear in others, or even our betters, we depreciate and diminish them with the utmost malignity, in order that we may not have to acknowledge the superiority of others.

If others have any vices we are not content to criticize them sharply and severely, but we exaggerate them hatefully.

Hatred grows into insolence when we desire to excel the rest of mankind, and imagine we do not belong to the common lot; we even severely and haughtily despise others as our inferiors.

3. The poor yield to the rich, the common people to the upper ten, the servants to their masters, the ignorant to the scholars; but there is nobody who does not imagine that he is really better than the others.

Everyone flatters himself and carries a kingdom in his breast.

Everyone is selfcomplacent and passes censure on the ideas and conduct of others, and, if there is a quarrel there is an eruption of poison.

Many discover some gentleness in others as long as they find everything pleasant and amiable; but how many keep their good humor, if they are disturbed and irritated?

4. To live happily the evils of false ambition and selflove must be plucked from our hearts by the roots.

If we listen to the instruction of Scripture we must remember that our talents are not of our own making, but free gifts of God.

If we are proud of our talents, we betray our lack of gratitude to God.

"Who makes you to differ?" says Paul. "Now, if you received all gifts, why do you glory as if you had not received them?"

We must watch and acknowledge our faults, and be truly humble. For then we shall not be puffed up, but have great reason to feel dejected.

5. On the other hand, whatever gifts of God we notice in others, let us value and esteem both the gifts and their possessors, for it would betray great wickedness in us to rob them of their God-given honor.

The faults of others we are taught to overlook, not indeed to encourage them by flattery.

We should never insult others on account of their faults, for it is our duty to show charity and respect to everyone.

If we pay attention to the honor and reputation of others, whoever they may be, we shall conduct ourselves not only with moderation and good humor, but with politeness and friendship.

For we shall never arrive at true meekness by any other way than by humiliating ourselves and by honoring others from the depth of our hearts. Rom. 12:10; Phil. 2:4; I Cor. 4:7.

V. *We should seek the good of other believers.*

1. How extremely difficult it is for you dutifully to seek the advantage of your neighbor, unless you quit all selfish considerations and almost forget yourself.

How can you perform the duties which Paul teaches to be works of love, unless you renounce yourself, and devote yourself wholly to others?

"Love suffers long and is kind, love envies not; love vaunts not itself; love is not puffed up; love does not behave itself unseemly; love seeks not her own; love is not easily provoked"; and so on.

2. If this be all that is demanded, that we do not seek our own, yet we must not exert little pressure on our own nature which is so strongly inclined to love self exclusively and does not easily permit us to neglect self and our own affairs.

Let us rather seek the profit of others, and even voluntarily give up our rights for the sake of others.

Scripture urges and warns us that whatever favors we may have obtained from the Lord we have received them as a trust on condition that they should be applied to the common benefit of the church.

The legitimate use of all the Lord's favors is liberally and kindly to share them with others.

You cannot imagine a more certain rule or a more powerful suggestion than this, that all the blessings we enjoy are divine deposits which we have received on this condition that we distribute them to others.

3. According to Scripture our personal talents may be even compared to the powers of the members of the human body.

No member of the body has its power for itself, nor applies it to its own private use, but only for the profit of the others; and equally, no member of the church receives any advantage from his own activity, but through his cooperation with the whole body of believers.

Whatever ability a faithful Christian may possess, he ought to possess it for his fellow believers, and he ought to make his own interest subservient to the well-being of the church in all sincerity.

Let this be our rule for goodwill and helpfulness that whenever we are able to assist others we should behave as stewards who must some day give an account of ourselves, and let us remember that the distribution of profits must be determined by the law of love.

For we must not first of all try to promote the good of others by seeking our own, but we must prefer the profit of others.

4. The law of love does not only pertain to the sizable profits, but from ancient days God has commanded us to remember it in the small kindnesses of life.

God commanded his people Israel to offer him the first fruits of the corn, as a solemn token that it was unlawful for them to enjoy any blessings not previously dedicated to Him.

If the gifts of God are not part of our sanctified life unless we dedicate them with our own hands to their Author, we must be guilty of sinful abuse if we leave such a dedication out.

5. But in vain we would attempt to enrich the Lord by a distribution of our talents and gifts.

Since our goodness cannot reach the Lord, as the Psalmist says, we must exercise it towards "the saints who are on the earth."

Alms are compared in the Scripture to sacred offerings to show us that the exercises of charity under the gospel have taken the place of the sacrifices under the law of the Old Testament. I Cor. 13:4-8; Ps. 16:2, 3.

VI. *We should seek the good of everyone, friend and foe.*

1. That we may not become weary of doing well, for which the danger is near, the apostle has added that "love suffers long, and is not easily provoked."

The Lord commands us to do good unto all men without exception, though the majority are very undeserving when judged according to their own merits.

But Scripture here helps us out with an excellent argument when it teaches us that we must not think of man's real value, but only of his creation in the image of God to which we owe all possible honor and love.

The image of God, moreover, is most carefully to be regarded in those who are of the household of faith, because it has been renewed and restored in them by the Spirit of Christ.

2. If anyone, therefore, appears before you who is in need of your kind services, you have no reason to refuse him your help.

Suppose he is a stranger; yet the Lord has pressed his own stamp on him and made him as one of your family, and he forbids you to despise your own flesh and blood.

Suppose he is despicable and worthless; yet the Lord has deigned him worthy to be adorned with his own image.

Suppose that you have no obligation towards him for services; yet the Lord has made him as it were his substitute, so that you have obligation for numerous and unforgettable benefits.

Suppose that he is unworthy of your least exertion; but the image of God which recommends him to you deserves that you surrender yourself and all your possessions to him.

If he has deserved no kindness, but just the opposite, because he has maddened you with his injuries and insults, even this is no reason why you should not surround him with your affection, and show him all sorts of favors.

You may say that he has deserved a very different treatment, but what does the Lord command but to forgive all men their offenses, and to charge them against himself?

3. This is the only way to attain that which is not only difficult, but utterly repugnant to man's nature: to love those who hate us, to requite injuries with kindness, and to return blessings for curses.

We should forever keep in mind that we must not brood on the wickedness of man, but realize that he is God's image bearer.

If we cover and obliterate man's faults, and consider the beauty and dignity of God's image in him, then we shall be induced to love and embrace him. Heb. 12:16; Gal. 6:10; Is. 58:7; Math. 5:44; Luke 17:3 and 4.

VII. *Civil goodness is not enough.*

1. We will not practise real selfdenial unless we fulfill all the duties of love.

These are not fulfilled by him who merely in an external way performs his services without omitting even one, but by him who acts from a sincere principle of love.

For it may happen that a man discharges his duties to the best of his abilities, but if his heart is not in them, he falls far from the mark.

There are people who are known to be very liberal, yet they never give without scolding, or pride, or even insolence.

We are sunk to such a depth of calamity in this awful age that scarcely any alms are given, at least by the majority of men, without haughtiness and contempt.

The corruption of our times is so enormous that it would not have been tolerated by the pagans.

2. Christians certainly ought to display more than a smiling face, a cheerful mood, and polite language when they practise charity.

First of all, Christians ought to imagine themselves in the place of the person who needs their help, and they ought to sympathize with him as though they themselves were suffering; they ought to show real mercy and humaneness and offer their assistance as readily as if it were for themselves.

Heartfelt pity will banish arrogance and reproach, and will prevent contempt and domineering over the poor and the needy.

When a member of our physical body is diseased, and the whole body has to labor to restore it to health, we do not despise this diseased member, or hold it under obligation, because it needs all this assistance.

3. The mutual help which the different parts of the body offer to each other is by the law of nature considered to be no favor, but a matter of course, which it would be cruel to refuse.

Therefore, if a man has performed one service, he should not reckon himself discharged of all other duties. A rich man, for instance, who has given away part of his property and leaves the burdens for others, cannot consider himself to be excused.

Every man, however important he may be, should realize that he is a debtor to his neighbor, and that love demands that he give to the limit of his ability.

VIII. *No happiness without God's blessing.*

1. Let us discuss more in detail the main aspect of selfdenial, its relation to God. It is needless to repeat the many remarks that have been made before, but it will suffice to point out how real selfdenial makes us calm and patient.

First of all, Scripture draws our attention to this that if we want ease and tranquility in our lives, we should resign ourselves and all that we have to the will of God and at the same time we should surrender our affections to him as our Conqueror and Overlord.

To crave wealth and honor, to demand power, to pile up riches, to gather all those vanities which seem to make for pomp and empty display, that is our furious passion and our unbounded desire.

On the other hand, we fear and abhor poverty, obscurity and humility, and we seek to avoid them by all possible means.

We can easily see how restless people are who follow their own mind, how many tricks they try and how they tire themselves out in their efforts to obtain the objects of their ambition and avarice, and then again to avoid poverty and humility.

2. If godfearing people do not want to be caught in such snares they must pursue another course: they should not hope, or desire, or even think of prosperity without God's blessing.

We may believe and trust that everything depends on divine blessing alone.

It may look to us that we can easily attain honor and riches through our own industry, or strenuous exertion, or through the favor of others; yet, it is certain that all these things are nothing in themselves, and that we shall not make any headway by our insight or by our labors, but in so far as the Lord shall prosper both.

3. On the other hand, his blessing will find a way to make us happy and prosperous, whatever adversities may come.

And though we may be able to obtain a certain measure of wealth and fame without divine blessing, as we may daily observe in godless people who acquire great honors and enormous riches, yet we shall see that those who are under the curse of God have not the smallest particle of happiness.

Therefore, we cannot gain anything without divine blessing; and if we do, it will prove a calamity to us.

Let us then not be foolish and wish for things that will make us more miserable.

IX. *We should not be anxious to obtain riches and honors.*

1. If we then believe that the whole cause of desirable prosperity is found in the divine blessing alone, and that without this we may expect only miseries and calamities, it must be plain also that we should not anxiously strive for riches and honors by relying on our own diligence or cleverness, or by depending on the favor of men, or by trusting in the notion of good luck; but that we should always expect the Lord to direct us to the lot he has provided for us.

The result of this will be, that first of all we shall not be in a rush to seize riches and honors by forbidden actions, by deceitful and criminal tricks, by robbing and injuring our neighbors;

but that we shall limit ourselves to the pursuit of these interests which will not lure us away from the path of innocence.

For who can expect the help of divine blessing in fraud, robbery, and other evil acts?

2. As divine blessing comes only on him who is pure in his thoughts, and righteous in his deeds, so it influences everyone who seeks to steer away from irregularity and corruption.

Further, we shall feel restrained from the intense desire to grow rich and from the false ambition to seek honors.

For would it not be shameful to trust in divine assistance, if at the same time we should crave matters that are against his Word?

Far be it from God to prosper with his blessing what he curses with his mouth.

3. Finally, if we do not succeed according to our wishes and hopes, we shall, however, be kept from impatience, and from detesting our condition, whatever it may be; because we shall understand that this would be rebellion against God at whose pleasure riches and poverty, honor and contempt are distributed.

In conclusion, he who retains God's blessing in the way we have described, will not passionately pursue the things which man in general covets, and will not use base methods from which he expects no advantage.

Moreover, a true Christian will not ascribe any prosperity to his own diligence, industry, or good fortune, but he will acknowledge that God is the author of it.

If he makes but small progress, or even suffers setbacks while others are making headway, he will nevertheless bear his poverty with more calmness and moderation than any worldly man would feel when his success is average and contrary to his expectations.

4. A true Christian possesses a consolation which affords him more sweet satisfaction than the greatest wealth, or power, because he believes that his affairs are so regulated by the Lord as to promote his salvation.

This was in the mind of David who followed God and surrendered himself to his rule, and who declared, "I am as a child weaned of his mother; neither do I exercise myself in great matters, or in things too high for me." Psalm 131:1 and 2.

X. *The Lord is just in all his ways.*

1. This is not the only case in which godfearing people should be quiet and patient, for they ought to try to live that way in all circumstances of life.

No one has rightly denied himself unless he has wholly resigned himself to the Lord, and is willing to leave every detail to his good pleasure.

If we put ourselves in such a frame of mind, then, whatever may happen to us, we shall never feel miserable, or accuse God falsely because of our lot.

2. How necessary it is to train ourselves this way will appear, if we consider the numerous accidents to which we are exposed.

Diseases of all kinds come upon us, the one after the other: now the pestilence engulfs us, now the disasters of war are harassing us.

At another time frost or hail devours our crops, and we are threatened by scarcity and poverty.

Sometimes our dearest ones, husband, wife, parents, children, and other relatives, are snatched away by death; or, our home is consumed by fire.

On account of such events people will curse their life, and the day of their birth; they will blame the sun and the stars, and even reproach and blaspheme God, as if he were cruel and unjust.

3. But a faithful believer will even in all circumstances meditate on the mercy and fatherly goodness of God.

If he sees his relatives taken away from him and his home made lonesome, he must not cease to bless the Lord, and he had rather consider that the grace of God, which dwells in his home, will not leave it desolate.

Or, if he sees his grainfields and vineyards destroyed by frost, or hail, and famine threatening him, he will not become discouraged and dissatisfied, but he will persist in this firm confidence:— we are under the guardian care of our God, we are "the sheep of his pasture," and, therefore, he will supply us with the food we need.

If he shall be afflicted with illness, he will not be broken down with bitterness, and give way to impatience, and complain against God, but he will consider the justice and goodness of his Eternal Father and grow in patience while he is being chastened and corrected.

4. In short, knowing that whatever may happen is ordained by the Lord, he will receive it with a peaceful and thankful heart, that he may not be guilty of proudly resisting the rule of Him, to whom he has once committed himself, and all his belongings.

Far be it from the heart of a Christian to accept the foolish and wretched consolation of the heathen philosophers who tried to harden themselves against adversity by blaming Fortune, or Fate, for it.

They thought that it was foolish to be displeased with our lot, because there is a blind and cruel power in the world which deals blows to everyone, worthy and unworthy.

But the principle of true devotion is that God alone is the Guide and Ruler of all prosperity and adversity, and that he is never in undue haste, but that he distributes all good and evil with the most equal justice. Ps. 79:13.

CHAPTER III

Patience in Crossbearing

I. *Crossbearing is more difficult than selfdenial.*

1. Moreover, it is fitting for the faithful Christian to rise to a still higher level where Christ calls every disciple to "take up his cross."

For all whom the Lord has chosen and received into the society of his saints, ought to prepare themselves for a life that is hard, difficult, laborious, and full of countless griefs.

It is the will of their heavenly Father to try them in this manner that he may test them.

He began with Christ his firstborn son and he pursues this manner with all his children.

For though Christ was his most beloved Son, in whom the Father was always well pleased, yet we see that he was not treated with indulgence and tenderness, so that it may be truly said that he was not only continuously afflicted, but that his whole life was a perpetual cross.

2. The apostle explains the reason, that it was necessary for him to "learn obedience by the things which he suffered." Why then should

we free ourselves from that condition to which Christ, our chief, had to submit, especially since his submission was on our behalf, to give us an example of patience?

For the apostle teaches that it is the destiny of all God's children to "be conformed to him."

And it is a real comfort to us when we endure many miseries, which are called adversities and calamities, that we partake of the sufferings of Christ, in order that we may pass through our different tribulations as he escaped from an abyss of all evils to the glory of heaven.

3. For Saint Paul tells us that if we "know the fellowship of his sufferings" we shall also understand the "power of his resurrection"; and, that while we are "participating in his death," we are also being prepared for sharing his glorious resurrection.

How much this helps to lighten the bitterness of the cross!

For the more we are afflicted by adversities the more surely our fellowship with Christ is confirmed!

By this fellowship the adversities themselves not only become blessing to us, but they are also aids to greatly promote our happiness and salvation. Matt. 16:24; Matt. 3:17; 17:5; Heb. 5:8; Rom. 8:29; Acts 14:22; Phil. 3:10.

II. *The Cross makes us humble.*

1. Our Lord was not compelled to bear the cross except to show and prove his obedience to his Father. But there are many reasons why we should live under a continual cross.

First, whereas we are naturally prone to attribute everything to our human flesh, unless we have, as it were, object lessons of our stupidity, we easily form an exaggerated notion of our strength, and we take for granted that, whatever hardships may happen, we will remain invincible.

And so we become puffed up with a foolish, vain, and carnal confidence which arouses us to become haughty and proud towards God, as if our own power would be sufficient without his grace.

This vanity he cannot better repress than by proving to us from experience not only our folly, but also our extreme frailty. Therefore he afflicts us with humiliation, or poverty, or loss of relatives, or disease, or other calamities.

Then, because we are unable to bear them, we soon are buried under them.

And so, being humbled, we learn to call upon his strength which alone makes us stand up under such a load of afflictions.

2. Even the greatest saints, though realizing that they can only be strong in the grace of God, and not in themselves, are nevertheless more sure than they ought to be of their own bravery and persistence, unless he leads them by the trials of life into a deeper knowledge of themselves. This proud idea induced even David to say: "In my prosperity I said, I shall never be moved; Lord, by thy favor thou hast made my mountain to stand strong. Thou didst hide thy face, and I was troubled."

For he confesses that prosperity had so stupefied and benumbed his senses that he disregarded the grace of God on which he should have depended, relied on himself instead, and imagined that he could not fall.

3. If this happened to such a great prophet, who of us should not be fearful and cautious?

Though in prosperity many saints have flattered themselves with perseverance and patience, yet they learned that they had deceived themselves when adversity broke down their resistance.

Warned by such evidences of their spiritual illness, believers profit by their humiliations.

Robbed of their foolish confidence in the flesh, they take refuge in the grace of God.

And when they have done so they experience the nearness of the Divine protection which is to them a strong fortress. Ps. 30:6 and 7.

III. *The Cross makes us hopeful.*

1. This is what Paul teaches, that "tribulation worketh patience, and patience, experience."

For God's promise to believers that He will help them in their trials, they experience to be true when they persist in their patience supported by his strength, and not by their own.

Patience, therefore, affords a proof to the saints that God will actually give them the help he has promised whenever there is need.

And this also confirms their hope, for they certainly would be ungrateful if they did not rely for the future on the truth of God, which they have found to be sure and unchangeable.

Now we see what a stream of benefits flows from the cross. For if we discard the false opinions of our own virtue, and discover our hypocrisy which leads us astray with it flatteries, our natural and pernicious pride tumbles down.

When we are thus humbled, we are taught to rely on God alone, and we shall not stumble, or sink down in despair.

From this victory we shall gather new hope, for when the Lord fulfils his promises, he confirms his truth for the future.

2. Though these were the only reasons, they are sufficient to show how necessary are the trials of the cross.

For it is no small profit to be robbed of our blind selflove so that we become fully aware of our weakness; to have such an understanding of our weakness that we distrust ourselves; to distrust ourselves to such an extent that we put all our trust in God; to depend with such boundless confidence on God that we rely entirely on his help so that we may victoriously persevere to the end; to continue in his grace that we may know that he is true and faithful in his promises; and to experience the certainty of his promises so that our hope may become firmer. Rom. 5:3 and 4.

IV. *The Cross teaches obedience.*

1. The Lord has still another reason for afflicting his children, to try their patience and to teach them obedience.

Indeed, they cannot show any other obedience to him than the one he has given them; but he is pleased in this manner to exhibit and to test the graces which he has conferred on his saints, that they may not remain hidden and become useless.

When God's servants openly manifest his gifts of strength and firmness in their suffering, Scripture says that he is trying their patience

Hence such expressions as "God tempted Abraham," who proved his devotion from the fact that he did not refuse to sacrifice his only son.

Therefore Peter states that our faith is tried by tribulations, just as gold is tried by fire in a furnace.

2. Who can deny that it is necessary that this most excellent gift of patience, which a believer has received from God, be developed by practice, so that he becomes sure and convinced of it?

For otherwise men would never esteem it as it deserves.

But, if God himself acts justly when He prevents such virtues from becoming obscure and useless by offering us an occasion to exercise them, then this must be the best of reasons for trying the saints, for without affliction they would have no patience.

3. By the cross they are also instructed, I repeat, to obedience, because in this way they are taught to follow God's desire, and not their own.

If everything proceeded according to their wishes, they would not understand what it means to follow God.

Seneca informs us that it was an ancient custom to exhort people to bear adversity with patience by the maxim: "Follow God."

This implied that man submitted to the yoke of God only when he willingly accepted chastisement with the meekness of a child.

Therefore, if it is reasonable that we should show ourselves obedient in all things to our heavenly Father, then we certainly should not deny him the right to use every way to accustom us to practice this obedience. Gen. 22:1, 2; I Peter 1:7.

V. *The Cross makes for discipline.*

1. Often we do not understand how necessary this obedience is for us, unless we also consider how eager our flesh is to shake off the yoke of the Lord as soon as we have been treated with some tenderness and indulgence.

For it is with us just as with unwilling horses which first are pampered in idleness, and then grow fierce and untamable, and have no regard for the rider to whose reins they formerly submitted.

In other words, what the Lord complains of in his people Israel is continually seen in every one of us: When we are grown "fat," and "covered with fatness," we kick against him who has fed and cherished us.

The kindness of God ought to have led us to consider and love his goodness, but since we are so ungrateful that we are rather constantly spoiled by his indulgence, it is very necessary for us to be restrained by some discipline from breaking out into wilfulness.

2. Therefore, that we may not become haughty when we acquire wealth; that we may not become proud when we receive honors; that we may not become insolent when we are blessed with prosperity and health, the Lord himself, as he deems fit, uses the cross to oppose, restrain, and subdue the arrogance of our flesh.

And he does this by various means which are useful and wholesome for each of us.

For we are not all equally afflicted with the same disease, or all in need of the same severe cure.

This is the reason why we see different persons disciplined with different crosses. The heavenly Physician takes care of the well-being of all his patients; he gives some a milder medicine and purifies others by more shocking treatments, but he omits no one; for the whole world, without exception, is ill. Deut. 32:15.

VI. *The Cross brings repentance.*

1. Moreover, it is necessary that our most merciful Father should not only prevent our future weakness, but also correct our past offences to keep us in the path of obedience. Therefore, in every affliction, we ought immediately to review our past life.

When we do so we shall certainly find that we have deserved such chastisement.

Nevertheless we should not draw the conclusion that we are first of all exhorted to patience because we should remember our sins.

For Scripture furnishes us a far better reason when it informs us that in adversity "we are chastened by the Lord, in order that we should not be condemned with the world."

2. Therefore, even in the bitterness of our trials we should acknowledge the mercy and kindness of our Father towards us; since even then he does not cease to promote our welfare.

For he does not afflict to destroy or ruin us, but rather to deliver us from the condemnation of the world.

This thought will lead us to what Scripture teaches in another place: "My son, despise not the chastening of the Lord, neither be weary of his correction; for whom the Lord loves He corrects, even as a father the son in whom he delights."

When we recognize the rod of a father, should we not show ourselves docile children rather than rebelliously imitate desperate men who have been hardened in their evil doings?

God would let us perish if he would not call us back to him by his corrections when we have failed, as the Apostle pointedly remarks, "If ye be without chastisement then are ye bastards, and not sons."

3. We are extremely perverse, if we cannot bear with him, when he shows his lovingkindness towards us, and his great concern for our salvation.

Scripture points out this difference between believers and unbelievers; the latter, as old slaves of their incurable perversity cannot endure the rod, but the former like children of noble birth, profit by repentance and correction.

Now we must choose where we prefer to stand.

But having treated of this subject elsewhere let it suffice that I have touched on it here briefly. I Cor. 11:32; Prov. 3:11, 12; Heb. 12:8.

VII. *Persecution brings God's favor.*

1. It is a source of singular consolation for us, when we suffer persecution "for righteousness' sake."

For then we ought to remember how greatly we are honored by God when he decorates us with the tokens of his service.

I call it persecution for righteousness' sake not only when we suffer in defense of the gospel, but also when we are opposed in upholding any just cause.

When we defend the truth of God over against the falsehoods of Satan, or protect good and innocent people against injustice and injury, it may be necessary for us to incur the hatred and indignation of the world, so that our lives, our possessions, or our reputation may be endangered.

But we should not be grieved when we exert ourselves in the service of God, and we should not count ourselves miserable when with his own mouth he calls us most blessed.

It is true that poverty by itself is misery; and the same may be said of exile, contempt, shame, and imprisonment; and finally, of all calamities death is the last and the worst.

But when God breathes his favor on us, all things work together for our happiness and our well-being.

Let us therefore be content with the approval of Christ rather than with the false opinion of our flesh.

Then we shall rejoice like the Apostles, whenever He shall "count us worthy to suffer shame for his name."

2. What of it?

If we in our innocence and with a good conscience are robbed of our goods by the villainy of the wicked, and are reduced to poverty among men, we shall thereby increase our true riches with God in heaven.

If we are banished from our country, we shall be received into the intimate fellowship of God.

If we are tormented and despised, we shall be the more firmly rooted in Christ for fleeing to him.

If we are covered with reproach and shame, we shall receive the more glory in the Kingdom of God.

If we are massacred, we shall be received into the eternal glory.

We ought to be ashamed of deeming the everlasting values of less account than the shadowy and fleeting pleasures of the present life. Matt. 2:10; Acts 5:41.

VIII. *Persecution should bring spiritual joy.*

1. Since Scripture comforts us time and again in all maltreatments and misery which we may experience in the defense of a righteous cause, we may, therefore, be accused of extreme ingratitude if we do not receive these hardships from the hand of the Lord with resignation and spiritual joy; especially since this type of affliction, or cross, is most peculiar to believers.

For by our suffering Christ will be glorified in us according to the saying of Peter.

And since a haughty treatment to noble and independent minds is more intolerable than a hundred deaths, Paul warns us that not only persecution, but also reproaches await us, just "because we trust in the living God."

And in another place he arouses us to follow his example and to go through "evil report and good report."

2. Moreover, we are not required to be cheerful while we shake off all sense of bitterness and sorrow.

The saints could not find any patience in cross bearing, if they were not disturbed by sorrow and harassed with grief.

For instance, if there were no hardship in poverty, no agony in sickness, no distress in insults, no horror in death, what courage or moderation would it be to regard these afflictions with indifference?

But since each of them by its own bitterness bows down our hearts as a matter of course, the faithful will show their real strength by resisting and overcoming their grief, however much they may have to labor.

They will be patient when they are keenly provoked, and they will be restrained by the fear of God from any outbursts of intemperance.

Their joy and cheerfulness will be apparent when, wounded by sadness and sorrow, they will rest in the spiritual consolation of God. I Pet. 4:14; I Tim. 4:10; II Cor. 6:8.

IX. *Our Cross should not make us indifferent.*

1. The struggle of believers against their natural emotions of sorrow while they try to build up patience and moderation, has been fully described by Paul in these words: "We are troubled on every side, yet not distressed; we are perplexed, but not in despair; persecuted, but not forsaken; cast down, but not destroyed. II Cor. 4:8, 9.

It is clear that bearing the cross patiently does not mean that we harden ourselves, or do not feel any sorrow; according to the old notion of the Stoic philosophers that a greathearted man is some one who has laid off his humanity, and who is not touched by adversity and prosperity, and not even by joy and sorrow, but who acts like a cold rock.

What profit is there in this proud wisdom?

They have pictured an image of patience which has never been found among men and which cannot exist, and in their desire to find a patience of a singular type they have removed it from human life.

2. At present there are among Christians modern Stoics who think it is wrong to groan and to weep, and even to grieve in loneliness.

Such wild opinions generally come forth from men who are more dreamers than practical men, and who, therefore, can not produce anything else but fantasies.

3. But we have nothing to do with such a harsh and rigorous philosophy which our Lord and Master Jesus has condemned in word and example.

For he mourned and wept for his own calamities as well as for those of others, and He did not teach his disciples any different way.

"The World," said he, "shall rejoice, but ye shall weep and lament."

And that no man might call sadness a vice, he has pronounced a blessing on them that mourn.

4. And no wonder, for if he condemned all tears, what must we judge of the Lord himself from whose body flowed tears of blood?

If every fear be labeled unbelief, what name shall we give to that anxiety of which we read that it depressed and amazed Him?

If all sorrow is displeasing, how can we be pleased with his confession that his soul was "sorrowful even unto death?" John 16:20; Matt. 5:5; Luke 22:44.

X. *The Cross makes for submission.*

1. These things should be mentioned so that devout minds may be kept from despair; that they may not hurriedly give up their desires for patience because they cannot lay off their natural inclination towards sorrow. For despair will be the end of those who let their patience slip into indifference and who contend that a man is strong and courageous when he makes himself a senseless block. On the contrary, Scripture praises the saints for their patience when they are severely afflicted by their adversities,

but not broken and overcome by them; when they are bitterly distressed, but nevertheless filled with spiritual joy; when they are weighed down by anxiety and become exhausted, and yet leap for joy because of the divine consolation.

2. At the same time there is a conflict in their hearts because our natural feelings avoid and fear what is hostile to our experience.

But our zeal for devotion struggles through our difficulties so that we become obedient to the divine will.

This conflict is expressed by the Lord when He addressed Peter as follows: "When you were young, you girded yourself, and walked where you would, but when you are old, another will gird you, and carry you where you would not."

It is not probable that Peter when he was called to glorify God by his death, was led to it with reluctance and aversion; in this case his martyrdom would be entitled to little praise.

But, however much he might submit with the greatest eagerness of heart to the Divine will, yet, because he had not shaken off his human feelings, he was distracted by an inner conflict.

For when he was thinking of the bloody death which was in store for him, he was stricken with fear and he would have gladly made his escape.

But, when he considered that God had called him to it, he suppressed this fear and submitted to it without reluctance and even with cheerfulness.

3. It must be our desire, therefore, if we want to be disciples of Christ, to fill our minds with such a great reverence for God and with such an unrestrained obedience that we may triumph over all contrary inclinations, and submit to his plan.

In this way we shall remain constant in our patience, whatever afflictions we may bear, and even in the greatest distress of our mind.

For adversity will always wound us with its stings.

When we are afflicted with disease we shall, therefore, groan and complain and pray for recovery.

When we are oppressed with poverty we shall feel lonely and sorry.

When we shall be defamed, despised and offended, likewise we shall feel restless.

When we have to attend the funeral of our friends, we shall shed tears.

4. But we must always come back to this consolation: The Lord planned our sorrow, so let us submit to his will.

Even in the throes of grief, groans and tears, we must encourage ourselves with this reflection, so that our hearts may cheerfully bear up while the storms pass over our heads. John 21:18.

XI. *The Cross is necessary for our salvation.*

1. Now that we have shown that the main consideration for bearing the cross is the Divine will, we must finally point out briefly the difference between philosophical and Christian patience.

For very few of the philosophers have reached the high understanding that we are subjected to afflictions by the divine hand, or have come to the conclusion that it is our duty to submit to his will.

And even those who have gotten so far do not mention any other reason than that resignation is a necessary evil.

What is this but stating that we must submit to God, because any effort to resist him is vain?

For, if we obey God only from necessity, we will cease to obey as soon as we can escape from him.

2. But Scripture commands us to consider the Divine will in a different light; first, as consistent with justice and fairness; then as directed to the perfection of our salvation.

The Christian exhortations to patience are, therefore, as follows: Whether we are afflicted with poverty, or exile, or imprisonment, or reproach, or disease, or loss of relatives, or any other similar calamity, we must remember that none of these things happen without the will and providence of God; and moreover, that he does nothing but with regular justice.

Do not our innumerable and daily sins deserve many more severe and grievous chastisements than those which he inflicts on us in his mercy?

Is it not very reasonable that our flesh should be subdued, and that we should be accustomed to a yoke, so that our carnal impulses should not get the best of us, and drive us into intemperance?

Are not the justice and truth of God worthy to be endured because of our sins?

We cannot without iniquity murmur or rebel.

We shall no longer hear that cold refrain of the philosopher that we must submit to necessity.

But we hear that lively and efficient appeal: We must obey because it is wrong to resist.

We must suffer patiently, because impatience is rebellion against the justice of God.

3. Because we really like nothing but what we imagine will profit and prosper us, our most merciful Father comforts us by this teaching that he promotes our salvation by inflicting the cross upon us.

If it be plain that adversities are good for us why should we not then endure them with grateful and peaceful hearts?

For, if we bear them patiently we do not surrender to necessity, but we submit for our benefit.

The upshot of these considerations is, that the more we are oppressed by the cross, the fuller will be our spiritual joy.

And, unavoidably, to this joy is attached thankfulness.

If praise and thanksgiving to the Lord can come forth only from a cheerful and joyful heart — and there is nothing which ought to repress such emotions — then it is evident that God will temper the bitterness of the Cross by the joy of the Spirit.

CHAPTER IV

Hopefulness for the Next World

I. *There is no crown without a cross.*

1. With whatever kind of trials we may be afflicted, we should always keep our eye on this goal, that we accustom ourselves to the contempt [of the vanities] of the present life in order that we may meditate on the future life.

For the Lord knows that we are by nature inclined to love this world blindly, and even carnally, and, therefore, he uses an excellent means to call us back, and to arouse us from our sluggishness, that our heart may not be too much attached to such a foolish inclination.

2. There is not one of us who does not strive passionately through the whole course of his life for the heavenly immortality, and who does not try to reach it.

For we are really ashamed that we are not better than the dumb animals whose condition would not at all be inferior to ours, if it were not for our hope in eternity after death.

But, if we closely examine the ambitious plans, enterprises, and actions of every individual, we will find that they are all on the level of this earth.

Hence our stupidity that our mind, dazzled with the outward splendor of riches, power, and honor, cannot see beyond them.

The heart also, filled and distressed with avarice, ambition, and other evil desires, cannot rise above them.

In one word, the whole soul, wrapped up in carnal delights, seeks its happiness on this earth.

3. To counteract this, the Lord by various and severe lessons of misery, teaches his children the vanity of the present life.

That they may not promise themselves a life of ease and comfort, he permits them, therefore, to be frequently disturbed and molested by wars or revolutions, by robberies, and other injuries.

That they may not hanker with too much avidity after passing and uncertain riches, or depend on what they possess, he reduces them to poverty, or at least limits them to mediocrity, sometimes, by exile, sometimes by sterility of the land, sometimes by fire, sometimes by other means.

That they may not become too complacent, or delighted in married life, he makes them distressed by the shortcoming of their partners, or humbles them through wilful offspring, or afflicts them with the want, or loss of children.

But, if in all these matters he is more merciful to them, he shows them by diseases and dangers how unstable and passing all mortal blessings are, that they may not be puffed up with vain glory.

4. We, therefore, truly reap advantage from the discipline of the cross only, when we learn that this life, taken by itself, is full of unrest, trouble, and misery, and not really happy from any point of view; and that all its so-called blessings are uncertain, passing, vain, and mixed with endless adversity.

In consequence of this we should at once come to the conclusion that nothing in this world can be sought, or expected, but strife, and that we must raise our eyes to heaven to see a crown.

But it must be admitted that our heart is never seriously inclined to wish for and to meditate on the future life unless it has first thoroughly learned to forsake the vanities of the present world.

II. *We are inclined to overestimate this present life.*

1. There is no golden mean between these two extremes; either this earthly life must become low in our estimation, or it will have our inordinate love.

Therefore, if we have any concern about eternity, we must put forth our most diligent efforts, to free ourselves from our temporal chains.

Now, since the present life has numerous attractions, and much pleasure, beauty and sweetness to delight us, it is most necessary for our highest interest that we should frequently be called away from it, that we may not be carried away by its glamour.

For what would be the outcome, if we were constantly happy in the enjoyment of the blessings of this life?

We cannot even by the incessant round of evils be aroused to give enough thought to its miseries.

2. That human life is nothing but a vapor, or a shadow, is not only known to the learned, but even the common people have many a proverb to that effect.

They consider this knowledge so useful, that they have many striking phrases and rhymes about life and its vanity.

But there is scarcely anything which we more carelessly consider, or sooner banish from our memory; for we go about everything, as if we want to make ourselves immortal.

If we watch a funeral, or walk among the graves, and thus clearly see the image of death before our eyes, we philosophize, I confess, about the vanity of life.

And even that does not happen every day, for often we are not moved at all.

But when we are, our philosophy is only short-lived, it vanishes as soon as we go away, and does not leave the smallest trace behind.

It passes out of existence like the applause for an entertaining program.

3. We not only forget death, but the fact that we are mortals, as if no word concerning this has ever reached us, and we continue our foolish dream that we are to live forever.

If any man in the meantime reminds us of the proverb that man is only a creature of a day we are willing to acknowledge this truth, but with such lack of attention that the idea of perpetual life keeps on lingering in our minds.

4. Who, then, can deny that we need to be warned not only by words, but that we should be convinced by every possible evidence that the present life is full of miseries!

For, even if after we have become convinced of this, we hardly know how to stop our perverse and foolish admiration of it, as if life were nothing but one great accumulation of blessings.

But, if it is necessary for us to be taught by God, it certainly is also our duty to listen to him when he speaks, and arouses us from our sluggishness, that we may turn our backs upon this world, and try to meditate with all our heart on the life to come.

III. *The blessings of this present life should not be despised.*

1. Nevertheless, our constant efforts to lower our estimate of the present world should not lead us to hate life, or to be ungrateful towards God.

For this life, though it is full of countless miseries, deserves to be reckoned among the divine blessings which should not be despised.

Therefore, if we discover nothing of God's goodness in it, we are already guilty of no small ingratitude toward him.

But to believers especially this life should be a witness of God's kindness, since all of it is destined to advance their salvation.

2. For, before he fully reveals to us the inheritance of eternal glory, he intends to show him-

self as our Father in matters of minor importance; and those are the blessings which he daily showers upon us.

Since this life, then, serves to teach us the divine kindness, should we dare to scorn it as if there were no particle of good in it?

We must, therefore, have enough sense and appreciation to class it among the bounties of the divine love which should not be cast away.

For, if Scriptural evidences were wanting, which are very numerous and clear, even nature itself urges us to give thanks to the Lord for having given us the light of life, and its many usages, and the means necessary to preserve it.

3. Moreover, we have far more reason to be thankful, if we consider that this life helps to prepare us for the glory of the heavenly kingdom.

For the Lord has ordained that those who are to be crowned in heaven, should first fight the good fight on earth, that they may not celebrate their triumph without actually having overcome the difficulties of warfare, and having gained the victory.

Another reason is that here on earth we may have a foretaste of the divine kindness, so that our hope and longing may be kindled for the full revelation of it.

4. When we have come to this conclusion that our life in this world is a gift of God's mercy, which we ought to remember with gratitude, because we owe it to him, it will then be time for us to consider its misery.

For only in this way will we be delivered from an excessive joy of life to which we are by nature inclined, as we have observed before.

IV. *What is earth, if compared with heaven!*

1. Whatever glory we must subtract from the sinful love of life, we may add to the desire for a better world.

It is, indeed, true for pagans that the greatest blessing is not to be born, and the next, to die immediately.

For without knowledge of God and true religion, what else would they see in life but unhappiness and misery?

Nor was there anything unreasonable in the behavior of the Scythians who mourned and wept at the birth of their relatives, and who solemnly celebrated at their funerals.

But their customs did not avail them in any respect, for without knowledge of true faith in Christ they did not understand how something which in itself is neither blessed nor desirable could be conducive to the benefit of the devout believers.

And so, the views of the pagans ended in despair.

2. It should be the purpose of believers, then, when they estimate this mortal life, that they understand that, as it is, it is nothing but misery.

For then only will they try diligently and with increasing cheerfulness and readiness to meditate on the future eternal life.

When we come to a comparison of heaven and earth, then we may indeed not only forget* all about the present life, but even despise and scorn it.

For, if heaven is our fatherland, what is this earth but a place of exile, and this life but a journey through a strange land?**

If leaving this world means the entrance into real life, what else is this world but a grave?

What else is dwelling on this sinful earth, but being plunged into death?

If deliverance from the body means complete liberty, what is this body but a prison?

If to enjoy the presence of God is the peak of happiness, is it not misery to be without it?

---

* The French has: *pass by lightly*; the Latin has *neglect*.
** The Latin has the first; the French the second main clause.

For, until we escape out of this world, "We are absent from the Lord."

Therefore, if the earthly life be compared to the heavenly, it should undoubtedly be despised and counted as a failure.

3. But the present life should never be hated, except in so far as it subjects us to sin, although even that hatred should not properly be applied to life itself.

However, we should become so weary and scornful of it that we may desire its end, though we should also be prepared to remain in it, as long as it pleases the Lord.

In other words, our weariness should keep us from fretting and impatience.

For this life is a post at which the Lord has placed us, and we must stay at it until the Lord calls us away.

Paul, indeed, laments his lot that he is kept in the bondage of the body longer than he would wish, and he ardently sighs for deliverance.

At the same time he rests in the will of God, and states that he is ready for either, to stay, or to leave.

He acknowledges that he is bound to glorify the name of God, either by life, or by death;

but that it belongs to the Lord to determine what is most expedient for his glory.

4. Therefore, if it is fitting for us "to live and to die for the Lord," let us leave the limits of our life and death to his decision and good pleasure.

At the same time let us ardently desire and continually meditate on death while we despise [the vanities of] the present life in comparison with future immortality.

And, let us on account of our enslavement to sin wish to leave this life, whenever it will please the Lord. II Cor. 5:6; Rom. 7:24; Phil. 1:20; Rom. 14:7 and 8.

V. *We should not fear death, but lift up our heads.*

1. It is terrible that many who boast themselves to be Christians, instead of longing for death, are so filled with fear of it that they tremble whenever the word is mentioned, as if it were the greatest calamity that could befall them.

It should not surprise us, indeed, if our natural feeling should be alarmed at hearing of our separation from this life.

But it is intolerable that there should not be sufficient light and devotion in a Christian's breast to suppress all that fear with an over-whelming consolation.

For, if we consider that this unstable, depraved, perishable, frail, withering, and corrupt tabernacle of our body is dissolved, in order that it may hereafter be restored to a durable, perfect, incorruptible, and heavenly glory, — will not our faith then induce us to wish ardently for what nature dreads?

If we remember that by death we are called back from exile to home, to our heavenly fatherland, shall we then not be filled with comfort?

2. But it will be said, there is nothing in this world that does not want to be permanent.

It must be admitted, but for that very reason we should look forward to a future immortality, where we may obtain such a realm of stability as is not found on this earth.

For Paul clearly teaches believers to go with anxious longing toward death, not to be stripped of our body, but to be clothed with a new garment.

Shall brute animals, and even lifeless creatures, down to blocks and stones, aware of their present vanity, be looking forward to the resurrection at the last day, that they may be delivered from vanity, together with the children of God; and shall we, gifted with the light of natural reason, and with the far superior enlightenment of the Spirit of God; shall we, when we consider our future existence, not lift our minds above the corruption of this world?

3. But, it is not necessary or suitable for my present purpose to argue against such utter perverseness as fear of death.

In the beginning I have already declared that I would not enter on a complicated discussion of commonplace topics.

I would persuade such timid hearts to read Cyprian's treatise on *Mortality*, unless they should deserve to be referred to philosophers, that they may blush when they discover how even pagans despise death.

But this we may positively state that nobody has made any progress in the school of Christ, unless he cheerfully looks forward towards the day of his death, and towards the day of the final resurrection.

4. For Paul stamps this mark on all believers, and Scripture often calls our attention to it, when it wants to provide us with a motive for true joy.

"Look up," says the Lord, "and lift up your heads, for your redemption draws nigh."

Is it reasonable to expect that the things which he planned to arouse us to ecstacy and wide-awakeness should cause us nothing but sorrow and consternation?

If this is the case, why do we still glory in him as our Master?

Let us, therefore, return to a sounder judgment, and notwithstanding the opposition of the blind and stupid desires of our flesh, let us not hesitate to long passionately for the coming of our Lord, as the most stirring of all events.

And let us not only long for it, but even groan and sigh for (the day of judgment).*

For he shall come to us as a Savior, to deliver us from this bottomless maelstrom of all evils and miseries, and he shall guide us into the blessed inheritance of his life and glory. II Cor. 5:4; Titus 2:13; Luke 21:28.

VI. *The Lord will come in his glory: Maranatha.*

1. It is true beyond doubt that the whole family of believers, as long as they are living on the earth, must be "accounted as sheep for the slaughter," in order that they may become more and more like Christ their Head.

Their condition, therefore, would be extremely deplorable, if they would not raise their

---

* Added in French.

thoughts toward heaven, rise above the passing show, and look beyond the horizon of this world.

2. Let the impious flourish in their riches and honors, and enjoy their so-called peace of mind.

Let them boast of their splendor and luxury, and abound in every joy.

Let them harass the children of light with their wickedness, let them insult them with their pride, let them rob them by their greed, let them provoke them with their utter lawlessness.

But when the believers see this, let them lift their eyes above this world, and they will not have any difficulty to maintain their peace of heart under such calamities.

For they will look forward to the day when the Lord will receive his faithful servants into his kingdom of peace.

Then he will wipe every tear from their eyes, clothe them with robes of joy, adorn them with crowns of victory, entertain them with infinite delights, exalt them to his glory, and make them partakers of his own happiness.

3. But the evildoers who have been great in this world, he will hurl down into the abyss of shame.

He will change their delights into torments, and their laughter and mirth into weeping and gnashing of teeth.

He will disturb their rest with dreadful agonies of conscience.

He will plunge them with their adulteries into the unquenchable fire, and put them in subjection to the faithful whose patience they have abused.

For, according to Paul, it is a righteous thing with God to award punishment to them that trouble the saints, and to give rest to those who are troubled, when the Lord Jesus shall be revealed from heaven.

4. This is our only consolation.

If we are deprived of this we shall have to sink into despair, or comfort ourselves with the vain pleasures of this world.

For even the Psalmist confesses that he was confounded when he kept on wondering about the present prosperity of the wicked.

And, he could not regain his composure until he entered the sanctuary, and marked the latter end of the righteous and the unrighteous.

To conclude in a few words:

The cross of Christ triumphs only in the hearts of believers over the devil and the flesh, over sin and wickedness, when they lift their eyes to behold the power of the resurrection. Rom. 8:36; I Cor. 15:19; Is. 25:8; Rev. 7:17; II Thess. 1:6 and 7; Ps. 73:2ff.

CHAPTER V

The Right Use of the Present Life

I. *Let us avoid extremes.*

1. Just as Scripture points us to heaven as our goal, so it fully instructs us in the right use of earthly blessings, and this ought not to be overlooked in a discussion of the rules of life.

For if we must live, we must also use the necessary instruments for life.

We cannot even avoid those matters which serve our pleasures rather than our needs.

But that we may use them with a pure conscience, we should observe moderation, whether we mean the one, or the other.

2. This the Lord prescribes in his Word, when he teaches us that for his servants the present life is like a pilgrimage in which they are traveling towards the heavenly kingdom.

Even if this earth is only a vestibule, we ought undoubtedly to make such a use of its blessings that we are assisted rather than delayed in our journey.

It is not without reason, therefore, that Paul advises us to use this world as if we did not use it, and to buy possessions in the same frame of mind as when we sell them.

3. But as this is a moot question, and as we run the danger of falling into two opposite errors, let us try to proceed on safe ground, so that we may avoid both extremes.

For there have been some people, otherwise good and holy, who saw that intemperance and luxury time and again drive man to throw off all restraints unless he is curbed by the utmost severity.

And in their desire to correct such a pernicious evil they have adopted the only method which they saw fit, namely to permit earthly blessings only in so far as they were an absolute necessity.

This advice showed the best of intentions, but was far too rigid.

For they committed the very dangerous error of imposing on the conscience of others stricter rules than those laid down in the Word of the Lord.

By restricting people within the demands of necessity, they meant abstinence from everything possible.

According to them it would be scarcely permissible to eat and drink anything but dry bread and pure water.

Others sought even greater rigidity, like Crates of Thebes, of whom it is told that he threw his treasures into the sea out of fear that unless they were destroyed he himself would be ruined by them.

4. On the other hand, there are many nowadays who seek a pretext to excuse intemperance in the use of external things, and who desire to indulge the lusts of the flesh.

Such people take for granted that liberty should not be restricted by any limitations at all; but to this we can never agree.

They clamor that it ought to be left to the conscience of every individual to use as much as he thinks fit for himself.

5. We must grant, indeed, that it is not right, or possible to bind the conscience of others with hard and fast rules.

But, since Scripture lays down some general principles for the lawful use of earthly things, we certainly ought to follow them in our conduct. I Cor. 7:30 and 31.

II. *Earthly things are gifts of God.*

1. The first principle we should consider is that the use of gifts of God cannot be wrong, if they are directed to the same purpose for which the Creator himself has created and destined them.

For he has made the earthly blessings for our benefit, and not for our harm.

No one, therefore, will observe a more proper rule than he who will faithfully observe this purpose.

2. If we study, for instance, why he has created the various kinds of food, we shall find that it was his intention not only to provide for our needs, but likewise for our pleasure, and for our delight.

In clothing he did not only keep in mind our needs, but also propriety and decency.

In herbs, trees, and fruit, besides being useful in various ways, he planned to please us by their gracious lines and pleasant odors.

For, if this were not true, the Psalmist would not enumerate among the divine blessings "the wine that makes glad the heart of man, and the oil that makes his face to shine."

And the Scriptures would not declare everywhere that he has given all these things to mankind that they might praise his goodness.

3. Even the natural properties of things sufficiently point out to what purpose and to what extent we are allowed to use them.

Should the Lord have attracted our eyes to the beauty of the flowers, and our sense of smell to pleasant odors, and should it then be sin to drink them in?

Has he not even made the colors so that the one is more wonderful than the other?

Has he not granted to gold and silver, to ivory and marble a beauty which makes them more precious than other metals or stones?

In one word, has he not made many things worthy of our attention that go far beyond our needs? Ps. 104:15.

III. *True gratitude will restrain us from abuse.*

1. Let us discard, therefore, that inhuman philosophy which would allow us no use of creation, unless it is absolutely necessary.

Such a malignant notion deprives us of the lawful enjoyment of God's kindness. And, it is impossible actually to accept it, until we are robbed of all our senses, and reduced to a senseless block.

On the other hand, we must with equal zeal fight the lusts of the flesh, for, if they are not firmly restrained, they will transgress every bound.

As we have observed, licentiousness has its advocates: there are people who under the pretext of liberty, will stop short of nothing.

2. First of all, if we want to curb our passions we must remember that all things are made for us, with the purpose that we may know and acknowledge their Author.

We should praise his kindness towards us in earthly matters by giving him thanks.

But, what will become of our thanksgiving, if we indulge in dainties, or wine, in such a way that we are too dull to carry out the duties of devotion or of our business?

Where is our acknowledgment of God, if the excesses of our body drive us to the vilest passions, and infect our mind with impurity, so that we can no longer distinguish between right and wrong?

Where is our gratitude towards God for clothing, if we admire ourselves, and despise others because of our own sumptuous apparel?

Where is it, if we prepare ourselves for unchastity, with the elegance and beauty of our dress?

Where is our acknowledgment of God, if our thoughts are fixed on the glamour of our garments?

3. For many so madly pursue pleasure that their minds become enslaved to it.

Many are so delighted with marble, gold and painting, that they become like statues.

They are, as it were, transfixed into metal, and begin to resemble colorful idols.

The flavor of meats, and the sweetness of odors, makes some people so stupid that they have no longer any appetite for spiritual things.

And this holds for the abuse of all other natural matters.

Therefore, it is clear, that the principle of gratitude should curb our desire to abuse the divine blessings.

This principle confirms the rule of Paul, that we may "not make provision for the flesh to fulfil its lusts."

For, if we give our natural desires free rein, they will pass all the bounds of temperance and moderation. Rom. 13:14.

IV. *Let us live with moderation.*

1. But, there is no surer and shorter way (to gratitude) than to turn our eyes away from the

present life, and to meditate on the immortality of heaven.

From this flow two general principles:

The first is, "that they that have wives be as though they had none; and they that buy as though they possessed not; and they that use this world as not abusing it," according to the precept of Paul.

The second is that we should learn to bear poverty quietly and patiently, and to enjoy abundance with moderation.

2. He who commands us to use this world as though we used it not, forbids not only all intemperance in eating and drinking, and excessive pleasure, ambition, pride, and fastidiousness in our furniture, home, and apparel, but every care and affection which would drag down our spiritual level, or destroy our devotion.

It was in olden times truly observed by Cato, that there is great concern about the appearance of the body, but great carelessness about virtue.

There is also an old proverb, that they who pay much attention to the body generally neglect the soul.

3. Therefore, though the liberty of believers in external things cannot be restricted by hard and fast rules, yet it is surely subject to this law, that they should indulge as little as possible.

On the contrary, we should continually and resolutely exert ourselves to shun all that is superfluous, and avoid all vain display of luxury.

We should zealously beware that anything the Lord gave us to enrich life become a stumbling block. I Cor. 7:29-31.

V. *Let us be patient and content under privation.*

1. The other principle will be that people who are poor should learn to be patient under privations, that they may not be tormented by a passion for riches.

Those who regard this moderation have made no small progress in the school of the Lord, and those who have not made this progress have scarcely given any proof of their discipleship in Christ.

2. For not only is a passion for earthly things accompanied by almost all other vices, but he who is impatient under privation will commonly betray the opposite vice when he is in luxury.

This means, that he who is ashamed of a simple garment will be proud of a glamorous one.

He who is not content with a sober meal feels uneasy because he desires a sumptuous one, and will even be intemperate as soon as there is an occasion.

He who grows restless and dissatisfied while he puts up with privation and humility will not be able to guard against pride and arrogance, if he rides to honor.

Therefore, let all those who want to be sincere in their devotion, earnestly try to follow the Apostolic example, "both to be full and to be hungry, both to abound and to suffer need." Phil. 4:12.

3. Scripture also mentions a third principle by which the use of earthly things is limited, and this was mentioned when we spoke of the precepts of selfdenial.

For while all such things are given to us by divine kindness, and are meant to be for our benefit, they are at the same time like deposits entrusted to our care, and of these we shall have to give an account some day.

We ought to manage them, therefore, in such a way as if we incessantly heard this warning in our ears: "Give an account of your stewardship."

4. Let us also remember who demands this account.

It is he who so highly recommends restraint, sobriety, frugality and modesty.

It is he who abhors excess, pride, showiness, and vain display.

It is he who will not approve our management of his blessings unless we are urged on by love.

It is he who with his own mouth condemns all pleasures which lead us away from chastity and purity, and which make us foolish and stupid. Phil. 4:12; Luke 16:2.

VI. *Be faithful in your divine calling.*

1. Finally we should note that the Lord commands every one of us in all the actions of our life, to be faithful in our calling.

For he knows that the human mind burns with restlessness, that it is swept easily hither and thither, and that its ambition to embrace many things at once is insatiable.

Therefore, to prevent that general confusion being produced by our folly and boldness, he has appointed to everyone his particular duties in the different spheres of life.

And, that no one might rashly go beyond his limits, he has called such spheres of life vocations, or callings.

Every individual's sphere of life, therefore, is a post assigned him by the Lord that he may not wander about in uncertainty all the days of his life.

And so necessary is this distinction, that in his sight all our actions are measured by it, and, often very differently from the judgment of human reason, or philosophy.

2. There is no greater heroism even among philosophers than to deliver one's country from tyranny.

But the voice of the heavenly Judge openly condemns the private man who kills a tyrant.

It is not within our plan to enumerate examples, but let it be sufficient to know that the principle and basis of right conduct in every civil case is our calling by the Lord.

He who disregards his calling will never keep the straight path in the duties of his work.

Sometimes he may perhaps succeed in doing something that appears to be praiseworthy.

But, however good it may look in the eyes of man, before the throne of God it will not be acceptable.

And besides, there will be no consistency in the various parts of his life.

3. Our present life, therefore, will be best regulated, if we always keep our calling in mind.

No one will then be tempted by his own boldness to dare to undertake what is not compatible with his calling, because he will know that it is wrong to go beyond his limits.

Anyone who is not in the front ranks should be content to accomplish his private task, and should not desert the place where the Lord has put him.

It will be no small comfort for his cares, labors, troubles, and other burdens, when a man knows that in all these matters God is his guide.

The magistrate will then carry out his office with greater willingness.

The father of a family will then perform his duties with more courage.

And everyone in his respective sphere of life will show more patience, and will overcome the difficulties, cares, miseries and anxieties in his path, when he will' be convinced that every individual has his task laid upon his shoulders by God.

If we follow our divine calling we shall receive this unique consolation that there is no work so mean and so sordid that does not look truly respectable and highly important in the sight of God! (Coram Deo!) Gen. 1:28; Col. 1:1ff.

A Most Confusing Game

"I would have asked you to make love to me when you answered the door . . . but I wondered what you would have done to me—"

"I don't know," Ann answered. "Depends on how you asked. Maybe you should give it a try." She kept her voice deliberately suggestive, challenging him with her eyes.

"Oh, no," he said. "Not until I know that you're the one at my mercy."

"Do you really think that could ever happen?"

"I don't see why not," he answered. His hand moved from her arm to her shoulder.

She couldn't speak with her heart in her throat.

CAROLYN THORNTON
a Southern native, now lives in Hattiesburg, Mississippi. Her widespread travels throughout the South and her deep-rooted interest in Southern traditions and heritage are reflected in her novels and magazine articles.

Dear Reader,

Silhouette Special Editions are an exciting new line of contemporary romances from Silhouette Books. Special Editions are written specifically for our readers who want a story with heightened romantic tension.

Special Editions have all the elements you've enjoyed in Silhouette Romances and *more*. These stories concentrate on romance in a longer, more realistic and sophisticated way, and they feature greater sensual detail.

I hope you enjoy this book and all the wonderful romances from Silhouette.

Karen Solem
Editor-in-Chief
Silhouette Books

CAROLYN THORNTON
By The Book

Silhouette Special Edition
Published by Silhouette Books New York

America's Publisher of Contemporary Romance

To Liz Scott, thank you

SILHOUETTE BOOKS, a Division of Simon & Schuster, Inc.
1230 Avenue of the Americas, New York, N.Y. 10020

ISBN: 0-671-53646-X

First Silhouette Books printing February, 1984

10 9 8 7 6 5 4 3 2 1

Map by Ray Lundgren

America's Publisher of Contemporary Romance

Printed in the U.S.A.

BC91

Books by Carolyn Thornton

Silhouette Romance

The Heart Never Forgets #19
For Eric's Sake #229

Silhouette Special Edition

Love is Surrender #11
Pride's Reckoning #57
Looking Glass Love #81
Smile and Say Yes #138
By the Book #145

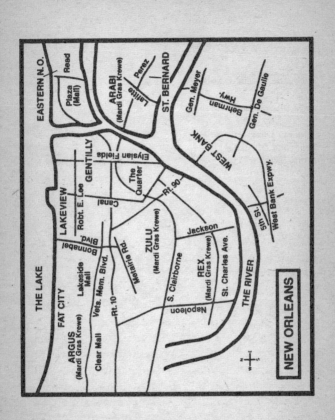

Chapter One

"If one more man asks me if he can help me with research for my romance novels, Dana, I swear I'm going to make him eat my last book—page by page. And I'm going to tell him *that's* the kind of research I need done since I'd like to know what goes through a billy goat's mind when he eats junk food."

Ann Straus's editor looked down at the shrimp with fettucine on the gold-rimmed plate in front of her, trying not to smile at her author's irritation. "Maybe you should take the man up on his offer," Dana Clare suggested. "We could use another best seller like *Love Is Desire*. Readers adore your racy love stories."

Ann set her fork down and picked up her water goblet. "Men I meet on the road with this horrendous publicity tour can't spell 'racy,' much less the word 'love.'"

"You've been single too long," Dana replied, signaling the Trianon waiter to bring more wine.

"If that's meant to point out the difference in our ages—"

"It's not. It's not." Dana held up her hands in mock surrender. "Besides, you're only—what?—four or five years older than I am."

"Six," Ann corrected, knowing it would be seven in a few months, when her thirty-first birthday would roll around.

"All I meant was, haven't you ever thought of getting married?" Dana smiled at the waiter, waiting for him to fill both wineglasses before she turned to Ann for her reply.

"That's all I *ever* think of," Ann said. "Can't you tell from my novels? Every one of them ends happily ever after, which, in my book, means *married.*"

Dana rested her chin on her hand, ready for some girl talk with her famous writer. "I always wondered why you never married."

"Believe me, I've been ready several times, but either I loved him and he didn't notice me, or I got bored with him and he drooled over me." Ann put down the water goblet and tasted the wine. "Timing's always been wrong."

"But you must have come close to getting married at least once."

Ann nodded.

"What happened?"

Ann sighed. "My first love ended in boredom. Met him in high school, dated him through college, et cetera, et cetera. You know the scenario."

Dana nodded. "I think everybody goes through that."

"After that I went through a string of men I didn't want to see twice. When I finally met someone halfway interesting, I would have married him the second week if he had asked. Fortunately, he didn't."

"Why was that fortunate?"

"As I got to know him, I realized I was in love with the idea of love and marriage more than I was with him." She picked up her fork again and began twining the pasta around the prongs. "It wouldn't have worked. We were poles apart."

"I still find it hard to believe you're single," Dana said, spearing a shrimp. "I always wanted to be honey-haired beauty like you, just to find out if blondes really do have more fun."

"I've never been anything else, so I wouldn't know."

"But blond," Dana said, twirling a strand of her dark brown hair. "I imagine you have men falling all over you."

"Oh, that happens." Ann frowned. "But that's usually because they're tripping over their canes."

Dana giggled.

"And the ones who still haven't lost their sight from old age never see past the blond hair. That's the type who can't get my name straight, even if I hang one of my books around my neck. They see the hair and the fact that I'm female. Period. Not too flattering."

"True. But—"

"I intimidate a lot of men." Ann sighed, thinking of the last eligible man she'd gone out with.

"How?" Dana asked. "You're so down to earth."

"Not many men I come in contact with make more money than I do."

"Oh. There is that."

"For some reason," Ann continued, "that's a big putdown to men's egos—which I think is ridiculous. They're looking at the megabucks and not me."

Dana nodded, beginning to see how Ann Straus found so much time to spend turning out best-selling novels at the rate of four a year. "It must be lonely."

"You guessed it," Ann said. "But it has to be in order to write. And all this travel—I don't have the time to form relationships."

"I wouldn't think so," Dana commiserated.

"A casual weekend or week-long fling is not my idea of commitment."

"Mine either," Dana said, spearing another shrimp.

"Sometimes I wish it were."

Dana glanced at Ann, but didn't comment.

Ann savored a bite of fettucine, thinking. "Yes." She nodded. "It is lonely. But sometimes"—she paused, frowning, looking at Dana as if her editor might have the answer—"I wonder if my books and all the travel aren't some sort of defense I create."

Dana gave Ann a look that encouraged her to continue.

"Sort of an insulation against all the wrong men. A nice way of putting them down—you know—'I'm in the middle of my novel so I can't see you tonight.' Or: 'I'm flying to Pittsburgh tomorrow so I have to be home and in bed, alone, by ten.'" She shook her head, thinking of how much time she'd spent in the air these past three months. "You have to admit," she said, smiling at Dana, "it's more creative than telling a guy something like—'I can't go out with you because I have to wash my hair.'"

Dana laughed, shoving aside her plate and concentrating on the wine left in her glass. "I guess you would also get quite a following of groupies, all those people who can't wait for your next book to come out."

Ann shrugged, trying to capture the last noodle on her fork. "Most of my readers are women. You've told me that from your market research. And I do meet some fascinating men from time to time." She paused and added, "Most of them are married."

"They're the worst kind," Dana agreed, "unless they happen to be married to you."

"You're lucky," Ann declared, lifting her glass to her editor. "Gerald is a doll."

"Yes," Dana cooed, giving Ann a goosey look.

They both laughed.

"To marriage," Ann said, clinking her glass with Dana's. "And the right man."

The two women drank in silence while the waiter cleared their plates away and brought the dessert trolley. Both set their sights on the vanilla mousse, watching with fascination as the waiter smeared a mocha sauce over the bottom of the plate, piled on the mousse, and topped it off with fresh strawberries and melba sauce.

"Actually," Ann said, then interrupted herself as she tasted the whipped cream concoction, "uhhhmmmmm. That is heaven." She put another spoonful into her mouth and continued, "Actually, I'm quite happy with my life. And if it comes right down to it and I get no offers, I could be quite content living the rest of my life alone, not by choice, but I kind of like kicking around the house by myself at all hours, especially when I'm trying to write."

"Yes, but there's just something about a man," Dana said, swirling a strawberry in mousse sauce, "the way he wiggles his bare toes against your own, or blows little kisses between your shoulder blades, or—"

"Stop. Stop!" Ann laughed. "You're going to depress me if you remind me of all the stuff that I'm missing." She smiled. "It's much easier to be happy in ignorance."

"Okay," Dana agreed, pausing with her spoon halfway to her mouth. "Do you realize we have spent this entire meal without discussing business?"

"Lord, it was nice!" Ann grinned wider. "What's on your mind?"

"I wanted to tell you about this trip you're making to Miami Beach."

"That writers' group I'm speaking to?"

Dana nodded with her mouth full. "Gwynn in publicity has also been in contact with a Justin Frye there in Miami about autographing books at a chain of bookstores in the area."

"Is he the owner?"

Dana shook her head. "As I understand it he's some kind of public relations person for the chain.

The stores are called The Page Turner. There are three of them."

"Oh."

"Anyway, The Page Turner must be a big enough operation that they can hire a public relations firm to promote the business. When Gwynn was calling around the Miami area to stir up some publicity for you, the stores invited you to sign books."

Ann nodded, pulling out her appointment calendar from her purse, making notes to herself about how much time she could spare before she had to get home. She flipped through the pages, singling out the christening date of her godchild, Matthew, on a Sunday that seemed closer than the last time she had checked the appointment book. "How many extra days will it take?"

"Two at the most," Dana said. "Gwynn has penciled in the Friday and Saturday after the speech until you can confirm it with her."

"That doesn't give them much time. Will they be able to handle the advance publicity adequately on this short notice?"

Dana shrugged. "Gwynn will have to fill you in on the details, but apparently this Justin Frye person knows how to get results overnight. He knows a lot about market research and is known well enough in the area for having contacts where they count."

Ann nodded, writing in the dates. "Gwynn has arranged the hotel for me, I hope."

"Confirmed," Dana answered. "At the Fontaine-bleau Hilton."

"Lovely," Ann said, knowing if she fell flat on her

speech with the writers' group and nobody showed up for the autographing, a room at the Fontaine-bleau would make the trip worthwhile. She finished writing messages to herself in the fawn-colored appointment book, then looked up. "Anything else?"

Dana shook her head. "Nothing except I'm supposed to prod you about the last manuscript in your contract. Please have it to me by the end of the month."

"I have that under control," Ann said, frowning at a scribbled entry in the front of her appointment book. "Possile-que," she mumbled.

"What?"

"Possile-que," Ann said, looking up. "I wonder why I wrote that down."

"What does it mean?"

"Beats me," Ann said, turning the book around. "Oh. Here's some more. Now I remember." She smiled. "P-o-s-s-l-q. Persons of the Opposite Sex Sharing Living Quarters. It's a term that came out of the census."

"Why in the world would you write that down?"

"I write everything down." Ann smiled. "I have notebooks in my head, by my bed, in my car, my purse, briefcase, desk, refrigerator."

"Refrigerator?"

Ann lifted her shoulders and grinned. "The eggs and milk and cheese get bad if I'm away too long, so I keep manuscripts wrapped in plastic on the shelves to justify the electric bill while I'm not occupying the house."

Dana laughed. "You're kidding me."

"No. Actually, it's like a vault. I read once that some author stored carbons in the freezer in case the house burned. Until I send you the original, I keep the copy in the freezer in case anything drastic happens. It's like insurance."

"That makes sense." Dana shook her head. "But POSSLQ. How could you ever use that bit of information?"

"Easily, such as in the question, 'Is it possile-que that you could pour me some more wine?'"

After Dana had signed for the bill and each woman had indulged in one last sweet—a chocolate-covered strawberry from a tree of delectables the waiter placed on their table when he returned the signed check—Ann walked with her editor into the lobby of the Helmsley Palace Hotel. "Will you be heading back to Sixth Avenue?" Ann asked.

"I have a new author to phone this afternoon," Dana said, "to let her know we're accepting her book. I love making those calls. You can almost see the shock on their faces when you tell them their first book is going to be published."

Ann smiled, remembering her first book—some twenty titles ago.

"How are you going to spend the rest of your time in New York?" Dana asked.

"I thought I'd see a play tonight—*Amadeus*. I'm going to be reviewing a local theater production of the play in a few months and I thought it might be fun to make good or bad references to the New York production."

"Are you flying home tomorrow?"

"Late. I still have a few more appointments in the

morning. Which reminds me. I must call Gwynn
about Miami Beach before I leave. Will she be in her
office this afternoon?"

"I think so. You've got the number?"

Ann nodded, bundling into her lynx as she
watched the snow flurries falling outside. She shiv-
ered. "To think I was in the Caribbean with eighty-
degree temperatures two weeks ago! How do you
stand this cold?"

Dana pushed her fingers into her gloves. "We're
actually experiencing a break in the cold weather.
It's twenty-nine degrees today. Besides, you'll be in
the sunbelt again in a few days. Just look at the tan
you have already. That's indecent this time of year."

"I know." Ann hung her head as if she were being
banished to a corner for misbehavior. "I'm learning
how to suffer through all of this sunshine." She
grinned.

Her editor smiled with her. "Call me if I can do
anything for you while you're still in the city."

"Will do." Ann saluted. "Thanks for lunch. It
was—fattening. But that's the best kind."

Dana laughed and waved as she stepped through
the doors into the Helmsley Palace courtyard to hail
a taxi.

Ann dug her gloves out of her pockets and took
her time pulling them on. All she had to do was
make one phone call to Gwynn about this trip to
Miami Beach. The longer she delayed that, the
shorter the time she would have to spend alone in
her hotel room.

Ann enjoyed walking the icy streets of New York,

looking at strangers' faces as if one day she would run into someone she knew. No one seemed to notice her searching glances. Each was intent on reaching his destination with as little time as possible spent lingering in the cold.

The window displays between the Helmsley and her hotel held her attention briefly, but the cold pushed her forward through the streets, then finally past the doorman at the St. Regis. Ann smiled, said hello, and walked through the lobby to check for messages at the desk before taking the elevator to her floor.

Once in the room, she locked the door behind her, dumping her briefcase and gloves on the nearest chair, piling her fur coat on top of that, and unzipping her boots to give her toes the luxury of wiggling against the carpet.

Out of habit she stepped to the window and looked down on the busy New York traffic, watching the people huddled against the cold. She blew against the windowpane, creating a fog of frosty glass, then drew two dots for eyes, a nose, and a mouth, downturned.

Ann turned on the TV and flopped on the bed, trying not to notice how big, and empty, it was. She picked up the phone thinking she might as well phone Gwynn about the Florida arrangements.

Ann phoned the offices of her publisher, asking for her publicist, Gwynn, and was put on hold for five minutes. She glanced at the clock. It was barely two o'clock. That meant if she took as long as thirty minutes on the phone she would still have four hours to kill before she left the hotel to see *Amadeus*. If she went out of the hotel in search of dinner, alone, that would take up at least another hour. If it were a quiet restaurant and she carried along her notebook, she might be able to scribble notes to herself between courses and prolong the meal to an hour and a half. If she gave herself a leisurely hour to wash her hair and get ready, that would leave her only about an hour and thirty minutes with nothing to do. Maybe she would look through her address book and see if there were any New York names in it she might want to call.

"Yes—Gwynn," Ann said, smiling as she came on the line. "It's Ann Straus. How are you?"

"Fine. And how is our famous author? Dana said she was having lunch with you while you were in town this trip."

"I've been busy," she answered, overlooking all the free time she had today. "You're the one who's seen to that."

Gwynn laughed.

"I'm calling about Miami Beach. What are all these arrangements you've made for me to coincide with that group I'm going to be speaking to?"

"Wait a minute," Gwynn said, and Ann could imagine her jamming the phone against her ear with her shoulder while she twisted her swivel chair around and consulted the proper stack of material in her small office; Gwynn always had five things going at once. "Let me see. Yes. Here. What did Dana tell you?"

"That I'm booked into the Fontainebleau Hilton.

Thank you. I love that hotel. She said after the speech, you've scheduled an autograph session at The Page Turner bookstore."

"Three stores."

"Yes, she mentioned that. And something about a—oh, what was his name?"

"Justin Frye. He's a PR man for the stores. Has a dreamy voice on the phone."

Ann smiled. Everyone who knew her was always trying to play matchmaker. She could tell Gwynn had similar ideas in mind from the softening tone of her voice. "But can he get the proper pre-publicity accomplished between now and then?"

"Just tell me you can meet the dates we've tentatively suggested and I'll get on the phone to him this afternoon. He has a small operation there in Miami, but he handles some giant accounts."

"He doesn't have much time between now and then."

"Let him worry about that," Gwynn returned. "I'm not. If he's anything like he sounds over the phone, this man can conquer the world if he wants to. Persuasive is how I'd describe him."

"Aggressive is how he sounds."

"Uhm, maybe, in a business way. But he has a personal manner that cloaks his razor sharpness in cordiality, and you find yourself being talked into whatever he has in mind."

"Are you sure you've talked to this person only over the phone?"

Gwynn laughed. "Yes, and he's quite pleasant, too. Don't get that kind of idea."

"But I have to. That takes all the fun out of it if I can't imagine there's more to this person than meets the voice."

"If you want to do any imagining, he's the one to do it with. He has the most romantic voice."

"Spare me," Ann said, knowing from past experience that men with romantic voices had wives, kids, debts, and wore platform shoes. "All I care about is whether he can do his job adequately."

"This is the first time I've dealt with him," Gwynn admitted, "but I get the impression that 'adequate' is not a word you can pin on him. I think he gets results, probably with everything he touches."

"What have I got to lose?" Ann asked, thinking a few days at the Hilton might give her a chance to complete the ending to her latest novel.

"Absolutely nothing. The bookstores hired him, so they're the ones who should be concerned with his results."

"Okay. I'm ready for some sunshine anyway after this snow."

"This is not snow," Gwynn denied. "Snow is when the streets are impassable and commuters take up all the available hotel space and nobody moves."

"When you come from Louisiana, this is snow," Ann declared. "We get it only once every five or ten years in New Orleans. Schoolkids have to look it up in the encyclopedia."

Gwynn laughed. "I can't say I wouldn't mind some Florida sunshine now myself, especially when there might be someone like Justin Frye thrown in to share it with."

Ann shook her head. She had gotten her hopes up

in the past when meeting media people. In fact, anytime she traveled to a new area there was always that chance that "he"—whoever the right "he" for her might be—would be in that city. She had given up looking. "What do I have to do?"

"Nothing. Justin has made all the arrangements for you and will set up the times for the autograph sessions after I call him this afternoon. Just get to the Fontainebleau Hilton for your speech and he'll contact you."

"Sounds easy enough. Thanks for setting it all up for me."

"No problem," Gwynn assured her. "Someone as successful as you doesn't need to worry about details. I'm glad to do it for you. Let me know how it all turns out."

"I will," Ann promised and hung up.

Success, she thought. *What good is it when there is no one to share it with?*

A station ID interrupted the program on the TV network Ann had tuned in. Three o'clock. That meant she had at least two hours to kill.

Ann looked across the hotel room at the stack of reading material she had carried with her for spare moments like this. As busy as her life was, airports and airplanes were becoming the best places for her to catch up on her reading. She had been immersed in her work all this week and didn't feel like reading for business, and reading for pleasure in her business always turned into business.

She could try to put in a few pages on the novel. The problem there was she was coming up to the end, where all the loose pieces had to be tied together. It was also supposed to be a weepy, romantic kind of reunion for her main characters. Right now she felt anything but romantic. Weepy she could handle, but her readers wouldn't appreciate the kind of mood she was in right now.

What she needed were the warm rays of sunshine and miles of sand, and maybe a flesh-and-blood hero, who really knew what love was all about, to inspire the proper ending to the book. It was getting more and more difficult to keep creating new love scenes based on experience that bordered on ancient history. But damn it all, she'd just been too busy the last year and a half to take time out for her personal life. Besides, there had never really been anyone with whom she wanted to get intimate.

Ann plucked at a loose thread in the coverlet of the bed, recalling her idle remark to Dana at lunch. Sometimes it seemed as if her existence wouldn't be nearly so lonely if she could indulge in a casual affair.

Enough men asked—people she met on airplanes, people she met in restaurants and hotel lobbies, people who used the excuse of her book at the autograph parties to strike up a conversation. Companionship was never a problem. The opportunities sometimes overwhelmed her.

But the kind of companionship offered by the casual stranger wouldn't ease the loneliness. If anything it would add to it. What could be lonelier than a stolen moment with no forwarding address attached? Why should she invest time and the essence of her self in someone she would never see or hear from again?

How many of those names and phone numbers that had been thrust into her hands over the years were real? She just couldn't imagine herself indulging in a purely physical relationship. It was love or nothing for her. Lately, that had added up to a lot of nothing.

She looked at herself in the mirror and forced a smile. "I'm happy," she told her reflection. The image blurred.

"This is ridiculous!" She became firmer with herself, pounding her fist down on the bed, blinking the wetness out of her eyes. "I *am* happy!"

Soaking her head under the shower might clear away some of the mustiness of her thoughts. "I am happy. I am happy. I am happy," she grumbled, getting off the bed and stomping into the bathroom. If she said it out loud often enough, she might brainwash herself into believing it.

The problem was, she decided, as she turned on the taps in the tub, she had a couple of free hours on her hands for a change. That had been almost unheard of during the past few months. Free time gave her a chance to think, along with an unwanted opportunity to take stock of her situation as a single person. Once she threw herself into the work again she'd be fine.

The long hours and the demanding schedule was insulation against the emptiness of her life. She knew it better than anyone. But she was afflicted with a glamorous life that permitted no time for herself. She could be in Cancún one week and Luxembourg the next. Every once in a while she made short stops at home in New Orleans—long enough to type out another best seller; long enough to tell her friends what an exciting life she led; just long enough to feel the solitude creeping in again before it was time to jet elsewhere and hide her loneliness in an absurdly busy schedule.

Maybe she should have an affair, if for no other reason than research for a new book.

She wrinkled her nose at the thought. That wasn't her style. Besides, she wouldn't know how to go about it.

Chapter Two

$\mathcal{A}$nn unlocked the door to her hotel room. Another key, another hotel, another city.

This time Ann had felt more at home than she usually did when traveling. The Fontainebleau Hilton was one of her favorite hotels. She had stayed there often enough to make a few friends on the staff and this time had been given a corner suite at the south end of the property. The room was furnished with wicker and bamboo in an open, airy, tropical splash of warm, earthy colors. It was the same type of furniture she had chosen for her own home.

She bolted the door behind her and dropped her purse and keys on the vanity counter outside the bath. Slipping off her sandals, she stepped into the living/sleeping area.

At least the lights were good, something she didn't often find with her frequent traveling. Someone had provided a typewriter for her to use during her stay and she had already been able to dash off fifteen pages. When she was engrossed in her writing routine, Ann felt more confident and happy with her life. She liked to see progress in stacks of pages typed and ready for the mail. She was not the kind of writer who only liked to get the book written; the process of seeing words flowing onto a blank sheet of paper excited her.

But that was how she felt most days. Today was not one of them.

She had awakened at dawn, as if some built-in alarm had gone off in her head. Looking out the expanse of windows on two corners of her room from where she lay under a cocoon of covers, the sky appeared leaden and overcast. A rainy Sunday alone in Miami Beach would seriously jeopardize her plans to soak in the sun and hide behind the pages of a glossy magazine.

She had jumped out of bed for a closer look at the weather situation. By that time she was fully awake. Opening the door onto her balcony, she was greeted with a warm breeze from the ocean, where the fingers of dawn were spreading out from the horizon. Ann had glanced at the clock then and seen the time.

She stepped out on the balcony, looking southeast, where distant lights were moving on the horizon. The cruise ships were steaming back to port, all in a proper row, preparing to disembark one shipload of vacationers and take on another group for a week or two in the Caribbean.

Some gulls were crying on the sand, and she could see a few people taking advantage of the early hour to walk or jog along the shore. As the seconds passed by, the dawn sky promised a perfect day.

Ann dashed back into the room, hurriedly dressed in shorts and sun top, splashed water on her face, and slipped into her sandals. This was her favorite time of day. A long walk along the beach, before the heat toasted the sands and everyone and their mothers-in-law populated the strip, would clear her mind and energize her enough to force her to sit down at the typewriter for a few hours. By the time she put in enough hours punching the keys, she would deserve a soak in the sun and would still have nearly the entire day ahead of her.

The walk had been good for her, stretching her muscles, freeing her mind, building up her appetite. She had walked a good two miles along the strip. By the time she had come back to the Fontainebleau's beach the attendants were setting up the orange-and-white-striped huts beside the redwood platforms next to the ocean. Two small catamarans with rainbow-hued sails had been dragged onto the beach, poised for launching in the surf.

The sun was at its most glaring angle and the tide was rolling in. Ann's legs began to sting from the sun; she hadn't taken time to smear on tanning lotion before she had left the room.

The Beach Broiler on the edge of the Hilton's lagoon-style pool was open and Ann stopped long enough to order a fresh-fruit breakfast. Then she had walked into the hotel's drugstore to buy a collection of the Sunday papers, which she had spread out over the bed and leisurely read during the next two hours. The typewriter remained silent.

Now it was dusk and she hadn't written a word.

Ann stared at the typewriter, thrusting her hand into the pocket of her shorts for the few seashells she had picked up on this evening's stroll along the shore. Miami Beach was far from the best beach to collect shells. The two small ones she had picked up were marked with brown and white splotches. She could already tell that when they dried out the richness of the patterns would disappear.

The red button on her phone was lit up. Ann pounced on it; someone had left a message. She called down to the front desk and gave her name and room number.

The message was from Justin Frye. Ann had the girl read it twice. "Wanted to take you to dinner, but assume you have other plans. Will contact you early this week."

"Didn't he leave a number where he could be reached?" Ann asked, thinking company for dinner would be nice after spending the entire day alone.

"No, I'm sorry, he didn't."

"Thank you," Ann said, hanging up the phone and picking up the thick Miami phone directory.

Her fingers raced down the listing of Fryes, but there were too many beginning with the initial J. for her to make a successful guess. Besides, if he had really wanted to be reached he would have left a number. He was probably relieved that he had been unable to reach her. Leaving his name and the brief message would be adequate proof for him that he had attempted to do some business socializing with her on a day that most people considered their day off.

Ann glanced at her typewriter. It was not beckoning to her. The idea of another meal alone held little appeal also. Maybe she would just order room service and go over the points she wanted to cover in her speech tomorrow. That would take all of fifteen minutes, with revisions—twenty, tops. She had made the same speech before with enough variations to suit each particular occasion. Usually, she would finish the speech quickly and her question-and-answer session would fill up the rest of her allotted time, and then some.

Ann sank back against the bed pillows and asked herself: *if I could have anything in the world right now or be doing anything at all, what would make me happiest?*

"I don't know why I always ask that question," she said out loud. "The answer's always the same. A man. Pure and simple." Right now she'd settle for someone at the other end of the telephone, anyone whom she could call up to ask, "Guess what I did today?" Someone who could in turn tell her what he did with his Sunday.

Enough of this wallowing in self-pity, she decided, forcing her mind out of the rut it seemed to linger in lately. She would take an hour getting ready for dinner and have an elegant meal by herself. Hadn't she proved in the last few years she didn't need anyone, least of all a man? Tonight was one of those times when she would prove it again, to herself.

The speech the next day went smoothly. She was able to throw in some witticisms that had the audience laughing and smiling long after the last question was asked. Even better for Ann was the feeling that the information she had given in her whimsical speech would be beneficial to those few in the audience who seriously wanted to write the same way Ann Straus did. Two people in particular had come up to her after the speech to ask more involved personal questions relating to the kind of writing they were currently doing.

Ann smiled and gave them answers to the things they asked and delightedly accepted their offer of lunch. She loved writing and enjoyed talking about it even more. It was seldom she could talk with someone who understood the love/hate affair she had with her typewriter. And it was always inspiring to hear her ideas on writing bouncing off of eager listeners.

She had returned to her hotel room late in the afternoon and typed out an entire chapter. She worked through dinner, but didn't mind because the late lunch had left her satisfied. Besides, Justin Frye had missed her when he'd called again and left no number where he could be reached in return. This night she didn't want to eat alone, not even in her room. The day's work had been satisfying, and a night of mindless television would be sufficient company.

She was beginning to think Justin Frye was all talk and no action. He probably liked giving the impression he was too busy to call more than once a day, and if you missed his call it was your loss, not his. Ann could do without that kind of arrogance. If he talked with Gwynn he should have known her speech was today. It would be so easy to leave a number where he could be reached. Or he could take time out from his busy schedule to phone her after hours.

But he was probably the kind of man who got down to his serious business—of playing—after hours. That she could do without, as well.

Ann spent the evening watching television after ordering an ice-cream dessert from room service. It was well after midnight when she drifted off to sleep, the television still blaring its message all during the night.

An alarm was buzzing in her head.

No, not an alarm, the phone on the bedside table nearest her ear. Ann picked up the phone. A wake-up call, she decided.

"You're a hard lady to reach," the voice said.

Ann frowned. Had someone at the desk tried to reach her earlier and she hadn't heard the phone? She sat up in bed, looking at the clock. Ten A.M. Then she remembered she hadn't left a wake-up call.

"It all depends on who's trying to reach me," she answered, thinking this had to be the imperial Justin Frye. He didn't waste time with preliminaries. He just started in with a reprimand.

"This is Justin Frye," he confirmed. "Didn't you get my messages?"

"All two of them," she answered, disturbed now that she had slept so late and had to wake up to this kind of confrontation. "You could have left a phone number where you could be reached and I would have acknowledged them."

"Oh, Lord," he swore, "a temperamental author."

"Not temperamental, but tired. I'll have you know you woke me up. I was up until very late last night. . . ." She paused. Let him draw his own conclusions about that. "And I haven't had time to put on my Ms. Nice Guy act—not that I think you deserve it."

"My mistake," he answered.

Was it ever! Ann thought, wondering how Gwynn, in New York, had ever gotten the impression this was the persuasive whiz kid of public relations in Miami.

"Sorry," he apologized. "Sugar always makes things nicer in the morning."

"Not if you don't have a coffee cup to put it into," she retorted.

"Shall I buy you one?" he asked, and she thought he might be grinning.

"No, thank you," she said. "By the time I could get ready for a cup of coffee it would be nearly lunchtime."

"Lunch, then?"

"I'm busy," she lied.

"Then dinner," he said. "I have some things we need to go over before the autographing. That's why I've been trying to reach you."

"Look," Ann said, softening her tone to match his own less demanding one, "I'm not thinking straight yet. You just woke me up," she reminded him, "and I haven't had time to remember what I have or do not have to do today. Call me back in an hour and I'll let you know." Before he could reply she hung up, smiling to think she had just fit his image of being the temperamental author.

Precisely one hour later, after Ann had showered, washed her hair, and dressed in a striped pair of flared seersucker shorts and matching blouse, the phone rang.

"Miss Straus," said the voice, one which Ann would have recognized immediately as belonging to Justin Frye, except this time he sounded suave and sexy.

"Yes?" she answered, still somewhat belligerent since she had allowed him to provoke her earlier over practically nothing.

"Justin Frye here," he said, as if they had not spoken previously.

"Yes?" she said again.

"I wondered if you might be free for dinner," he said, continuing in a voice that was beginning to show Ann how Gwynn had been duped by his buddy-buddy nature. He did have a lovely voice.

She had nothing to do. "I'll check my appointment book," she answered nevertheless. "Hold on." She held the phone away from her and opened the drawer to the night stand, pulling out the thick Miami telephone directory and flipping the pages within hearing of the receiver. "What's today?" she asked, coming back on the line.

"Tuesday," he answered, "the thirtieth day of November, eleven-forty-seven A.M. Eastern Standard Time."

"Oh, here it is," she answered. "I was looking at the wrong week. This didn't look like it was the Yucatán."

He didn't answer. She took that as a signal she

couldn't try his patience much longer. "No, I'm not busy."

"Excellent," he said. "There are some wonderful restaurants there in the Fontainebleau."

"Yes, I know. I've stayed here before." She had also sampled the restaurants on her own since Saturday. It would be nice to see something else of the city and sample the cuisine available outside the hotel.

"Good. Then I won't feel badly making you eat alone."

"What do you mean?" Wasn't he just now in the middle of inviting her to dinner? What had she missed?

"I just noted a previous engagement in *my* appointment book for this evening." She heard the rustle of pages over the phone. "Yes. One of those unavoidably boring dinners. I can't see how I'll manage to get out of it."

"Oh," Ann said, an unexplainable pang of loneliness throwing clouds over her sunny-spirited day. Even if they had fought each other and ended up with indigestion, it would have been preferable to the boredom of traveling alone that she had come to experience so much lately.

"Actually," he continued, "there's really not much reason why we need to get together before the autographing. You've probably done these things hundreds of times before without coaching. I'll pick you up on Friday morning around nine o'clock. I have some ads placed in this week's newspapers, and Gwynn . . . By the way, is she as cute in person as she sounds over the phone?"

"Not knowing your definition of cute," she answered, "I wouldn't know."

"Anyway, Gwynn sent me all the promotional material, displays, and book jackets we'll need at the three Page Turners."

"Oh," Ann said again, thinking that at this stage, disagreeable company would be better than none at all. He could have left that information in a phone message and not even bothered to call and get her hopes up for a dinner engagement.

She bit her tongue to keep from telling him what she thought of him. He'd already branded her as temperamental; she didn't need to strengthen that reputation.

"I just wanted to welcome you to Miami Beach," he remarked, ending his speech.

"Thank you," she said, clenching her teeth to avoid adding, "for nothing."

"If you need anything while you're in town," he said, "don't hesitate to call me."

He would be the last person she turned to for help. "That's generous of you," she said, without pointing out that he had still not told her how to get in touch with him, probably deliberately. "What if I decide I want a bull elephant to ride on through the city streets? Can you deliver?"

"Possibly," he answered. "Could be good publicity, particularly if there's real incentive in the stunt. Do you have any Godiva tendencies?"

"Crave them," she returned. "Chocolates are my weakness. How did you guess?"

His end of the phone was silent for a few seconds.

"Sorry about dinner," he said.

The man creates fairy tales, she thought. He didn't seem the type to believe in them. "Me, too," she answered, knowing that was true.

"Perhaps another night?" he asked.

"Yes," she answered, thinking she had nothing to do tomorrow or Wednesday evening.

"Maybe we could share a quick hamburger after the autographing."

"Maybe," she answered, wondering what other invitations he planned to dangle in front of her.

"I'll call you on Friday morning," he said, "to let you know where you can meet me."

"How about here in my hotel room?" she suggested, always uneasy about meeting a stranger face to face beneath the second palm tree near the third elevator in the main lobby of hotels.

"What's your room number?"

She told him.

"That's in the south section," he said, displaying a thorough knowledge of the hotel property. "No sense in both of us trudging all that distance to the main lobby. I'll call you on Friday morning and you can meet me in the lobby."

She decided she could wait.

Ann spent the remainder of the week watching old movies on TV, guessing at the answers to the ridiculous questions on the game shows, writing a little and excusing the low output by the lack of a schedule (she always worked best when there was too much to do at once), and spending long hours walking the beach. The beach was the part she enjoyed the most. The sand against her bare feet and the wind whipping at her hair set her mind free to wonder why she couldn't form a decent relationship with a decent man.

She didn't want much, just someone who was warm, caring, well educated, well read (all of her books, naturally), handsome enough to be the envy of other women, well traveled, self-assured, someone who was making more money than she was—not because she wanted to die a millionairess, but because she needed someone dynamic and powerful enough to challenge her, and she equated that with more money.

Where in the world was that man? When in heaven would she meet him? Did he even exist?

She kept walking and thinking, every once in a while picking up a small shell that interested her. She dodged the seaweed and let the surf splash against her feet.

After every walk she would return to her room, give half an effort to writing a page or two, occasionally succeeding, but more often giving up in frustration at the amount of time on her hands that wasn't being put to productive use. She just couldn't work adequately when she had too much time on her hands.

She needed self-imposed deadlines, obstacles hurled in her path to make her find the hours to work. Deadlines forced the words onto the page. She had written more in thirty minutes on a bus trip to the ruins of Chichén Itzá than she was doing now with thirty hours in a day at her disposal. She wrote more in airports and waiting rooms than she did with the borrowed typewriter sitting quietly on the hotel desk, because she had known there was a deadline with her flight leaving in thirty minutes or an hour.

She would be glad when this autographing was finished so that she could run home and settle into her routine again in familiar surroundings. During the last five years she had been so devoted to her career that she had forgotten how to enjoy the time that was left over.

Friday morning eventually dawned somewhere between the late-late show and the early-early movie. Ann was up before eight o'clock, and ended up sitting a little anxiously beside the phone thirty minutes before Justin Frye was scheduled to call. New places and new people always made her a bit nervous until she could grasp the total situation and find a friendly face.

She didn't expect that to be Justin Frye's face, either.

Precisely at nine the phone rang. *At least he's punctual,* she decided, reluctantly giving him points for not keeping her in suspense over whether he had changed his mind about escorting her personally to the bookstores.

She let the phone ring two more times.

"Miss Straus?"

She hesitated. What would he do if she said she was the maid? "Yes?"

"Justin Frye here. Did I wake you?"

She glanced at the clock. Nine A.M., as he had arranged. What did he think she did? Lie around in bed and eat chocolates all day? "Not at all," she said, straightening her back. "I've been up for hours." One hour and ten minutes to be exact. When a man told her nine o'clock, she was going to be ready. Her time was valuable to her and she treated it equally so with the men she met, although she wasn't certain Justin Frye deserved such a consideration. She should have told him she had just gotten in from a wild night on the town, then kept him waiting—for at least an hour.

However, she was getting stir-crazy and was ready to leave the room—even if she had to meet with him.

"Do you need a few more minutes to powder your nose?"

Powder my nose? she thought. What archives did he crawl out of? The only kind of powder she felt was appropriate in this case was gunpowder, preferably placed with a short fuse somewhere in the near vicinity of Justin Frye.

"I've been ready for quite a while," she said, "waiting for you."

"Oh? Am I late?" He paused and she imagined him checking his watch. "It's straight up nine right now."

Damn the man! She fumed. He knew he was right on time. And damn the man for getting her to admit she'd been sitting on the edge of her chair waiting for someone to rescue her from this sybaritic hotel room.

"Where are you?" She changed the subject.

"Right at the head of the escalators," he told her, "wearing a navy suit and tie."

How plain. He'd stand out like a crayon in a box of lead pencils. "What, no flower in the lapel?"

"Will a fern frond do?" he asked.

She suppressed a laugh.

"There's a plant right next to the phone here. I'll stick that in my buttonhole so you won't miss me."

"All right," she answered. "I'll be there in about five minutes. I'm wearing a lavender sweater with ribbons running through the weave, tan slacks, carrying a briefcase and my hair is dark blond, light brown, take your pick."

"Blond sounds nice."

Ann smiled. She liked to stretch a point, too, and consider herself blond. "Five minutes," she said again and hung up, wondering what it was that had set her off on the wrong foot with Justin Frye in the first place.

She made a mad dash to the bathroom, rebrushed her teeth and reapplied her lipstick, took one last look in the mirror at her casually curling hair, then gathered up her keys and briefcase before leaving the room.

It was a fine winter day, with a temperature in the mid-fifties, reminding her of what spring would feel like in a few months back home. But according to the morning *Miami Herald,* New Orleans expected a high of thirty-seven today.

Even without the ridiculous palm frond in the same pocket as a silk handkerchief, Ann's attention would have been caught by the man standing at the head of the escalators. He would be difficult to miss standing over six feet tall. Out of the corner of her eye she noticed she wasn't the only woman eyeing him with interest.

His hair was cut in layers and lay against his neck.

It was a wind-blown style that made Ann curious to run her fingers through and rumple. His eyes were the sharpest gray she had ever seen. They were direct, catching her blue eyes and singling her out from the crowd before she had even set foot on the escalator. It made her nervous and she hesitated while stepping on the moving stairway, feeling like a child for taking so long to position her feet on the step and not the crack.

She was smiling as she met him, holding out her hand in greeting before she had stepped off the escalator. He took her hand in his and the contact of his solid male strength against her small hand excited her. She forgot about the escalator and stumbled at its end, tripping forward to be caught in his arms and steadied while she laughed at her graceless introduction and blushed.

"I would have known you without the fern," she said, plucking the frond from his pocket.

"I would have known you, too," he admitted, "or wanted to enough to make certain we met."

Ann smiled, thinking: *Flattery, my dear sir, just might get you everywhere.* How had Gwynn guessed that he could be such a charmer without even seeing him? Ann wondered how she had managed to get off on the wrong foot with him and blow the chance of dinner with him earlier in the week.

"Have you eaten breakfast?" he asked, still retaining his grasp on her hand.

"I never eat breakfast, unless I've been up for hours."

"I thought you'd been waiting for me 'for hours,'" he reminded her.

"Oh, longer than that," she said, smiling sweetly as she evaded his perceptive comment.

He accepted her parrying with a nod of his head and the slightest of smiles, then released her hand and asked, "Shall we go? I have a doorman watching my car at the main entrance."

Ann let him lead her through the lobby of the sprawling resort hotel, past the registration desk, which was beginning to draw a line of people waiting for rooms, and out the glass doors where his aging but acceptable Porshe was parked.

During the drive to the bookstore, Ann didn't talk much. She played the part of the tourist, craning her neck to look out the windows at the hundreds of hotels they drove past along the strip. She hoped her silence gave him the impression of intelligent preoccupation with her thoughts. In reality she was afraid to say anything for fear of being bested, again, verbally by Justin Frye.

He was one of the most quick-witted men she had met in a long while. The problem with that quick wit was it didn't always play to her advantage.

At The Page Turner, a cozy boutique-style bookshop with a pull-up-a-chair-and-browse atmosphere, Justin introduced Ann to the manager and assistants and then stepped back while they talked with her.

Readers clutching Ann Straus books in their hands clustered around her from the moment the doors of the store opened. Ann glanced up between signatures to smile in surprise at Justin Frye. Whatever preparation he had done, he had done well for this promotion. She had never seen so many of her readers in one place the way they were crowding in around her this morning.

When she looked for him she didn't see him. It surprised her even more that he could arrange for such a phenomenal party and then disappear. Did he always have such confidence that the things he set in motion were so well arranged that he could leave them and know that they would snowball into a success?

Three hours and writer's cramp later, Ann closed the last copy of her book that the store had in stock and looked up to see Justin Frye watching her from across the room.

A sensuous feeling, as of a fine Champagne settling over her senses, stirred within her. Timing. The man had it down to a science.

Her speculative stare was broken when he made his way across the room and leaned down to whisper in her ear. "I thought they'd never run out of books. Do you realize we're an hour over schedule?"

She shook her head. The time had passed too quickly answering questions the readers had for her about where her ideas came from and who the dreamy character was that the last hero was based on.

"I have sandwiches in the car. You'll have to eat on the way to the next store, so I guess I can't even take you to lunch."

Ann picked up her briefcase and told the managers good-bye as Justin pushed her out of the bookshop and pointed her in the direction of the car.

Chapter Three

For Ann, signing books at the second Page Turner store was even more exhausting. It was a Friday afternoon and the women who read her books were beginning to get off work for the weekend, stopping in the store on their way home to have Ann Straus autograph their books. Ann had to admit Justin Frye had done an excellent job arranging her promotional autographing.

Too excellent, she thought, as she shook out her hand, trying to loosen up her stiff joints. She hadn't written so much in longhand since the first book she had written years ago. The hamburger she had wolfed down on the drive between the two stores had given her indigestion. Thoughts of how large a crowd Saturday's signing would draw after this afternoon's group didn't make her feel any more relaxed.

All she wanted to do was get back to her hotel room, kick off her shoes, and stretch out on the bed.

But when Justin Frye ushered her toward the door and asked, "Where would you like to go for dinner?," she didn't rail at him for assuming she would have dinner with him. She smiled and said, "Anywhere you say." Then she justified her docile response to this domineering man by telling herself she was too tired to argue—this time.

As if he read her mind, he put his arm along the back of the seat before he turned the key in the ignition and looked at her. "You look exhausted."

"Thank you, and you look beautiful, too."

"Temper, temper," he cautioned.

"Sorry," she retorted, glaring at him. "But I happen to be exhausted. You run a tight schedule."

"I was going to warn you."

"When?"

"All those days ago when I tried to invite you to dinner with me. But you were being so finicky about your damned schedule I decided you didn't deserve to be forewarned."

"Nice of you," she grated.

"Hey!" He shrugged, the beginnings of a grin altering the line of his lips. "I'm a nice guy. I keep trying to tell you that."

She rolled her eyes toward the roof of the car, wondering why she had decided to have dinner with him. It would be so easy this time to tell him she just wanted room service and sleep. Maybe she should change her mind and tell him she decided to go on a starvation diet starting now.

He seemed to understand her better than she knew herself at this moment. Reaching up, he tugged at a strand of her hair and said, "It's just after five now. Why don't I drop you off, let you get some rest, and pick you up around eight-thirty for dinner?"

"What? No hamburgers on the drive back to the hotel?"

"If you want a snack—"

She shook her head. "Spare me if it's anything like lunch."

"We could eat earlier than eight-thirty if you're that hungry."

"No." She smiled. "I like to build up a huge appetite." Let him worry about the bill when she went through appetizer, salad, soup, wine, entrée, and dessert. Maybe she'd even order an after-dinner liqueur. That should make up for all the past nights he'd had a chance to take her out and hadn't.

"Eight-thirty, then," he confirmed, stopping the car in front of the hotel and leaning across her to open the door without getting out.

She glanced at him and before she could form the words, he was adding, "And I'll pick you up at *your* room." She frowned. Now what was his intention? Did he think that after such a short acquaintance with her he was going to invite himself into her room—and possibly her bed—as easily as a snake climbed an apple tree?

"I'll be ready," she replied, planning to have her purse and keys in hand when she opened the door to him.

Rest and a shower perked Ann up and increased

her appetite, justifying her threat to Justin Frye. She was ready by eight, just in case he should try to catch her off guard with an early arrival.

He knocked on the door exactly at eight-thirty, making Ann wonder if he had been standing out in the hall for the past five minutes watching the second hand on his watch.

"Are you ready?" he asked, acting as if he didn't even care what color carpet lay behind the door to her room.

With keys and purse in hand, Ann stepped into the hall and closed the door behind her. "Absolutely starving," she promised him.

He took her to the Dockside Terrace Restaurant at the marina, where they sat at an intimate table for two in fan-backed peacock-throne chairs. Ann felt right at home amidst the tropical-style furnishings, but wasn't certain whether the decor suited Justin Frye.

As she watched him tasting the wine he had ordered, she decided there would probably be very few situations or places where Justin Frye would be out of place.

Ann thanked the waiter for filling her glass with wine and picked it up by the stem, swirling the contents gently as she studied Justin Frye across the table. He looked up and caught her eye. She smiled. "Tell me about Justin Frye. Who is he?"

He toasted his glass to hers. "Cheers." He tasted the wine before answering. "Just a man."

Just? she thought. After seeing the result of "just" this man's work today, she didn't think it could be as simple as that.

"What do you want to know?" he asked.

Ann put an elbow on the table and ran a finger over her chin. "Tell me about your business. How long have you been in public relations?"

"God!" He laughed. "That would be dating me."

She lifted her brows. He didn't look too ancient. Forties probably, but early or late she couldn't say.

"I used to write for one of the suburban newspapers here in Florida." He smiled in response to her surprise at this information. "I have a good idea of the obstacles you're up against as a novelist. I still write."

"What kind of writing?" she asked, always pleased to discuss her craft with another writer.

"Primarily brochures for the agency. I keep telling myself I'm going to take a few months off at some point, find a deserted island, and turn out the Great American Novel."

"It doesn't work that way," she argued, "at least not for me it doesn't—not that I'm writing Great American Novels," she qualified, "but I have to write every day in bits and pieces. I don't know how to handle big blocks of time at once—probably because I've never had the luxury," she added as an afterthought to herself and picked up her glass of wine to take another sip. "How did you make the switch from newspaper writing to public relations?"

He traced his finger around the rim of his glass. "Luck, I suppose," he answered, "in a negative way."

"How?" she prompted.

"I was fired from the newspaper, and there was an

opening in an ad agency during the time I was job-hunting."

Ann wondered what he could have done to justify losing his job. Whatever it was wouldn't surprise her. In the little time she had been with him she had come to see him as a leader, one who was a professional in the game of life. He saw an opportunity and seized the moment, taking time later to think about the results of his actions and learn from them, good or bad. Amateurs, on the other hand, thought about the moments offered them too long and lost them.

"But I thought you were the head of your own agency."

"I am now. One of the biggest accounts at the agency I was with decided to pull their business. They talked with me, saying they liked what I had done for them and told me if I wanted to go into business for myself they'd be my first account. And here I am."

Not only could he woo women at a distance, like he seemed to have done over the phone with Gwynn, but he could command the respect of giant companies, as well. What was it about him that made her like and dislike him at the same time?

Dynamic, yes. She would be the first to admit it. Handsome, true. It had been a long while since she had sat in a restaurant with a man whom she knew other women would envy her for. But likable? That didn't fit.

"What about your family?" Ann asked, adopting a phrase that usually revealed whether a man was married or not. It gave him a chance to say, "Oh, the little woman was my high-school sweetheart—a side-line cheerleader when I was a star football player. We live in a nice house with a swimming pool and a second mortgage and the three children all attend private schools."

"I have two teen-aged daughters, thirteen."

"Twins?"

He shook his head. "One's adopted."

"Oh," she said, leaning against the fan-backed chair with her glass of wine in hand. Indirect tactics hadn't given her the answer she wanted about his marital status. She'd have to try a more direct approach.

"Doesn't your wife get upset when you have to take other women out to dinner?"

"We've been divorced nearly five years," he answered.

Ann leaned forward again. She wanted to ask about any girl friends, but didn't. Five years. That would account for his car's vintage—pre-divorce.

"What about you?" he asked. "Are you married?"

She sat back again, giving him her Lady of Mystery smile. "I thought you were supposed to know all about me."

"Uhm," he admitted, sipping some wine, "I should, and normally I would have researched you thoroughly, but I didn't even read the jacket on your latest book."

"It's a good thing you're no longer a newspaper reporter."

"Why is that?"

"If there's one thing I can't stand, it's someone who shows up to interview me and doesn't know the first thing about me."

He nodded. "That's a bad sign for an interviewer. But I'm not here to write your life story. I only invited you to dinner."

Ann smiled as it occurred to her what it was she was beginning to enjoy about this evening with Justin Frye. For once she wasn't being treated as the famous romance novelist. He wasn't hanging in awe on to her every word, trying to impress her with his knowledge of her work. He was simply taking her at face value, treating her like a person. It reminded her of the days when she hadn't been a success, before anyone knew or cared who Ann Straus was.

In return, she didn't feel as if she had to be on her guard, protecting each word that came out of her mouth to be certain it was interpreted correctly according to the image her publisher had gradually built around her.

"But I will admit," he said, his eyes hard for her to read because of the shadows falling across his face, "that now that I have met you I'm going to read your new book."

She turned up her nose at him. "I don't think it's your style. What do you read, anyway?"

"Anything I can get my hands on, when I find the time."

"Uhm." She nodded. "I have trouble myself picking up a book and finishing it these days. It's quicker sometimes for me to try to write one than read one, my time is so limited by my traveling."

The waiter arrived with a dish of fried zucchini

and cocktail sauce, which he set in the middle of the table between them.

"Try one," Justin said, pushing the bowl slightly in her direction.

Ann picked up one of the crisply fried pieces of squash and dipped it in the sauce. "Delicious," she admitted, reaching for another. "But don't think you can fill me up on this and expect me not to eat a full-course meal besides." She gave him a wicked glance that said she could eat a truck right now.

"I could use a few expenses against my income tax," he said, their hands brushing as he reached for a zucchini slice. "So order one of everything if that's what you want. The sky's the limit."

"Funny," she said, beginning to feel light-headed from the wine on a near empty stomach, but loving the feeling enough after the long day to accept another glass of wine. "I thought we were having seafood. But tell me what kinds of books you like to read best." She swirled another zucchini slice into the sauce, wanting to learn more about this man by the books he chose.

"I like Irving Wallace and Arthur Hailey, sometimes John D. MacDonald. When I'm reading non-fiction I lean toward political literature."

"Oh," she said. That was a subject she was in awe of but felt she wasn't knowledgeable enough to discuss. Now what would they talk about? "Do you enjoy your job?"

"For the most part," he answered.

"Do you always expect to be doing this?"

He looked across the table at her. "Do you?"

"Writing, yes," she answered. "Not necessarily

always this kind of book. I write travel articles, too, you know."

"No," he answered. "I didn't."

She waved a zucchini slice at him and took another sip of wine. "You really should have read my book jacket. At least it would have told you that."

"I'll rectify that tonight. I promise."

"You don't have to read my book." She shook her head, wondering when the waiter was going to come back to refill her wineglass. Justin noticed her glass was empty and took the bottle from the wine cooler to refill the glass. "Thank you," she told him. She continued, "It's not your style of reading from what you just told me."

"I read everything. Why wouldn't I like this, especially now that I've met you?"

"Too mushy," she answered, eyeing the remaining zucchini in the bowl and wondering how greedy she would look if she kept eating it. "Granted, I do have male readers, but I write for a female audience. However," she said, propping her elbow on the table and resting her chin on her hand as she went on to say something she'd been meaning to tell someone for some time, "I do think men could learn a lot from a book like mine."

"In what way?" he asked, his own eyes just as intent on the remaining zucchini.

"Lovemaking," she answered, deciding she wanted the zucchini. And glancing down at her glass, she decided she needed more wine as well.

Justin Frye was staring at her now. The race to see who would get the most zucchini was forgotten. "What are you writing? Porno?"

"You see!" she said, shaking a zucchini slice at him before nibbling at it. "That's exactly what I mean! Men. That's how you all think. Sex. Pornography. But a woman doesn't see it that way."

His eyebrows went up, but he kept his mouth shut as he refilled her glass.

"If you took time to read a book about love and romance, like mine, for example, written by a woman with a woman's feelings, you might learn something about what women want and how they like to be treated," she concluded, stuffing the rest of the zucchini into her mouth and swallowing it, a signal that she had made her point and the subject was closed.

"Sex manuals," he commented.

"We're not talking sex," she corrected.

"What, then?"

"Love. Romance. It doesn't always have to end up with s-e-x. Not that it can't, as well, but there's a lot more to love and romance and what a woman needs from a man than a bed."

"Sandy beaches are nice, too," he suggested, "so are kitchen floors and bearskin rugs and—"

Ann waved her hand at him and sat back against the fan chair. "Spare me the details of your teen-age acrobatics. You're missing the point."

He shook his head. "I wasn't reminiscing about my youth," he said, his eyes darkening.

"Oh," she said, suddenly breathless. She must remember she was dealing with a creative person here. If his lovemaking was anything like the rest of what she was learning about him, it would be anything but routine. And she had to admit that making love on a moonlit beach was a fantasy she'd like to try out for real one day.

The bearskin rug had possibilities, especially if a roaring fire went with it, and a light snowfall outside a Swiss chalet . . . a bottle of wine . . . Justin Frye . . .

"What point am I missing?"

"Point?" She blinked, trying to remember what they had been talking about. She looked down at the wine in her glass and set the drink down.

"About what I'm supposed to learn from reading one of your books."

"Not you specifically, just men in general."

"Maybe you should give me an example," he prompted, taking the last strip of zucchini from the bowl.

Ann blinked again and glanced down at the wine-glass, trying to bring it into sharp focus. She shouldn't have drunk so much so quickly on an empty stomach.

The waiter arrived with two bowls of conch chowder and saved Ann from replying. Right now she couldn't even remember the plot of her last published book, much less an example of what a man could learn from it. The book she had been signing all day long had been written a year ago. And the one that she was trying to finish wouldn't be a good one to comment on because he wouldn't be able to read that one for at least six months.

How had she allowed her mouth to run away with this subject, anyway? She was just testing a theory she had never even voiced before. All she knew was when she wrote she created the ideal hero on paper, simply because she had never run into him in the flesh. Her writing expounded on her search for the perfect man. "If you had read my books," she said, deciding a vague reply was as intelligent as she could sound right now after all that wine, "or even my book jacket, you would know what I mean. A lot of myself comes through in my writing."

"It would have to," he agreed. "Writing has to be one of the most revealing professions around."

She nodded. "Don't read my book. You won't like it."

He looked at her and smiled, taking that as a dare. He tasted his soup, then watched while she tasted hers. "Where do you get your ideas?" he asked after a while.

"Everywhere," she answered. "I tell everyone that once they've met me, no one's safe—not even you."

"I think I'd be pretty dull material for one of your books if they're as racy as I've heard they are."

She put on her Mysterious Lady mask again and smiled. "You wouldn't be dull by the time I finished with you—on paper, of course. I play 'what if?' games a lot. So don't believe everything you read."

"Didn't you just tell me that I should do exactly that, and take notes in the process to learn something about how to handle a woman the way a woman wants to be treated?"

Ann pretended to concentrate on eating her soup without spilling it to avoid answering him. Was it just because she was beginning to have too much to drink, or was it the man himself who made it difficult for her to find a way to respond to his retorts? She looked at him while he was preoccupied with his own bowl of cheesy conch soup and decided it was a little of both.

With his wind-blown brown hair he wouldn't make a bad hero. He certainly had the looks for it, judging by the couple of glances she had noticed other women giving him tonight. She'd even admit to herself, but not him, that he had the lean grace of a well-cared-for body that she respected in a man. Tall, too. She was tired of dwarfs who only came up to her shoulders when she was in heels and made her always feel as if she should pick them up to kiss them good-night.

She wanted a man's approval and understanding. A man who was as perceptive as Justin Frye would be able to read a lot into her personality by taking one of her books to heart.

She had handed her books to dates in the past who thought her writing was nice and impressive. But no one saw the messages in her stories; they didn't realize she had handed them a blueprint to her heart when she had given them a book. They saw it as something on a slightly higher level than a party favor. And based on the superficial comments they gave her, most barely read more than the book jacket and first and last page.

Ann sighed. She didn't know why she kept thinking that one of her imagined heroes was going to come to life and step out of the pages of her book one day. Her writing was just too idealistic. She should simply face the fact that anyone who had to follow the romance guidelines revealed in her writing wouldn't have any initiative of his own. She didn't want a carbon copy of herself. She wanted someone who would be able to lead her.

She played with her soup. She should face the fact that she didn't know what she wanted. That was probably why she was successful; her books were a continual search for the ideal romantic situation and the perfect mate. One of these days she was going to have to realize such a fantasy didn't exist. She was going to have to learn to work with the real-life material at hand.

"This is a lovely restaurant," she said, craning her neck to look at the birdcages hanging from the ceiling and admiring the mix of tropical plants tucked into corners. "The food's terrific, too. Do you come here often?"

He smiled, knowing she was deliberately changing the subject. "It's a popular place on weekends, when all the cruise ships come into port. The crews know this is the in place to come and it's hard to find a free table."

"I can see why," she said, wondering how long she could draw out this conversation on a geography she knew little about. "Dodge Island is just over the bridge, isn't it?"

He nodded, going back to his soup. "What about the characters in your books?" he asked. "Do you base those on real people?"

"On bits and pieces of people," she told him, relaxing back into her chair as she talked on a subject that she had answered in interviews countless times. "My most successful characters are based on people I may have met or known briefly, before I get to know all their quirks and bad habits. That way

I create the perfect person in my mind based on all the good things I like about the person who inspired the character." She smiled, thinking of all the times she had told men she wanted to get to know better that she was going to base her next hero on them. It was a unique line and one designed to flatter the person she was with, but a statement she also reserved for those she really liked.

Unfortunately, most didn't see it quite that way and it didn't result in as many dates as she would have thought it would. And she had also learned, more than once, that after writing a book based on a person she barely knew, then getting to know that person better, she liked her own characters better than the real thing.

She was too picky, she decided. She'd written too many romances. It was going to be increasingly difficult for some man to write a true-life romance to her satisfaction. As she looked across the table at this man's handsome cleancut jaw, she wondered if such a man existed for her.

Take Justin Frye, for instance. Based on looks alone, he was the type of man she usually avoided for two reasons. One, the good-looking type she had always been drawn to usually turned out to be the most shallow of companions. So far, Justin hadn't managed to do that, but she'd barely given him enough time.

Secondly, his type was always taken by some other woman, or when she decided she'd like to get to know him better, he wouldn't be interested in her. So she had learned from past experiences not even to attempt a relationship with a Justin Frye type. If he didn't manage to bore her before the evening was out, he wouldn't be interested enough in her beyond the business side of their association to want to see her again. That was how real-life scripts always worked out.

"What are you doing tomorrow night?" he asked, those gray eyes startling her in their intense interest in her answer.

"Oh, I, uhm . . ." Her mind raced ahead trying to remember while her thoughts protested. He was only being polite. "I'm going home. Why?"

"Do you have to?"

"Why?" She held her breath. Did he want to see her again, even after she had been so adamant with him?

"I'd like to have dinner with you again before you slip away from me."

"You would?" She closed her mouth, trying to tell herself one of her heroines wouldn't be as shocked as she was to discover a man like Justin Frye cared enough to want to see her again, especially after all the time he'd had this week to take her to dinner and had said he was too busy to manage.

"Of course I would," he said. "You're a stimulating conversationalist."

I am? she thought. *"Provoking" would be a better term.* Most men didn't like a woman who challenged them on every issue. And she'd better learn not to do it so often, particularly when she didn't have an opinion on an issue. "Thank you," she said now, wondering what his gain would be in seeing her a second night. Could he be hatching some business scheme that he wanted her to play a part in? "But I have to get home."

"Surely you could stay one more day. Don't you pretty much set your own hours?"

She nodded, touching her wineglass and deciding against bringing it to her lips. There was something about Justin Frye and the way he was looking at her that made her want to remember everything about this evening. She picked up the water glass instead and said, "Ordinarily, but my godchild, Matthew, is being christened on Sunday and I have to be back in Louisiana for that." She sipped some water and set her glass down, wondering when he was going to reveal what business he might have to keep her in Miami for one more evening. A department store opening? An awards presentation at a boys' club sack race? The christening of a rowboat?

"I guess I'll let you go for that," he said. "Damn but I wish I hadn't blown this whole week. I never got to know you."

"You wish you had?" she asked, thinking maybe she did need another glass of wine to understand correctly what he was saying.

"Of course I do," he said, gazing directly across the table at her. "You're a damned intelligent lady."

"How can you say that after knowing so little about me?"

"Anyone who writes books has to be intelligent. There is power in words. And I have to respect someone who can sit down and turn out as many words as you do."

He must really have some big publicity stunt in

mind for her—like opening a new shopping mall that
needed a celebrity for the grand event. "Most men
don't see it that way. They think it's nice that I write.
I think they see it as some kind of hobby."

"Most men probably don't write themselves, either," he told her. "They don't know the kind of
struggle and work that go into filling up a blank
sheet of paper."

Ann smiled. He did understand, which was a
delightful change for her. Not only was he treating
her as a person, but also as a writer who commanded
his respect. "Thank you," she said, wondering if he
wasn't opening a new shopping mall. Maybe it was a
traffic island on Miami Beach. Whatever it was
would have to be so ridiculous that it would take
someone crazy to help Justin with the promotion. It
was too much to hope he could be interested in her
alone.

She sat back and waited for him to suggest his
scheme.

Their entrées arrived at that time. She and Justin
sat back, watching the waiter set coconut fried
shrimp in front of her and clams and oysters in front
of him. As the waiter hovered next to Justin, opening a second bottle of wine and refilling their glasses,
Ann surveyed Justin's looks.

He certainly had the outward makings of an Ann
Straus character. She needed some new inspiration
for the next book she would start as soon as the one
she was finishing was mailed off to New York.

His occupation would be easy enough for readers
to relate to. He also had a little glamor she could
throw in from time to time. As a hero he would be

ideal, right up to and including that layered, professionally styled hair that begged to have her fingers running through it, messing it up. *Watch yourself,* she warned herself. *He's too strong for your ego.* He'd have her intimidated in two minutes if she ever let her guard down around him. Just look at the way he treated her the past week, inventing some flimsy excuse about suddenly remembering another dinner engagement and not being able to take her out. He simply hadn't liked the sound of her over the phone and had grasped at anything to get out of taking her to dinner. Otherwise he would have invented a better excuse than a last-minute dinner engagement.

To test him, she picked up her wedge of lemon and squeezed it into the cocktail sauce that had come with her shrimp plate and asked, "Who was it you had dinner with earlier this week?"

"On Tuesday, you mean?"

She smiled at him, thinking he at least got the date right. But how inventive can one be in two seconds flat? "Yes, I believe that was when it was."

He set down his fork from the efforts he had been making to separate the oyster-and-spinach concoction from its shell and looked at her as he answered. "Ron McDonald from the Hips to Toes Hosiery account in New York. They're doing some test marketing for a new product in the Miami area and wanted my ideas."

Fast thinking. She nodded, picking up one of her coconut fried shrimp. "They?"

"He's president of the agency handling the account—an old friend of mine from school—actually, that's why I was brought in on this deal—

and two of his account executives. I'd forgotten they were flying into Miami that day sometime and would be calling me to set up the exact time for dinner. If you hadn't . . ."—He paused, looked down, picked up his fork again and concentrated on the oyster as he finished his sentence—". . . if I hadn't looked in my appointment book I would have completely forgotten it because we'd talked about the meeting weeks ago."

Ann played with her shrimp, dipping it in and out of the sauce. "Don't you always consult your appointment book?"

"No. My secretary usually keeps up with things for me. But this was written in a date book I carry with me and apparently I had neglected to let her know about these arrangements."

Ann picked the soggy shrimp out of the sauce and nibbled at it. "Lucky for you that you checked the book."

"That's one way of looking at it," he said, dividing his attention between her and the oyster on his fork. "In another way it was damned unlucky, especially since you say you're leaving tomorrow."

"I've been here all week," she pointed out.

He was motionless a moment and she had to smile because she'd won his attention over the oyster, which slipped off his fork and landed on his plate. He didn't even glance down at it. "That's what's so frustrating, but—" He hesitated.

"But?"

He exhaled, sat back in his chair, and looked at her a moment, calculatingly, as if he was trying to figure her out. He leaned forward and admitted,

"Let's just say the impression I got of you over the phone was not nearly as pleasant as the impression I'm getting now."

She smiled. So he had been glad to find an excuse—real or invented—to get out of having dinner with her earlier this week. Apparently his opinion had changed or he wouldn't have invited her out tonight.

"I'm sorry," she apologized. "But I was literally going stir crazy in that room, pleasant as it was, with my own company all week. And you did wake me up."

"Remind me not to do that again," he mumbled. Then he amended, "On second thought, remind me some morning to give you pointers on waking up pleasantly."

Her eyebrows went up and she looked down at her wineglass, pleased to notice it was still full. She knew she had heard him correctly, or maybe she just wanted it to mean what she thought it meant.

"On third thought, one morning might not do it. It could take several mornings, just for practice."

She smiled. He did mean what she thought she wanted him to mean.

"I don't need practice," she assured him, giving him her sexiest voice and her silkiest smile, "although I'm always open to new suggestions. Research, you know, for the books."

"Don't you ever stop and put that pencil behind your ear once in a while?"

She shook her head. "All of life is material for me and I'm afraid I'll miss something if I don't have my security pen and paper around."

"I'll have to see what I can do about that," he said, letting his oysters get cold as he lost interest in his dinner.

"Actually," she said, deciding it was time to lighten up the conversation before he challenged her to follow through on his suggestions and found out just how inexperienced she was, "I'm quite pleasant in the mornings. That's when I get my best ideas—for the books." She blushed, thinking he could interpret that any way he wanted to.

"I'll make a note of that," he said, the gray of his eyes deepening as he chose not to accept the innocent explanation of her morning preferences.

"As a matter of fact," she said, picking up another shrimp in the hope that the action would divert his attention back to a nice, safe, unsexy dinner topic. "I'm quite pleasant most of the time." Then she grinned with her little-girl-helpless look that made him laugh.

"I'm beginning to believe it," he answered, taking her cue and attacking the food on his plate again. "But I think it deserves some added research on my part to verify my observations."

Ann took time to finish another shrimp before she said, "I'll be signing books at this bookstore called The Page Turner in the morning in case you'd like to make an appointment to see me for a few minutes."

"I'll do more than that," he said. "I'll take you to the airport. What time's your flight?"

"Oh, but you don't have to do that."

"I want to," he assured her. "That way you'll have to have lunch with me, too."

"Oh," she said, picking up her fork and tasting the

fried potatoes on her plate. He was serious about wanting to see more of her. "Thank you. It would save me a lot of trouble."

"Either that," he said, smiling at her, "or more trouble!"

Ann knew she was blushing again. He was flirting with her and it had been a long while since she had met a man who made her feel so warm all over. Or maybe he was just an expert at choosing a dinner wine.

Chapter Four

$\mathscr{A}$nn was stuffed by the time the waiter arrived to take a dessert order. So she decided to forgo the extra calories. Justin, however, insisted she have the key lime pie, recalling her earlier declaration of how hungry she was. "I don't need to receive any bad press about starving visiting writers," he told her. "We'll go somewhere else for a drink."

She sat back in the peacock fan chair and thought how pleasant his company was becoming with each glass of wine. It wasn't taking much right now to build him into a larger-than-life hero for her next book that was kicking around in the back of her mind.

The longer she sat across from him and listened to him, the more things she found they had in common —ice cream in winter, writing letters to a journal on rainy nights, snorkeling and sailing, listening to classical music on hectic days, and just acting busy with an unbaited fishing pole in hand.

The longer she listened to him, the more she respected him as a man. He was a leader, one who acted and then made explanations. He was not one to follow the crowd or jump on a fad simply because it was the fashionable thing to do. Justin was the kind of man who created fads. But, most important, he knew how to handle people.

She had to keep reminding herself of that. He was in public relations, but that just meant he knew how to put a shiny new shoe forward. He could be feeding her all the compliments she wanted to hear right now. She would have to be careful in order to determine how much of what he was saying to her was genuine and how much was designed to impress her.

After she had finished her pie, he paid the bill, leaving a generous tip for the waiter, and they left.

It was a starry night and she could hear the gentle creak of the small craft rocking at their moorings as they strolled along the wharf to the place where he had parked the car. *This*, Ann thought, *is the stuff of which novels are born.* She looked at him out of the corner of her eye as she walked along beside him, rewriting this night with him in her mind.

He should be walking with his arm around her, she decided, penciling in the feeling of the warmth of him beside her. He was just the right height, too, tall but not towering. He was bound to be an expert kisser.

Just remember he's not real, she told herself. *He's giving you his best side because that's what he's paid to do.*

He didn't talk as he drove down Biscayne Boulevard past the Omni, and took a sidestreet that brought him to the inland passage. She could see the lights of Miami Beach flickering across the waterway.

Justin helped Ann out of the car and led her to the building on the corner, inauspiciously marked by the address "1800." When he opened the door and stood back for her to precede him, she saw that it was a private club with a dark cocktail lounge.

"What would you like to drink?" he asked.

"A glass of sherry," she answered, and watched him showing the girl his card membership. "I take it you come here often," she said when he had placed his order for a glass of white wine.

"Not too often," he said, waving to someone seated at the other side of the bar. "Seldom with clients."

"Oh?" *Flattery again,* she warned herself. "Why not?"

"It's a comfortable place. I like to feel it's my hideaway."

"Nice," she said, admiring the stained-glass window and trying to ignore the painting of the nude hanging behind him.

The barmaid brought their drinks.

"So," he said, "you're going home tomorrow for your godchild's christening. Then what happens?"

"Depending on how cold it is in New Orleans and

how long I can stand the winter, I'll be there awhile. I have to finish this book I've been working on. But that shouldn't take too much longer. I fly to Cancún and after that to Curaçao to spend a week with an entertainer I met aboard one of the cruise ships I sailed on last month. She invited me to her home and I'll need the break by then. Besides, she's a fascinating woman and I might want to base one of my characters on her."

"Does she know that?" he asked, toasting her briefly as he lifted his glass.

"Sure. Everybody who knows me knows that. Haven't I told you up front that you could turn up in one of my books?"

"You're serious."

"Of course. What is fiction, anyway, but a toning down of fact into a believable form. People have such fascinating stories to tell that I can't help myself from fashioning books around them."

He considered that a moment, then asked, "Where will you be after Curaçao?"

She shrugged. "I'd have to consult my appointment book. I think I have another book coming out sometime after that and it may involve another round of publicity tours. I don't think I have to go back to New York anytime soon, but I do have a meeting in Long Beach sometime in the spring, and Germany is in the back of my mind for later in the year. I can't remember right off hand. It's gotten so crazy, sometimes I don't know myself where I'm supposed to be."

He nodded. "I can understand why. Do you ever stay home?"

"Oh, sure, when I have to write. My word processor misses me from time to time."

"Does anyone else?" he asked, his eyes that dark gray that she now knew was a sign that he was devoting his entire attention to what she was saying.

She shook her head. "I stay too busy. When I'm home I am home. Literally, glued to my word processor. The only guest appearances I make are at the grocery store, and only then when I run out of tuna fish." She smiled to make it seem as if her lonely life was quite gay, and one of her choosing. She worked as much as she did because she had no other diversions to keep her from it. And the local publicity she had received when each new book was published made her a minor celebrity. It wasn't uncommon to be persued by autograph hounds when she went out to dinner. Ann was glad she wasn't a movie star who was easily recognized by the public. When she traveled, her name was frequently recognized, but her face wasn't. New Orleans was the only place where she found it impossible to travel incognito.

"If I turned up in New Orleans sometime, would you take time away from your writing to show me around?"

"I'd love to," she said, thinking with each sip of her drink that she'd love to show him around her house, as well as her city. "Do you go to New Orleans very often?"

"Whenever I can get the business to take me there."

"You must be doing quite well to have so many connections—New York, Miami, New Orleans."

He smiled and set his drink down, opening his mouth to say something when someone clamped a hand down on his shoulder and interrupted him. "Justin! How long have you been here?"

Ann turned to see a man closer to her age than Justin's standing behind him. The questions were directed to Justin, but the looks were all for Ann.

She smiled politely and looked down at her drink.

"Just got here," Justin answered. "Haven't seen you around lately. Where have you been keeping yourself?"

"That's what I was going to ask you," his friend said, "but now that I see the kind of company you're keeping I can understand why I haven't seen you."

There was a long pause and Ann knew the new stranger was forcing Justin to introduce her. She had turned and was watching the exchange as an observer, wondering why Justin wasn't rushing to include her in the conversation.

"You're new," Justin's friend said finally when no one broke the uneasy silence. "Justin always was one to pick real lookers."

What cave did this guy crawl out of? Ann wondered. She was "a real looker?"

"Ann," Justin finally said, "this is Ed Tyner. Ed, Ann."

"Glad to meet you," Ed said, transferring his hand from Justin's shoulder to Ann's own and sitting down on the empty barstool beside her.

Ann looked down at his hand on her shoulder and leaned closer to Justin. "Hello," she said, picking up her drink and looking away from him. People who reached out and touched her in such a familiar manner before they barely knew her name made her uneasy.

"Have you known each other long?" Ed asked, not taking the hint to remove his hand.

"Five hours," Ann said.

"A day," Justin corrected.

"Ah," Ed said, sliding his hand from her shoulder to the small of her back, "newly mets."

Ann turned to Justin and frowned. Justin shrugged, mumbling, "Something like that."

Ann wiggled on her barstool, leaning more and more in Justin's direction, hoping Ed would take his hand off her body.

"Do you live here in town?" Ed persisted.

"Ann's from out of town," Justin answered for her.

The barmaid approached Ed, asking what he would like to order. When he took his hand away from Ann to sign the tab, she slid her stool even closer to Justin and picked up her glass.

"Is he a good friend of yours?" Ann whispered to Justin while Ed was busy talking to the barmaid.

"Hardly," Justin answered. "If he insults you, don't take it personally. It's his nature. He could use some ice water thrown in his face from time to time."

"Not a bad idea," Ann said, sipping her drink. "Maybe you should have a glass standing by, just in case I need it."

Justin gave Ann an intimate look that implied if Ed didn't go away soon, they'd have to resort to their plan. She smiled at him, pleased to know he considered his friend's arrival as much an intrusion as she did.

"What brings you to town?" Ed asked after his drink had been set in front of him.

"Ann's a writer," Justin answered for her, his voice in clipped tones. "I brought her in for some publicity at The Page Turner."

"A writer," Ed said, sitting back and staring at her as if she were a purple cow in a blue field. "What kind of writer?"

"I write romances," Ann supplied, not at all interested in telling him her life's story when she had been having such a pleasant evening with Justin.

"Really? Tell me about yourself."

"If you don't mind," Ann said, deciding this stranger deserved some semblance of politeness from her, "I'd rather not discuss my work. It's my night off and my brain has reached its capacity for one day."

"Fine," Ed said, clamping his hand back on her shoulder as he leaned forward and suggested, "but if you ever need any help with research, good old Ed here wants to be the first in line as a volunteer."

"Really?" Ann asked, grinning, leaving the protection of Justin's side to snuggle up to his friend. That did it. She had heard that offer for the last time without doing something about it. This man was obnoxious enough to encourage her to do something about it. She glanced at Justin as if to say, "Do I have your permission?" Then she turned back to Ed and said, "I'm always looking for new twists with the research." She kept her voice low and seductive.

"Honey, you've come to the right place."

"Uhm," Ann said, looking him up and down as if he were a majestic eagle, minus feathers. "You could be right." She glanced over her shoulder at Justin, whose eyes had darkened in agitation. Since Ed enjoyed touching her so much she might as well give him a treat in return. "How about if we do a little experimentation right now?" She gave him another low-lidded look along with her suggestive smile and leaned slightly closer.

"Your place or mine?" he quipped, ignoring Justin.

The man's not even original! Ann thought. Then she answered, "Oh, here will do nicely." She put her hand on his arm and started making suggestive circles, moving toward his shoulder and across his back.

Ed loosened up to her seduction. "I think I'm going to like this."

Ann's grin widened and she touched his glass of Scotch on the rocks, moving it on the counter as if it were in the way of her moves on Ed. "I can't guarantee that," she cooed, "but I do think it will be memorable."

He laughed, his eyes daring her to keep it up as she walked her fingers around to his chest and slowly started unbuttoning his shirt, caressing the skin of his neck, unbuttoning, touching the skin at his throat, unbuttoning, snaking her hand farther inside his shirt, and unbuttoning.

The more she unbuttoned, the wider she grinned. "Now," she said when she had sufficiently loosened the shirt from his body, "just lean forward a little."

She slipped both hands inside the opened neck of his shirt and centered his shoulders in her direction.

He laughed again as she put her smiling face millimeters from his own and whispered, "Now close your eyes. Good." She massaged gently at his neck. "Just relax. Concentrate on what you're feeling."

She looked quickly at Justin and pointed to her glass, containing nothing but the half-melted ice cubes, and mimicked for Justin to get her a big glass full of ice.

Justin grinned and caught the barmaid's attention.

"Does that feel good?" Ann asked.

"You got it," Ed assured her.

"Not yet, but I will," she murmured, removing one hand from his shirt. "Just keep your eyes closed and open your mind to the sensations around you. I want you to really anticipate a warmth. Good. Good." She put her other hand in the glass of ice and picked some up, keeping her voice low and seductive. "Now," she whispered, "I want you to tell me just what you feel."

"I feel—" he began as his eyelids fluttered.

"No, no," she said, smiling, "keep your eyes closed and tell me what you're really tuned in to."

He closed his eyes again, smiling.

"Good," she crooned, taking her other hand away from him, "just relax." She loosened his shirt and with the ice cubes in her hand dropped them down the neck of his shirt. By now everyone in the bar was aware of what was about to happen and there was a hushed silence except for the piped-in music playing in the background.

"I feel—damn!" His eyes flew open. "What are you doing?"

Justin started laughing as Ed sputtered, hopping off of the barstool as he tried to shake the ice cubes out of his shirt. Rage and confusion distorted his features. Ann overheard comments of "Someone should have done that to Ed a long time ago." Laughter filled the room.

Ann shrugged, sipping from her drink, trying not to smile as widely as she wanted to. "You offered to help me with research. I don't often get volunteers for that kind of work, you know."

"I'm not surprised. That wasn't the kind of research I had in mind." An ice cube fell out of his shirt as he tried fanning the material to make it dry. A new wave of laughter swept through the room.

"But it's the only kind of research I need help with," she answered. "I wanted to see if I could make the ice cubes sizzle."

Justin laughed louder, and Ann turned to him, slightly concerned that he would be upset with her for embarrassing his friend. But he seemed to be enjoying the experiment as much as Ann was. She looked back at Ed, still mopping himself up, and said, "I either did something wrong or you just don't have any sizzle."

Justin was still chuckling as he asked Ann, "Are you ready to go?"

"I think so." She nodded, hopping off the stool without another second's thought, ready to wait beside the door until Justin could pay the bill. "Thanks for letting me experiment with you," she said to Ed. "Maybe we can try it again sometime!"

He didn't answer her as he looked from her to Justin and back again.

Ann waited until she and Justin had walked out into the parking lot before she said, "I hope he's not one of your best friends."

"Ed's okay," Justin said, taking her arm and steering her away from the car toward the walk along the water, "but I can't say I was glad to see him when he showed up tonight. You had both of us going there for a few minutes."

"I'm sorry," she said, "but I just couldn't resist."

"You're a dangerous lady," he said, still chuckling.

"I couldn't help myself," she said. "He just happened to have been at the end of a long line of men who have the aggravating habit of asking if they can help me with my research. And I didn't like the way he looked at me."

"I didn't like that, either," Justin said.

A warm rush of affection washed over Ann as she remembered his eyes darkening in jealousy when Ed had touched her. "You didn't?"

"And I didn't like the way he kept touching you. But I sure am glad he was the one who asked about the research before I had a chance to. I was saving that line to throw at you when I dropped you off at the hotel."

"You were?" She laughed.

"I guess it's a pretty obvious line for a romance writer."

She nodded, wondering what the words would have sounded like coming from him.

"I would have asked you at the door, where you

wouldn't have had any ice cubes around. But I'm wondering what you would have done to me."

"I don't know," she answered. "Depends on how you asked. Maybe you should give it a try." She kept her voice deliberately suggestive, challenging him with her eyes.

"Oh, no," he said, "not until I know you're the one at my mercy and there are no ice cubes within reach."

"Do you think that could ever happen?" she asked, looking up at the clear night sky and admiring the twinkling lights across the water in the distance.

"It has every possibility," he answered.

Ann glanced up at his dark eyes and then away, watching her feet as they kept pace with his. His tone was getting more intimate, so she attempted to steer the conversation back to the frivolity of her meeting with Ed. "I didn't like the way he was touching me, either. That plus the liquor you've been plying me with all evening just had me begging for mischief."

Justin stopped and his hand moved from her arm to her shoulder. His eyes had a soft look to them in the dim light of the moon. "Do you mind the way I'm touching you?"

She couldn't speak with her heart in her throat. She shook her head and smiled.

"And now?" he asked, both hands gently on her neck, fingers weaving into her hair.

Her heart was racing a twenty-second mile. "You don't have any ice cubes in your pockets, do you?" She laughed, hoping the joke would keep him away from her.

"Why don't you check for yourself?" he asked,

smiling at her, delaying the moment when she knew he would lower his lips to hers, enticing her more by the denial, waiting for her to meet him halfway.

What can it hurt? she asked herself. *One kiss and I'll leave him at my hotel door.*

She put her hands on his shoulders, struggling within herself to justify the kiss. It would signal the confirmation of a potential romance; it would take them one giant leap past a business relationship and open doors to a more personal one.

As he smiled at her, she wondered what difference it would make whether he kissed her. A kiss was a kiss was a kiss. Why shouldn't she just enjoy it of and by itself?

Kissing him didn't have to mean a surrender of her self. It would signal a beginning, if they both decided to see it that way.

She sighed. "You did this on purpose."

"What?" he whispered, not moving any closer, not drawing farther away.

"The moonlight, the wine . . . you."

He looked up at the sky, noticing the moon for the first time, then smiled back at her. "Anything to please you, my lady."

Yes, she thought, *that's just the problem.*

She felt his breath, warm against her lips. Then his lips pressed against her own with tender assurance. Like the man, there was strength, yet gentleness, in his kiss as he explored the opening between her teeth and slid within, teasing the tip of her tongue.

A calm settled over Ann as she moved closer against him, giving her mouth up to his seduction. His kiss was firm but not demanding, designed to give her pleasure. She had never known there could be such fire in a kiss, or known how much chaos a kiss could bring to her emotions.

It was not a long kiss, but it was intense. When he moved slightly away to look into her eyes, judging the effect of his mouth on hers, she could see uncertainty and desire conflict in his expression. He didn't want to stop kissing her, but he did, and simply continued to hold her as he smiled down at her.

A beginning, Ann thought, *that could die tomorrow when I leave town.* Or was Justin serious when he said he'd like to see her if he came to New Orleans?

She couldn't read the answer in his eyes. She wasn't certain he had an answer. Ann felt vulnerable standing against him. He had cast a spell over her. She was afraid to speak and break the quiet awe of the moment, yet she had so many questions she wanted to ask, feelings she wanted to share.

As if he understood, he slipped his hand around her back. Turning her, he pulled her tightly against his shoulder. Slowly they walked along the water's edge.

Ann sighed against him, purring like a cat. It was nice to have the support of a man against her side. It was even nicer to know that the man was Justin Frye.

She didn't know how long they ambled along the shore. If they had never run out of beach, the shoreline would have been too short. His silence gave her time to pretend, and she let her imagination run away with her, thinking that if she closed her eyes she could believe he was in love with her. Never mind about tomorrow. Tonight was just fine. If she didn't take time to question or reason or remember it would end tomorrow, she could pretend he was the man who had been waiting for long, lonely years to love her.

She stretched her neck forward and looked up at him, smiling.

"What?" he asked, curious about the glance she gave him.

"Nothing," she said, snuggling back against his side.

"There must have been something," he prodded.

She wrapped her arms around his side, hugging him, and sighed. Turning her face into his chest, she could smell the scent of pipe tobacco lingering in his clothes and another essence of his distinctive musky cologne. "No." She shook her head, loving the way he put his hand on her head when she started to draw away from him, keeping her face pressed next to his heart. "I just wanted to be sure I didn't imagine you."

She heard him laughing, but the chuckle was low and deep.

"Kismet, my lady," he whispered, his mouth close to her ear, "I was wondering the same about you."

She looked up at him, keeping her chin against his shoulder, her face radiant with the love she felt. Who cared if it was just a loving feeling that was merely a by-product of the wine and moonlight and a man?

"You're just saying that because it's what I want to hear."

"Maybe," he admitted, but his smile said he liked the thought as much as she did.

"Thank you," she said. "It's nice to be with you."

He pulled her tighter against him before relaxing his grip and resuming his loping pace.

Ann admitted to herself she was disappointed when his steps finally led them back to the car. He kissed her again before he opened the door for her. His kiss this time was a gentle one, affectionate and reassuring without a hint of passion.

Ann smiled at him and watched as he walked around the car to the driver's side, got in, and reached for her hand before starting the car. They held hands like teenagers on a first date all the way back to the Fontainebleau.

It was after three in the morning by the clock on the dash of his car as he pulled up in front of the entrance, where a bellboy was waiting to open the door for Ann.

"I had a wonderful evening," she said, turning to him as the bellboy held the door for her.

"Not so fast, my lady," he said, as she wondered how she would kiss him good-night with the kind of kiss she wanted to give him while the bellboy stood by and took notes. "Save your speech until I get you to your door."

"But this is my door," she protested. "You don't have to walk all the way with me to my room."

"I know I don't have to," he said, opening his door and tossing the keys to the boy with instructions to keep the car waiting nearby. "I *want* to," he concluded, reaching a hand in the car to help her out.

Ann smiled. Right now he was better than her own imagination could have created him.

They were silent as they walked to her room. But the silence was perfect. She knew she would see him again in the morning, in fewer hours than she cared to think about right this moment. Instinctively, she also knew he wouldn't be inviting himself into her bed. That made her happy because as vulnerable and trusting as he had ended up making her feel, if he asked to stay the night she wasn't certain she would say no.

She longed to be with him tonight, but this was just not something she did. For her sake it was better that he wouldn't be asking. She wanted to keep this night perfect in her mind.

He took her key and opened her door for her.

She wondered if she should invite him in, but had nothing to offer but an empty bed and that wasn't on the agenda. So she waited, with the door open, for him to take her for the last time into his arms and brand his kiss on her lips.

Kissing him, she let him know how relaxed she felt, tracing his lips with her tongue, inviting his deeper kisses, letting her fingers weave through his hair to find it was as fine as it looked.

"I'll pick you up tomorrow about nine again."

"By the escalators?"

He shook his head, playing with her hair as he looked at her. "Here. Would you like me to come earlier?"

She bit her lip, smiling at him. "Yes, but don't."

He smiled at her diplomacy, kissed her gently again, and said, "Goodnight."

Chapter Five

*A*nn had been lying awake trying to convince herself that if she didn't get up right now she'd fall asleep again and wouldn't be anywhere near ready when Justin arrived at nine o'clock to pick her up. But the bed felt so comfortable, and she had made a warm spot beneath the covers to protect her from the chilly air conditioning.

Five more minutes, she told herself, checking her travel alarm. She closed her eyes and tried to stay awake.

She was drifting between dreams when she heard a knock at the door and sat up, wide awake. Blast it all but she had fallen asleep and Justin was here and she was late. Worse than that, she thought, tumbling out of bed and looking around for her robe, he was going to see her at her worst.

After he had taken her to her room last night she had not even taken time to remove her makeup before crawling contentedly into bed. Her hair had to be washed, not to mention the fact that she wasn't dressed; he'd probably love that part.

She glanced hurriedly at the alarm as she put her arms through the sleeves of the robe and heard the knock at the door again.

It was only eight o'clock. What was he doing arriving early? One thing she knew for certain—he wasn't going to set foot across the threshold, even if she had to make him wait in the hall. He had said he would be here at nine o'clock, and that was when she would let him in.

She peeked through the security glass of her hotel door to see a bellboy standing, lifting his hand to knock again. "Yes?" she called through the door, knowing she hadn't ordered room service.

"Special delivery," the boy said.

She looked at him again through the peephole. He looked innocent enough, she decided, and unlocked the door to poke her head out into the hall.

"Miss Straus?"

"Yes," she said, opening the door wider, but using it as a shield to hide behind as he handed her an arrangement of orchids. "For me?"

"That's what the card says," he answered, grinning as she took it.

"Let me get my purse," she said.

"It's been taken care of, ma'am."

Someone sent her flowers *and* tipped the bellboy? "Thanks," she returned, closing the door and walking with the flowers into her room as she looked for the card.

It read:

I couldn't find violets. Will orchids do?

J.

"Violets?" She smiled, thinking she had never seen lovelier flowers. "Why would I want violets? I've never gotten violets in my life."

Then it didn't matter. He had thought of her first thing this morning and had taken the time to call a florist and have the flowers delivered so that they would be the first thing she saw this morning.

Stop mooning over the flowers, she finally told herself. *You have a lot to do if you're going to be ready on time.*

She dashed into the bathroom and got washed and dressed as quickly as she could, but even so, her hair was still in curlers when he knocked on the door an hour later.

"I'm coming, I'm coming," she practically sang as she headed for the door and then remembered that her hair was still filled with enough curlers to make her head feel as if she were wearing a diver's helmet. But what did it matter? she asked herself, still heading for the door. If last night continued where it left off, he would see her in much worse condition than at present.

She stopped, her hand on the doorknob, her fingers in her hair. Last night might not continue where they left off if she started taking for granted on day two of their meeting that he would accept her as she was, hair curlers and all. "Just a minute!" she yelled instead, tearing the curlers out of her hair and vigorously brushing her hair forward to get the tight curlicues out. Then she threw her head back to let the hair fall luxuriously around her shoulders. Of course, the wind would hit it on the breezeway between this building and the main hotel and it would be straight as an interstate highway. But at least for now she knew he would be seeing her at her best.

Her heart was thumping like a jackhammer as she opened the door to him and smiled, wondering for a moment if she should give in to her wildest imaginings and throw her arms around him and kiss him as she led him toward the bed.

"Good morning," he said, taking the matter out of her hands and pulling her into his arms. He ran his hands up and down her back, kissing her with an ardor that picked off somewhere well past where they had left off last night.

"Whoa!" she said, putting her hands up against his chest. Had she missed something somewhere? Maybe that practically chaste kiss at the door last night had not been the end of the evening. Maybe that had just been the beginning, but because of all the wine she had been drinking her memory was fuzzy.

But she didn't think anything else had happened last night. Surely she would have remembered.

"Good morning to you, too," she said, placing some distance between them, his sudden forcefulness making her nervous. "You'll smudge my lipstick. I'm ready to go."

He followed her to the vanity mirror, touching and rubbing her back as she tried to avoid his eyes in the mirror. She wiggled away from him to pick up a Kleenex and blot her lips before starting to repair her makeup. She hoped her hand wouldn't shake too much and draw a crooked line.

"I realize now I shouldn't have left you last night," he said.

His slow seductive tone didn't help ease her jitters. What had come over him? It was like seeing Dr. Jekyll and Mr. Hyde. If she didn't know better she'd think he'd been drinking, but there had been only the taste of toothpaste in the kiss.

Her defenses went up automatically. "Why? Did someone tow your car away while you were walking me to my door? I told you I could find my way here myself."

He looked at her and his eyes darkened. As she took the chance to look directly at him she thought his eyes looked much blacker than she had remembered. He didn't look as if he had gotten much sleep, but then she hadn't, either. How long a drive had he had, she wondered, between here and his home last night and back again?

"What's with you this morning?" he asked as he put his hand on her back and again she found an excuse to wiggle away.

She put her lipstick in her purse and turned to him. "I was going to ask you the same thing. You seem different, and I'm not sure I like the change."

His brows shot up and he frowned. "Me, too."

"Look," she said, "I don't know if this is part of

your lesson in teaching me how to have a pleasant morning, but if it is, I don't want to buy the entire course." Her anger mounted as she continued, "And if you think that you can just leave me nice and sweetly at my doorstep and a few hours later send me flowers . . . which"—she interrupted herself long enough to smile—"were lovely, by the way." The frown reappeared on her face. "But flowers do not a love scene justify."

"Who said anything about love?"

"Nobody, but you're coming on too fast for me. Back off. I don't like all this morning macho business you're giving me. What ever happened to last night's gentleness?"

He blinked again and she wondered if he had slept at all.

"Look," she said, softening enough to put her hand on his arm and lower her voice, "maybe you're just tired. You couldn't have slept much."

"I didn't sleep at all."

"Maybe you're just wound up from lack of sleep, but I liked you better last night when you were being affectionate and not this, this—"

Where did I go wrong? Justin thought, reliving in his mind his bold and plundering pirate-like entrance. Wasn't that how she had written about the hero in *My Heart Surrenders?* Maybe he had fallen asleep over some essential pages in trying to finish the book before he saw her again this morning. Maybe he had read more into the character than she had intended. It was a good thing he wasn't an actor, because he had just been a flop in his first interpretive role. At least the flowers were well received, but they might have gotten a better response from her if he could have found violets like the hero had in *My Heart Surrenders*. "Sorry," he said, running a hand through his hair. "I guess it was the animal in me coming through. But isn't that the kind of man that appeals to you?"

"Wherever did you get an idea like that? Animals are okay," she assured him. "In their place. Early morning is not the time for jungle gymnastics. I'd much rather see a koala bear."

He chuckled and shook his head again, as if he were only half awake and had caught every other word she had said. "I apologize, but I got the impression—" He looked at her in a way that seemed to say it was the first time he had really looked at her this morning, then smiled. "Come here and let me try my good-mornings again, koala-bear style."

He gave her a bear hug this time, full of warmth and affection and tender kisses along her cheekbone and eyelids. Ann kept waiting for him to kiss her lips and tease her mouth into trembling desire. "Why don't you kiss me properly?" she finally whispered as he started nibbling her ear. Aroused, she was reminded of how close the bed was and how rumpled and inviting the covers looked.

"I don't want to smudge your lipstick," he answered.

"Ooohhh!" She laughed, playfully pummeling his chest and drawing away from him. "But that was much nicer. Too nice, in fact. Don't you have somewhere you're supposed to be taking me this morning?"

"Right," he said, "and we're going to be late if we don't leave right now."

She grinned, thinking he had stayed awake all last night because he couldn't sleep for thinking of her. No man, as far as she could recall, had ever lost sleep over her.

On that Saturday morning, there seemed to be a huge crowd drawn to The Page Turner's third store for her final autographing appearance. This time Justin didn't drop her off and drive away, but stayed hovering in the background between the shelves, watching her from time to time, and browsing through a book he had picked up to pass the hours.

She would sign a book and look at him, smiling when she caught him staring at her. His stares started turning into frowns, then raised brows, and finally puzzled glances with narrowed eyelids.

"What were you reading so intently while I was autographing?" she asked when the event ended and he was driving her back to the Fontainebleau to pack for her trip to the airport.

"*Love is Desire,*" he answered.

"My book?" she squealed, turning to him with delight written on her face. "What did you think?"

"I liked *My Heart Surrenders* better."

"You read that one, too?"

"Last night."

"After you left me?"

"Uh-huh."

Wow! Ann thought, glowing. He had been interested in her enough to want to know more about her, and if he couldn't take her to bed, he could at least curl up with her book.

She had learned not to ask for more specific comments than readers were willing to give. If he wanted to expand on what he had just said she would eagerly absorb every comment he made, but he didn't seem too inclined to go into detail page by page. "I wouldn't think it's the sort of thing you usually enjoy reading."

"It's not. But it is interesting having met you. How much of what you write is really about you?"

"Oh"—she smiled, talking now in generalities—"just about everything." Her thoughts, desires, emotions, and philosophy of life usually turned up between the lines of her books. She enjoyed weaving them around an imagination wilder than the everyday events of her life. If she tried to write realistically about herself, she'd bore her readers silly.

"That's what I thought," he said, looking over at her with that narrowed glance on his face.

The sun must be too bright for him, Ann thought, intrigued that he had spent so much time with her books.

"I thought we'd have lunch Under The Trees," Justin said as they pulled up in front of the hotel. "It's a good warm day—too nice to stay inside."

"I'd love it," Ann said, thinking just about anything he suggested would be equally well received. "But I think I'd better pack first before I have to pay for an extra night past check-out time."

"There's no problem with that," Justin said, getting out and handing the keys to the attendant as he walked around to Ann's side of the car to help her out. "I know the manager and I've already told him you need to stay a little later. The hotel's not fully booked and I told him how I was going to be keeping you occupied elsewhere this morning."

"Justin, thank you. That was thoughtful of you. So the manager said he really didn't mind?"

Justin chuckled. "He said someone on his staff had pointed you out to him in one of the hotel restaurants. He thought I was crazy for keeping you busy *away* from your hotel room."

Ann blushed and wished she could put a skip into her walk. She smiled to herself as he pulled the chair out for her.

"The spinach salad here is very good," Justin said as he perused the menu.

If he recommended sand cakes at this point, she would give them a try. "Delicious," she said, admiring his tan.

"And the Florida stone crabs are a good appetizer."

Ann wondered what he would look like in dark-rimmed glasses. They would give him a Dean Martin–Cary Grant image, especially if she substituted one of her novels for that menu he had in his hands. "Uhm."

"Do you like shrimp?" He lifted his eyes from the menu to judge her reaction.

"Who?" she asked, blinking, wondering what it was he had just said.

"Shrimp. Do you like it?"

"Love it." She blushed, hoping the heat from the patch of sunlight she was sitting in would disguise her embarrassment at being caught staring at him.

"Then let's have the barbequed brochette of shrimp."

"Fine with me," she said, rearranging the silverware in front of her.

She didn't say anything until after the waiter had come by their table to take Justin's order. He requested a carafe of house white wine and asked that it be served before the salads.

When he caught her staring again she pretended she was looking past his shoulder at the Caribbean steel band playing in a corner of the outdoor restaurant. But then she turned to him and smiled. Yes, she thought, if she had created the perfect hero in her mind, she couldn't have dreamed up anyone to better fit the physical image than Justin Frye.

Ann Straus really was like the heroines of her books, Justin thought as he looked at her as she glanced around the open-air café and admired the steel band playing Caribbean music. It was even more obvious after managing to read most of *Love Is Desire* today while she was signing books. She was a woman with high standards and a strong will. A man would have his hands full taming her. But she would be damn well worth the effort. He had been attracted to her from the minute he set eyes on her. The more he knew about her, the more he wanted her.

As Justin thought about her now, it didn't seem there was anything she hadn't done, judging by the experiences she had given the characters in her books. She couldn't possibly have imagined all those pages. Her writing was too vivid, too real for pretense. And the more time he spent with her, the more he saw of her in her heroines. Was there anything he could challenge her to, just like the strong, dominant, totally masculine heroes of her books did with her heroines? Could he even manage to do something simple, like out-drink her, the way her heroes in her books always did?

One thing was for certain: he was going to see her again. Next time he met her he would have all her books read and committed to memory. If this powerhouse of a woman wanted a real hero in her life, he was not only going to apply for the position, but he was going to meet all of her requirements and then some to win her. And it would take that kind of intensive research of her books to get her to notice him as someone unique from the host of males she must meet in her travels. She moved around so much with her schedule, he'd have to make the best use of the limited time he could manage between her trips. It wouldn't be too hard if he just applied all his public relations training. This was one woman who cried out for a novel approach from a man. She was a creative lady. Maybe he could turn her creativity back on her to win her. He had had luck before in giving his clients exactly what they wanted. What could be easier than giving this woman an exact copy of the heroes she wrote about, and probably desired for herself in real life?

"So where do you go after your godchild's chris-

tening tomorrow?" he asked now, figuring he'd
better make mental notes of her schedule to plan
their next meeting.

"Let me think," Ann said, putting her elbows
on the table. "I'm not sure of the dates without
pulling out my appointment book, but I'll be home
about a week and a half before I fly down to
Cancún."

"Why Cancún?"

"I want to do some research on the Mayan ruins of
Tulúm and Chichén Itźa to use as background for a
future book. Besides, Cancún is the latest rival to
Acapulco, and I thought it would make a good
romantic setting. And I like to get away from the
cold."

"Then what?"

Ann yawned. "Sorry," she apologized. "I hope I
catch up on my sleep sometime between now and
next week. Anyway, I'll be home a week or two after
that—I have to say hello to my word processor every
once in a while. It gets hungry if I don't keep feeding
it more disks."

"Why don't you travel with a typewriter?"

She shrugged, yawned again, and stretched her
shoulders to try to liven up her spirit. The few hours
of sleep last night and the long hours of signing her
name over and over in her books were catching up
with her. "No reflection on the company," she said
to apologize again for yawning. "Uhm, let's see."
She frowned in concentration. "I usually try to get a
typewriter set up while I'm traveling, like here, but
so far I haven't found one that suits me enough to
lug around from airport to airport. And I work best

when I have my word processor around. Everything goes faster."

"A word processor," he said, impressed. "That costs a lot more than a roll of newsprint or the old typewriter. But I've worked with them a little and know what you mean."

"It's great," Ann agreed.

"Uh-huh. Where do you go after Cancún?"

"Oh, home for a couple of weeks. Maybe longer, I can't remember. Then Europe. I forget which country comes first."

"You're doing a tour, then?"

She shook her head. "No, I'm researching locales again for a couple of book ideas floating around in my head. I want to get the details clear in my mind since it's been a few years since I've crossed the ocean. I can't remember which country I decided to see first. Then I'll come home again for a couple of weeks. July and August are fairly open at this point. But that could change at any time."

"Don't you ever stop?"

She nodded. "Long enough to finish a book or start one. It usually ends up getting written in airports and airplanes in various parts of the world."

Justin shook his head but refrained from commenting while the waiter brought the carafe and two glasses. "Don't you ever get tired of all the travel?"

"Yes," Ann answered, "like now." And she yawned again. One day she wanted to settle down. One day she wanted to give in to her real fantasy of having a nice, quiet home in the country with a dog and cat underfoot and a husband beside her, and kids screaming in the yard. But she couldn't admit that to Justin. He was still practically a stranger, and she had her image of a jet-setting author to uphold.

Justin picked up his glass and held it to toast her, thinking he would see if he couldn't just out-drink her and all her fast-living, heavy-drinking heroes combined. It was going to be a challenge since he didn't even like to drink very much, but it might improve her impression of him in her mind. "To you, dear lady, one of the most fascinating women I have ever met."

"Thank you." She lifted her glass, too, ready to clink it against his.

"And to New Orleans. I feel a business trip coming on in the next couple of weeks."

"Really?" she asked. She had heard that line before so many times and responded in kind with the expected answer. "Well, you must look me up when you come into town. If I'm home I'll take *you* to dinner."

She just couldn't get her hopes up that he really meant much behind those words. He was probably telling her that because it was her last day here and he still wanted to make one last, grand play for her.

Most of the men she met exchanged cards with her. A few followed up with phone calls, but none ever went out of their way to see her again. Not that they didn't want to, but it just wasn't worth the expense of a special trip to see her. Usually they turned up around convention time in New Orleans. Then they would call her and spend a pleasant evening together. Few had taken the time to see her on a regular basis.

She had to admit, though, that she was seldom

home. It was difficult enough for her to keep track of her own whereabouts. And there hadn't been more than two or three men whom she had seriously wanted to see again.

Now there was Justin Frye. In Miami. She wouldn't get her hopes up that he'd move his mountain to her moss-and-jazz city. But she did know that she would see him again, but maybe only when *her* trips took *her* back here to Miami and *she* called him.

The meal progressed through the stone crabs and spinach salad into another carafe of wine. No more mention of tomorrows was made between them as the approaching emptiness of the afternoon loomed ahead.

Ann dawdled with her glass of wine, letting him drink twice as much as she sipped. She wondered if he was going to try to get any work done this afternoon in his office, or did he consider that entertaining her was part of his work? Could that be the only reason he was being nice to her?

His suggestive glances and teasing comments, which flattered her and her writing, could only be because he considered the business over and he now wanted an easy playmate.

The more he drank and the more she pretended to match him sip for swallow, she didn't think there was going to be the slot machine's chance of three cherries turning up in a row for him to score with her this afternoon, if that was what he had in mind.

And that suited her just fine. She wasn't sure she liked the way he was drinking so much. Men. They really were just the way she imagined them—

alcohol-guzzling gamesmen who could only bring themselves to reveal their true feelings, particularly toward a woman, when they were too drunk to remember what they were saying. That left the woman forever wondering if what he said under the influence of the drink were true or not.

As the carafes of wine continued to turn up empty, Ann didn't even think he'd be able to recognize a cherry if he swallowed one whole, pit and all. She watched him drink and become increasingly bolder in his assumptions about her. His chance caresses—knees beneath the table, fingers brushing as glasses exchanged hands, and looks that still continued to make her sizzle—revealed a Dr. Jekyll–Mr. Hyde personality. Where was the man with whom she had enjoyed having dinner last evening? What had happened to his gentle, open vulnerability? What games was he playing now?

By the fourth carafe, Justin looked in no shape to drive her to the airport an hour from now, and she still had her packing to do. At least she had sat in the breeze beneath the garden trees long enough to feel the heat of the sun on her cheeks, and long enough to decide she didn't really care if she ever saw Justin Frye again, not if he liked to drink this much. The last thing she needed was an alcoholic on her hands.

As she sipped on her last glass of wine, she wondered how she could tactfully leave him. She didn't want to get into a situation in which he would offer to walk her to her room. She didn't want to offer to walk him to his car. The fact was, she was not too pleased to be seen sitting across from him right now. She wondered if he would notice if she simply got up to go to her room and never came back.

Why not just get up and leave? It served him right for embarrassing her in broad daylight with his midnight-style hangover. The only thing keeping her in her seat was the realization that she had never been rude enough to leave a man sitting in a restaurant, especially after he had bought her lunch.

Some things deserved "firsts," she decided, picking up her purse, leaning provocatively across the table and saying, "Would you mind excusing me a minute?"

"Just a minute?"

"Actually, five or ten would be better." She smiled. "Will you wait here for me?" That would keep him sitting there for a while, and if she hurried she could be out of the hotel before he knew what hit him.

"Sure," he answered.

She smiled and crinkled her nose provocatively. "Just wait here until I get back." *That should take a year or two,* she thought, still smiling, and left before he could talk her out of it.

Men, she thought, heading in the direction of the ladies' room in case he was watching her. When she was out of sight she doubled around to the beach side of the hotel to enter her side of the complex the back way. It just went to show, she could never judge a book by its cover.

Justin Frye, of all men, was the type her eyes gravitated toward. Once she got to know that type of man she soon learned he had only one thing on his mind—bed. Home, marriage, and children didn't seem to be in that type of man's vocabulary. When was she going to learn to leave the good-looking ones alone?

When was she going to meet a real man, one who had depth and humor and caring sensitivity and could admit his weaknesses as well as his strengths? Where would there be a man who cared more about her as a person instead of the money and the image the books had built around her?

She'd just written too many books about the perfect man. Too bad he didn't exist.

Chapter Six

*A*nother long-term-parking stub, suitcases that seemed heavier on arrival than departure, and the same old jet lag. Ann turned the key in the front-door lock of her house off of St. Charles Avenue and shoved the door open, sliding the suitcases inside the back room just enough so they would be within reach of the washer and dryer when she started to unpack.

Same old stuffy smells from a house that had been shut up too long, she thought, locking the door behind her and dropping her briefcase, purse, and carry-on luggage in a pile near the larger suitcase. She took the plastic bag she had been carrying between her teeth out of her mouth and tossed it on the countertop. Why she had even bothered to take home those orchids she couldn't explain, but she'd carried them on her lap the entire flight and struggled with all of her luggage through the airport trying to keep the orchids from getting crushed. She opened the plastic bag to take them out and place them in a saucer of water. They looked as if they'd been flown in from Africa—two weeks ago.

Oh, well, she sighed, it was the thought that counted. And why she was even thinking of that jerk, Justin Frye, she had no idea. If she had stayed longer with him in that restaurant she was sure he would have publicly embarrassed her. As it was, she had probably enraged him when he finally sobered up enough to realize she wasn't coming back to the table. That was his problem. He deserved to be stood up. It had probably never happened to him before. His ego could use the demeaning lesson. Maybe after this he wouldn't take things for granted with a woman.

Ann didn't believe that, but it helped her justify her rude behavior.

She had to try to keep herself from thinking about him. She was only going to see his good side, the side she wanted to see because she was a hopeless romantic. She had better stop making a habit of this and realize she was going to have to face reality one day. The problem was that she kept meeting real, but boring, men. Like this Justin-drinking-Frye. He was proof—about one hundred proof. Why couldn't she meet men who were interesting and knew how to handle liquor, like the men in her books? They always knew when to stop and weren't any less masculine in her heroines' eyes because of it.

She walked into the kitchen, where the circular

glass table was covered with a mountain of mail. She dreaded tackling the stack.

It was still early and her sense of organization wouldn't let her sleep until she got the laundry started and at least skipped through the mail enough to put things into stacks of bills, business junk, and the items she wanted to read. The magazines were already heaped in a neat pile to one side. Besides, flying always keyed her up too much to let her sleep.

When Ann finished unpacking and took another look at the covered kitchen table, she smiled. Bess was a terrific neighbor to take time out to watch her house and take in the mail for her. It was friends like Bess who made her look forward to coming home.

Home was like a haven, a delightful dull spot in the glamorous jet-set routine she lived every other week of her life. When she was home, Ann stayed close to her word processor, called on her friends, or had them over for dinner. She rarely took advantage of the wild nightlife New Orleans had to offer. That was for out-of-towners or for people who were dating. For Ann, New Orleans represented humdrum life. With her hectic schedule, she needed peace and quiet.

People often wondered how she could find moments of isolation in the big city. Yet here it was easy to remain lost in the crowd.

Ann checked her phone messages and took her shower. By that time the clothes were ready for the switch to the dryer, which would take about forty-five minutes. That would be her signal to stop sorting mail and head for bed, she decided, pulling the trash can near the table as she sat down to open envelopes and toss them into the "out" basket that would be hauled away by the city's garbage men.

It was after ten and the dry clothes had already been folded and put away, but Ann had decided to finish the initial sorting of the mail tonight. The phone rang, distracting her.

She went over to the kitchen counter and picked it up before it rang enough times for the answering machine to accept the call.

"Ann?"

His voice sounded familiar, but it couldn't be him, Ann thought.

"This is Justin Frye."

Ann sat down, her heart pounding at the sound of his voice, her eyes immediately going to the orchids she had placed in the center of the kitchen table.

"How are you feeling?" she asked.

"Not too good," he admitted. "Where did you go?"

"To the airport," she answered.

"I thought I was going to take you."

"I thought so, too," she said, "but you didn't look as if you were going to be in shape for a little drive."

"Yeah," he said. "I can't remember the last time I've had such a hangover. What happened?"

"You kept ordering and drinking wine. It does that to me every time, too. That's why I rarely drink a lot."

There was a pause before he said, "It's not very clear what I did or said to make you get up and leave the table, but I'd like to apologize. I don't normally drink so much."

A likely story, she thought, and said, "There's nothing that requires an apology."

"I still feel like an absolute fool," he said. "Anyway, I just wanted to call to see that you had gotten home okay."

"Oh," Ann said, her heart fluttering faster from his concern. Where had this soft, concerned side of him been before when the wine-drinking macho man had had lunch with her?

"Was your flight all right?"

"Fine," she said. "We even got in a few minutes early."

There was another pause before he said, "I can't believe I wasted the little time we had together this afternoon."

"Forget it," she said, her voice pulling the brisk, businesslike tones together for a self-assured woman-of-the-world image.

"Look, I've got some business to take care of in New Orleans next week. Do you think I could see you?"

Ann wondered if she could arrange any TV appearances so that she could say, *yes, Channel 6 Midday Thursday.* Tangling with this man was only going to cause her trouble emotionally. He was going to play her up and down like a yo-yo until he either got the message she wasn't going to hop into bed with him or that she was interested. And she was interested enough that she just might let her defenses down around him and accidentally fall for his line—for all the wrong reasons. It would be better not to see him again. Her mixed feelings about him would make it too easy for him to hurt her, and she had too much work to do to take time out for heartbreak.

"I don't know," she said, preparing her defenses in advance. "I have stacks of work to catch up on in the short time I'll be in town. I was just sorting through my mail when you called. And I'm working against a two-week-old deadline. Traveling always throws me off schedule, so I can't promise."

"Lunch maybe?"

Ann's brows went up. Lunch? It was as if he knew she wanted to stay away from any kind of romantic interlude. "Possibly. Why don't you call me when you get in town and I'll know better then." *And I'll have more time to dream up some excuses,* she thought.

Why should she see him? she asked herself. He was no different from all the rest. Business was bringing him to New Orleans and it would be nice to have some fun and games on the side. No one ever went out of his way to fly here specifically to take her out to dinner. She shrugged—that was probably too much to ask of any man.

"I'll do that," he said. "You'd better go back to your mail. I'm keeping you up."

"Okay. Thanks for calling."

"Take care," he said, ending the conversation.

It took two days for Ann to get settled back into her home and start writing again after weeks of traveling. By the third day she happily immersed herself in pages churned out from her word processor, marching steadily toward the page that would read "The End."

Each day as she wrote she wondered if he would call that night.

When he did phone the following Saturday, she found herself agreeing to meet him for dinner at Houlihan's in the French Quarter. By bringing her car, Ann reasoned, she could excuse herself from his company at any time instead of worrying about the awkwardness of saying good night at her door. He would probably expect to be invited in and once she had him on her home turf he might be harder than a barnacle to extricate. The excuse she gave, however, was that it might be difficult for him to find her house since he didn't know the city too well. But all it would take was one visit to see how convenient her house was to his hotel.

Since he was booked into the Royal Orleans, he was a short walk away from the Bourbon Street restaurant and Ann had given him plenty of time to arrive ahead of her. She found him at the bar, his tall distinctive figure standing out above the crowd.

She smiled, telling her heart not to fall too hard. *Quit reacting to that six-four physique and wind-blown brown hair,* she reminded herself. *The looks don't always match the true personality.*

But the gray eyes had a lot to say as they spied her near the door, drawing her to his side. Her heart pounded faster just thinking that all his attention was directed toward her. He was ignoring completely the looks and stares he was getting from the women seated near him.

Her eyes made a quick survey around the room, something she always did to see if there were familiar faces she needed to acknowledge. Tonight she didn't see anyone she knew or anyone she wanted to know. Justin Frye was literally the pick of the evening crowd.

He straightened at her approach, his eyes twinkling and a silly grin altering the straight line of his lips. She held out her hand to him and smiled. "Hello."

He took her hand and pulled her closer, kissing her briefly, but effectively, before releasing her to ask, "Would you like to sit at the bar or find a table?"

"It doesn't matter," she said, sliding onto the empty barstool. She needed something beneath her to keep her legs from wobbling. "This is fine."

He signaled to the bartender and ordered a banana banshee for her without asking what she wanted to drink.

Ann looked at him, eyebrows raised. "How did you know that's one of my favorite drinks?"

He shrugged, amusement playing on the features of his face. "Lucky guess."

Ann was certain there was more to it than that. She thought of their time together in Florida but couldn't remember ordering a banshee while she was with him. How had he known her taste?

"How's the writing?" he asked, paying the bartender for the drink and resuming his relaxed position.

"The pages are adding up," she answered. "But I

think I was about ready for a break. I'm glad you called." She smiled into her drink thinking she really meant that. It was good to see him again, this side of him at least. By the end of the evening she might decide she never wanted to see him again. "How's your business?"

"Business?"

"The business that brought you to New Orleans."

"Oh, that," he answered, nodding. "It's . . . uh . . . developing." He paused. "Yes, I guess you could describe it that way."

Ann played with the straw in her drink. "I hope it was worth the trip here."

"It was," he replied, his direct gaze making her nervous. "I read a few more of your books this week."

"You did?" He was going out of his way to flatter her, Ann decided. "Any new opinions you'd like to tell the author in person?"

"Uhm . . ." He hedged around the subject, intriguing her with his mysterious reply of, "Not *tell* so much as . . . uh . . . *show.*"

She looked at him, trying to interpret the look in his eyes. "I'm always open for new material," she told him, trying to make her voice as sexy as possible.

"How many books have you written?" he asked, sipping from his drink, which Ann guessed was a Scotch-and-water; he looked like a Scotch-and-water man.

"The question is not how many have I written, but how many are published," she corrected. "They're backlogged at my publisher's right now." He nodded, accepting her gentle correction, and she added, "I have eighteen in print. Another one is coming out in a few months."

His eyebrows rose at that. "I have quite a few more to read, then."

Why would he want to read all of her books? Romances couldn't possibly be his thing, and one of her books was usually as much as most men could take. It was flattering, but it did make her wonder why he was going to so much trouble to read everything she had written. What would he think of *The Golden Arrow?*

When Justin's name was called for dinner, Ann followed him into the fern-filled dining room. "Ann!" someone shouted to her. She turned toward the direction of the voice, waving in recognition of one of her favorite girl friends. "How long have you been in town?"

"This trip?" Ann quipped, as if she were visiting New Orleans instead of staying here. "About a week. How are you?" She hugged Cassandra Anderson and introduced her to Justin.

"Are you going to be in town long enough for us to get together for lunch or something?" Cassandra asked, looking over Ann's shoulder to appraise the man she was with.

"Possibly," Ann agreed. "It has been a while since we've had a good long talk."

"Long overdue," Cassandra agreed, her eyes still on Justin Frye. "I want to know everything."

"I can't tell you *everything!*" Ann exclaimed,

exaggerating the word for Justin's benefit to keep him guessing about her nonexistent secret life. Then she added, for Cassandra's benefit, "It would take too long, anyway."

Cassandra laughed with Ann, but she gave her friend a look that said that an explanation of Justin Frye would be enough. "When?" she asked Ann. Then she turned to Justin and explained for his benefit: "If you don't pin this girl down and make a definite appointment with her, and watch her write the time down, she slithers away from you. It's always the same excuse—the word processor has captured her and is holding her for ransom until she does 'x' number of pages."

"I've already guessed how busy this lady is," Justin commiserated. "In fact, it's the second thing I noticed when I met her. That's why I've learned to bring the mountain to Moses if I want to see her."

"What was the first thing you noticed about her?" Cassandra asked.

"How beautiful she is," Justin answered, not taking his eyes off Ann.

Ann looked at him, her eyebrows peaked. It was flattering that he should say that, but she knew it was probably just one of his tactics in this verbal game they were playing with each other. "Name a day," she said now to Cassandra.

"Tuesday. Lunch," Cassandra answered.

Ann thought a minute. "Fine. Where?"

"My house," Cassandra said, "and come early."

"I'll write it down," Ann promised.

"Will you see that she does that?" Cassandra

asked Justin. "I would like to see Ann again before I turn old and gray, and my head is still spinning from all of this in-town, out-of-town travel."

"Tuesday, lunch," Ann confirmed, knowing she wouldn't forget the chance to enjoy a lazy lunch and conversation with her best friend.

"Nice to meet you," Cassandra said, letting Justin lead Ann to their table.

Justin seated Ann and ordered another round of cocktails for both of them. "I hear the quiche here is terrific," Justin said.

Ann looked across the table at him. It was as if he were reading her mind. How could he know she always ordered quiche when she ate here? "It is," she confirmed. "Have you eaten here before?"

He shook his head and glanced over the menu. "I've only been to New Orleans a couple of times."

"Amazing," Ann said.

"Why?" He looked at her, a blank expression on his face, he hoped; otherwise, she might guess he had picked up those details from her books.

"Because this is one of my favorite restaurants."

"Really?" He smiled. "Maybe my luck is changing."

"Uh-huh," Ann said, looking to see if anything new had been added to the menu lately, but already sure she wanted the quiche with a spinach salad.

They had just ordered when other friends of Ann caught her eye and waved to her from across the restaurant. Justin turned to see who had caught Ann's attention and said, "Looks like you have quite a fan club here in town."

Ann lifted her shoulders. "It's the restaurant. My

friends are the ones who introduced me to the place, so it's only natural that I should run into them when I eat here. I'm sorry. But you picked the place."

He nodded. "Meeting all of your friends will just give me more insight into your personality."

Ann wondered briefly if that was good or bad. She leaned forward and asked a question about his career, if only to let him know that she was interested in what he had to say and who he was.

It didn't take long to read between the lines to know this man was a born leader, the type who acted first. She had guessed that from the last time they had met, but talking with him now reconfirmed her positive impressions about him.

He told her about his daughters, Beth and Sue, who were duly impressed when he had shown them the books Ann had written and told them he had met the author. They had been even more curious when he'd told them they weren't old enough to read the books.

His daughters, Ann learned, lived with Justin's ex-wife and her new husband. Justin didn't dwell long on the subject of his ex and she guessed their parting had been painful. It would have to have been since children were involved. Plus she read other sorrows into Justin's past marital history. His wife, it seemed, had left Justin for another man.

It was evident that the pain of the divorce had almost disappeared. The question of visitation rights didn't appear to be a source of argument. But, like a cocklebur beneath the saddle of a horse, she could tell he harbored some feelings of resentment.

He was a handsome man, one who was in charge

of his life—executive material. He understood, from the very nature of his own independent business, the kind of motivation it required to keep her at her desk when she would prefer hunting for violets on a fine, sunny spring day.

He didn't just praise her talent to flatter her and then promptly dismiss it as a hobby. Or, worse, he didn't tell her he was "jealous" of her writing. Any man who loved her would have to live with her writing; it was the essence of her soul.

Justin Frye seemed to understand that and appreciate it. In fact, he seemed to like her better because of it. Maybe it was because he had a writing background and understood some of the pressures she was up against.

"Do you get to see your girls very often?"

"Not often enough," he answered. "Weekends, when I can take the time, and a couple of weeks in the summer. But I've got the best end of the deal."

"How?"

"They think they're really big stuff when they spend the weekend in Dad's apartment. And when we're together I'm with them, not working on some report in a corner of the room. We do things together."

"That's terrific," Ann agreed. "How many parents these days spend time with their kids? Look at all the kids who are forced to grow up in day-care centers because today's economy dictates that both parents must work. Parents feel guilty about not being able to spend time with their children when they're young, yet they have no choice."

He nodded. "I don't feel as if I spend as much

time as I should with my girls. That's one of the reasons I try to spend quality time with them when we're together."

"What sorts of things do you do?"

"I take them sailing. I have a friend who owns a boat. Or we go to the zoo."

"Oh, I hear the new Miami zoo houses the animals in their native-style habitats."

He nodded again. "When they finish with the reconstruction, it's going to be one of the top zoos in the country."

"What else?" she asked, leaning forward, seeing how animated he became while discussing his children.

"Sometimes I take the girls shopping, but not too often because I don't want them to get the idea I'm buying their time."

Ann smiled. This man built a large part of his life around his children and took his role as a parent seriously. What had hurt him more, she wondered— divorcing his wife, or losing the chance to live with his children while they were growing up?

"I'd love to meet your children someday," she said. "They sound beautiful."

"I think so." He smiled and reached in his wallet to show her a picture of them.

One had dark, short-cropped, Buster Brown-style hair, glasses, and two missing teeth. "I have to get new pictures," he said, realizing how much the girls had changed since these photos were taken. The other, Sue, had straight blond hair and wide, freckled features.

Ann looked from the photo to the man beside her.

The blonde would be his natural daughter, but she could barely see a resemblance.

Justin smiled. "She resembles me in my youth."

Ann gave him a skeptical look. As far as she was concerned, he was still a youthful man. It had a lot to do with the kind of active life he led. This man would still be young at ninety.

"They're very good-looking children," she said, always slightly at a loss as to what a proud parent wanted to hear. Ann had always thought she would enjoy having children, but she had never found a husband and there hadn't been time for her to develop her social life the way she had developed her writing.

Children, like finding the perfect man, were easier for Ann to put off. *I'm happy,* she told herself silently, knowing it was a different happiness than what Justin shared with his daughters.

"It sounds very nice," Ann said, warming more and more to Justin Frye as he revealed himself. Most men tried to keep their family life separate from hers. They saw children as an intrusion, something to mar their macho image. A macho man wanted to forget about his children when he was putting the make on the current woman in question.

"This quiche is delicious," Justin said, dropping his eyes from their intent appraisal of Ann to finish what had been set before him a few minutes earlier by the waiter.

"Uhm," Ann agreed, her mouth full. "Thanks for recommending it."

"But I didn't recommend it," he said, picking up his wineglass and draining it. "You did."

She frowned. "Did I?" She looked at the wine still in her glass. True, she had had two banana banshees, but very little of this wine, and she felt as clear-headed as an April day. "When?"

Justin suddenly had a coughing fit; something had gone down the wrong way. "Sorry," he apologized, once he had recovered his voice, swallowing all the water in his glass. He smiled at her and signaled to the waiter, asking him to bring more water. "Would you like more wine?" he asked Ann. "No? Then how about some dessert?"

She nodded. "Something with ice cream would be nice."

Justin consulted the waiter over the menu and placed their order, then returned his attention to Ann.

She smiled, pleased to be having dinner with a man who knew how to treat a waiter with deference, yet remain in command. Many times in the past she had felt like taking the menu out of her date's hands and orchestrating the meal herself.

Dessert arrived and with it came another of Ann's friends who hadn't seen her in months. This time it was a man she had dated and dropped after two disappointing evenings.

Ann made introductions between Ron Carrington and Justin and submitted to Ron's obnoxious kiss on the cheek and his hands on her shoulders. Who was he trying to impress? Her? Justin? Or some woman in the background?

"Carrington, Carrington," Justin mused. "Plastics?"

Ann nearly choked on her wine. Justin had sized

the other man up in a short time and already knew how to put him down without the other man's realizing it. But it fit perfectly; Ron Carrington was a plastic person.

"No, office systems," Ron answered, trying to figure out who Justin was and why they had never met.

"Something about you seems familiar," Justin said. "I almost feel as if we've met before."

"What business are you in?"

"Justin owns his own public relations firm in Miami Beach," Ann said, knowing that if she left it to Justin he would downplay his position, and with Ron everything had to be overstated. She didn't stop to ask herself why she did it; she only knew she wanted Ron to realize Justin was a man of importance. "He has business connections in New York and now New Orleans."

"It's possible we've met," Ron said. "Do you travel much? I was in Atlanta last week and Houston the weekend before that."

Justin shook his head. "Couldn't have been that. But something about you seems very familiar."

Ron dropped names of people, corporations, and cities for a while. Justin just kept shaking his head, but his eyes were keenly studying the other man. "No, no, I haven't been out of Florida in a couple of months."

Ann relaxed in her chair and watched Ron try to impress Justin, even by hinting at his past relationship with Ann. She saw Justin's speculative side glances at her, but knew he wasn't totally buying Ron's story. There was a curious look on his face and she had to smile inwardly. Justin Frye was not sure of his position with Ann, but was gentleman enough not to ask about Ron unless she decided to divulge any insights into her past with him.

"This has to be the longest meal on record," Justin said once Ron had grown tired and had wandered off to be seated at a table of his own, alone, Ann was surprised to notice.

"I am sorry," Ann said. "Now do you see why I frequent the grocery stores when I'm home? If I did this sort of thing every day I'd never get any work done."

"I was hoping I could talk you into not getting much work done while I'm in town," Justin said. He turned in her direction.

"At least I left my word processor at home." She smiled. "But I never go anywhere without my notebook and pen. I feel naked without them."

His eyebrows shot up at her provocative remark. "Can we go somewhere other than Grand Central Station?"

He hadn't asked to take her to his hotel room. He hadn't invited himself to her house. He was still letting her make the rules. She was trusting him more and more and wanted to be with him. Maybe tonight, but just to talk.

"Why don't we go get my car and I'll drive you to your car?" she suggested, knowing he had rented a car because of his earlier offer to pick her up. "You can follow me over to my house. I won't promise the phone won't ring, but at least my entire life won't flash back and forth between us at the table the way it seems to be doing here."

"Sounds fine to me," he said, looking at the bill and pulling out a credit card to pay for it.

"As long as you understand," she said, immediately regretting her invitation, "that it's just to find a quieter place. I'm not offering you a place to spend the night."

He didn't say yes, he didn't say no. His look said the rules were fine, but that didn't mean he wouldn't try to bend them a little.

Ann thought they would find privacy as soon as they left the restaurant. But as they walked down Bourbon Street, another former date accosted them and in a somewhat inebriated state tried to resume his position as the man in Ann's life.

Justin, she could tell from his clenched jaw and tight smile, had reached the end of his patience. She couldn't blame him. All of these interruptions were beginning to annoy her. She sighed and smiled and extricated herself, thinking that if she had arranged to make a man jealous, she couldn't have done it any better.

Once they were on their own again, Ann didn't bother to apologize to Justin for the interruption. She had used the word "sorry" often enough tonight, and she was trying to alter the situation by inviting him home with her—to talk. She would turn on her answering machine so that if someone did call while he was there, she wouldn't have to answer the phone. He wasn't speaking at all now as they walked the last few blocks to her car.

Chapter Seven

Ann drove Justin to his hotel and waited while he got his car and pulled up behind her. Their strained silence during the drive to his car had given her even more cause to regret her invitation.

Her house was her private place. Very few people knew her real address and she had invited even less to visit her. Her close friends came often, but near strangers, like Justin Frye, rarely crossed the threshold.

It's too soon, she thought. She shouldn't have asked him home with her. They could have gone somewhere else for quiet, driven around town for instance. But that was so high-schoolish, definitely not Justin's style.

Inviting him home with her hadn't been her style, either. She kept so much to herself when she was in town that she didn't entertain often. Hostessing even one guest made her uneasy. It wasn't the same as having Cassandra come over or opening the door to Bess and watching her head straight for Ann's refrigerator, making herself right at home with its contents.

Quit worrying about it, she said to herself as she pulled into the sidestreet where her house was located. Turning into her short driveway, she pulled the car as far forward as she could so that there would be room for Justin's car as well.

She turned off her car lights and got out of the car, slamming the door behind her.

Where was he?

She stood a minute beside the car. He had been behind her when they started out. He must have gotten caught behind another car in traffic, but she had driven slowly enough so that he would catch her turn signals along the way.

She wandered to the edge of the driveway and looked down the narrow street. Traffic whizzed by on the busier St. Charles Avenue. Not one car slowed as if it were preparing for a turn.

Damn the man! He had led her on, acting as if he wanted to be alone with her when he was just as soon glad to be rid of her! The least he could have done was come right out and tell her that, face to face, instead of cowering behind her in traffic just so that he could lose her.

Men. She never could predict what they were thinking or feeling.

She unlocked the door and stepped inside her house. Empty again tonight, just the way she liked it, the way she was used to having it. At least she wouldn't have to worry whether she had enough ice cubes for drinks or questions to keep up the conversation.

Ann poured a drink. *Humility,* she told herself. When she was riding high and forgot the humility, something like this shattered her ego. Actually, the more she thought of it the more she embarrassed herself. She shouldn't have let Justin take her to a restaurant where she was so well known in the first place. She could have suggested another place or—

Forget it. It was over. Justin Frye had made it perfectly clear what he thought of her, leading her on and then dropping her. Why did that always happen with someone when she was just beginning to like him? Why couldn't she ever meet a perfect man like the kind she created in her books, the kind who only existed in her mind?

Because the perfect man did not exist outside books. There was no man alive, she was beginning to believe, who was strong, yet gentle, sure of himself, yet able to recognize his own vulnerability, and someone who could admit every once in a while that he was wrong.

She waited for a while in the kitchen, listening for the sounds of cars on the street, or even more hopefully for the sound of a car door slamming. But there was nothing, just the usual night sounds—a hoot from the steamboat *President* returning from a moonlight cruise, distant but recognizable, a siren somewhere even farther away, and the wind beating the banana tree against the side of the house.

She had to face it. He wasn't coming. He wasn't coming before he said he was coming.

She poured the rest of the drink into the sink and decided she might as well go to bed with a good book.

It just wasn't fair, she thought later as she crawled into bed, her eyes red and swollen from the tears she seldom allowed herself to shed. Why did she always end up alone? Everyone thought she had such a remarkable love life, but she could barely get a date, much less a man in bed with her.

But that wasn't what she really wanted, or it would have happened easily enough. There were always men to pick and choose to her heart's content. The problem was none of them ever touched her heart. None of them ever made her want to spend time just sitting quietly beside them. None of them challenged her enough to want to know them better.

Except Justin Frye, and this wasn't challenge so much as exasperation. He was the least predictable man she had ever met and it wouldn't bother her at all if she never met him again.

Then why was he making her cry?

The phone rang on the table beside the bed. Ann sniffed and tried to catch her breath. Her head was so blocked up from the crying fit that she wasn't certain she could speak. She tried swallowing with her mouth open to keep her ears from stopping up. She let the phone ring another time.

"Hello," she said, her voice sounding totally unlike her own.

"Ann, it's Justin."

Where the hell are you? she wanted to scream at him. But she didn't say anything because she was still trying to sniff and catch her breath without hiccoughing.

"I can imagine every blasted name you must be calling me right now."

"Uh-huh," she managed to say, not about to let that statement pass without a comment.

"Believe me, it's not half the measure of what I'm calling myself."

If he thought he could just call up and smoothly apologize and think everything was going to be hunky-dory from here on—

"I followed the wrong damn car."

"What?"

"I followed the wrong car. I was trying to be cool and hang back a little, just so you wouldn't get the idea I was too eager to be alone with you, and somehow I let the wrong car get ahead of me and ended up following it through God only knows where."

Somehow, he said to himself. He knew how it had happened. He'd finally figured out why Ron Carrington had seemed so familiar. Ann had written about him in the last book he'd read. There couldn't be any mistake about it—his egotistical talk about the Lear jet, the wild parties in every major United States city, the lovemaking. Especially the lovemaking. She couldn't have made all of that up. Her writing was so real that he'd had to put the book down and take a cold shower and even then he hadn't been able to forget her erotic passages. Thinking about her with that Ron character had taken his mind off his driving and he hadn't even realized he was no longer following her car.

If Ann could have spoken she would have laughed. Right now it was nice to know she could breathe again. He hadn't set her up as a fool. It was an accident that he hadn't managed to follow her here. Or was this just a good story created in the writer's mind?

"It's taken you long enough to call for directions," she said, looking at the clock. It was well over an hour since she had returned home.

"I know. I've been fuming for the last hour. I just now managed to find my way back to my hotel. You wouldn't believe the hell I've been through."

And you deserve it, she decided.

"The car I was following belonged to some teenagers who must have been a first date and they noticed somewhere along the way that I was tailing them. By the time they pulled up into a parking lot and I whizzed up behind them they were pretty worried—must have thought I was some kind of gangster or something. When I realized they weren't you, I was less than coherent and that didn't help ease their fears any."

Ann could picture him thinking the end of the long road beginning to a romantic evening at her home was about to take place, then finding two teen-agers getting out of what he must have thought was her car. She managed a giggle between hiccoughs.

"By then I was lost, pure and simple, and the directions they gave were less than accurate. Never ask a local for directions. I wound up somewhere in Metairie."

She hoped he wouldn't ask if he could still come over tonight. Her eyes were red and swollen and her makeup was smeared. "Why don't we call it a night and start over tomorrow?"

"If you give me directions, I'm sure I can find my way on my own," he said.

"I have my doubts about that," she said, wondering now if she put him off for the rest of the evening if he would not want to spend tomorrow night with her. He might decide she wasn't worth the effort. "But I've already gotten ready for bed, and I think it would be much nicer if you come here tomorrow evening for dinner. I'll cook, if you don't mind eating an experiment."

"Tomorrow's fine," he said, "but I wasn't planning to end tonight so early."

"I know," she said, nervous now that he might talk her into coming over anyway. She wanted him to, and she didn't want him to. If only he could come over and take her into his arms and not expect anything of her, but just to hold her and tell her not to cry anymore, and that everything would be all right. But he couldn't do that when she looked worse than Little Orphan Annie with hiccoughs. "Don't you ever get omens about some things?"

"Not really."

"I don't either," she admitted, "but I'm declaring tonight a first. Let's just write the rest of the night off and try again tomorrow."

His sigh echoed over the line. "I guess you're right. I can't blame you after the fool I've been tonight. Of all the ridiculous—"

"Hey!" She interrupted him. "It doesn't matter." All that mattered was that he hadn't stood her up, or planned it.

"What time tomorrow?" he asked, relenting.

"Six," she answered. If he came over early enough and they had a nice leisurely dinner, if he stayed past midnight it would feel as if he were overstaying his welcome. So he would have to leave early the way she figured it.

"I'll bring some wine."

"Lovely," she said, then gave him easy directions to get to her house from his hotel.

Ann made a pre-dawn phone call to her best friend, Bess, the next morning after worrying the remainder of the night about what she would cook for Justin.

"Bess, you have to help me," Ann implored after apologizing for waking her friend up on a weekend morning. "I'm fixing dinner tonight for a guest and don't know what to make."

"Wait a minute," Bess said. "I think I'm still asleep. You're doing *what* tonight?"

"Cooking."

"That's what I thought you said." Bess burst into hysterical laughter.

"Bess!"

"Sorry, but I still remember last time."

"I know," Ann commiserated. "That's why I'm calling you. You're such a great gourmet cook. Come up with something nice and simple, yet impressive." Last time she had invited a few friends over for dinner, she had thought spaghetti with meat sauce would be simple enough. But she had forgotten to buy the spaghetti, and the sauce had been sticky and thick, then watered down after someone had rushed out to the store. They had held dinner until the spaghetti could cook.

"How about Spam *delicioso?*"

"It sounds interesting," Ann said, ready to try anything as long as it was simple. "How do you fix it?"

"You open a can of Spam and place it under the broiler with some cheese."

"Oh." Ann sighed and put down her pen once she realized what Bess was saying. "Come on, Bess. I'm serious."

Bess laughed. "I was, too. Who is this guest?"

"Justin Frye."

"Is that the man you were going to see last night?"

"Yes. Will you help me?"

"Why don't I cook the meal and let you worry about entertaining him?"

"I thought of that," Ann admitted, "but I want to do it myself. Something easy, but different, not the old run-of-the-mill steak and potatoes, yet a cut above the instant-oatmeal package directions. Can't you think of anything foolproof?"

"Let me think about it," Bess said, "and I'll call you back."

Instead of calling Ann back, later that morning Bess knocked on her door, laden with grocery bags. "He must be special," Bess said. "I can't remember you cooking for a man in recent or past history, not one man alone."

Ann shrugged. "Can you remember me having a bona fide date with a man in recent history? I mean one of these situations where he calls me ahead of time and asks to see me?"

"We-e-ll," Bess hedged. "I see your point. You do stay busy. So why weren't you busy when this one called to ask you out? I've heard you give men excuses before—deadlines to meet, typing to do, a trip coming up or just plain exhaustion from overwork."

"I don't know," Ann said, peeking over the edge of the grocery bags to see what Bess had brought with her. "I planned to, but when he called I couldn't find a way to say no."

"Sure." Bess grinned, beginning to unpack the bags. "Well, let's get going with the seduction plans."

"Bess! I don't go around seducing men."

"I know," Bess said, folding the first empty bag as she talked. "But haven't you ever wanted to do something wild and crazy like that, especially with—what did you say his name was?"

"Justin Frye. And of course I have fantasies. Doesn't everyone?"

"They do, but most just don't admit it." Bess started on the contents of the second bag, carefully setting a wide container on the counter. "What could it hurt? An evening of pleasure with no strings attached."

"That's the problem," Ann said, frowning at the array of goods Bess had bought, wondering how she was going to turn so many different things into one successful meal. "I want strings."

"With Justin Frye?" Bess spun around, giving Ann her full attention. "This could be serious."

"That's not what I meant." Ann blushed. "I don't know the man well enough to be certain I *want* strings with him."

"I'm trying to help you get to know him better," Bess said, that devilish grin reappearing on her face.

"There must be other ways, Bess."

"There are. But this one's direct. Straight from the stomach with the meal to—"

"What kind of meal is this supposed to be, anyway?" Ann interrupted, deciding it was high time she changed the subject. She should have expected this with Bess and not asked her to help, but she didn't have a better best friend and she didn't know anyone who could cook as well.

"Details," Bess grumbled, "you always want details."

"It's the writer in me," Ann said, picking up the package of sausage and eyeing the can of tomatoes. "What is this supposed to be, anyway?"

"Jambalaya," Bess said, poking at all the vegetables that would go into the Creole stew. "I figured if you throw all this stuff together there's no way you can go wrong."

"You have more faith in me than I do. What's this?" Ann pointed to the container Bess had carefully removed from the bag.

"Oysters freshly shucked on the half-shell."

"Oysters!"

"Great aphrodisiac."

"Bess, I told you—"

"Men love oysters," Bess said. "Trust me."

"But I don't—love oysters, I mean. I trust you, or at least I did before you arrived with this bag aimed at seduction. What am I supposed to do with these oysters?"

"Easy. Fork a little spinach over them, grate a little cheese, and bake right in their shells. He'll be impressed."

"What do I do for an encore?" Ann asked, wondering why it took two grocery bags full of food to provide one meal for two.

"Ice cream for dessert, with Kahlua drizzled over it. Exotic. He won't be able to place the flavors."

Ann looked at her once-neat kitchen that suddenly looked as if it were in a scene for "cooking for camp" and shook her head.

"Okay, roll up your sleeves," Bess said, taking charge. "We're going to start this thing right now so I can supervise and you'll have it all but ready to reheat when he arrives this evening."

"You didn't get detoured by any teen-agers tonight, did you?" Ann asked Justin as she let him in the front door of her house several hours later. After a day with Bess, Ann now knew how harried Erma Bombeck felt.

"Not a one," he replied, smiling, walking through the door with a small cloth bag under his arm.

Ann eyed the bag. Presumptuous of him to think he might need provisions for staying the night, she thought, but didn't say anything.

"Very nice house," he said, admiring the high ceilings and sculptured moldings. "Quite a surprise from the way it looks outside."

"You should never judge a house by its paint," she said, smiling, beginning to feel nervous again. "Or a book by its cover," she added, wondering if she was babbling too much. "Come in."

He walked with her down the short front hallway into the living room. "Very surprising decor," he said as they entered the bamboo and rattan-filled room that was accented with two antique wood side tables. "You have a very inventive style—with everything."

"Sit down," Ann invited, sitting in the chair adjacent to the end of the couch where Justin chose to sit. "How long are you staying in New Orleans?" she asked, thinking that next she'd be asking him about the weather.

"I'm leaving in the morning."

It was too much to hope that he would be staying longer. Besides, she asked herself, why should she care?

"Would you like some wine?" Justin asked.

"Oh, but I forgot—"

"I brought some," he said, reaching into his bag and taking out a bottle of wine and a corkscrew.

Ann relaxed. She always worried too much about making guests comfortable in her home. She should just settle back and let them take over, the way Justin Frye was doing now. She watched him expertly uncork the bottle as if he were the sommelier of a fine French restaurant. "I'll get some glasses," she said.

"I brought two," he replied, reaching into the canvas bag and pulling out two crystal goblets.

Ann smiled, charmed. She took the glass he

handed her and waited while he filled his own glass and set the bottle aside. "To each new beginning," he said, toasting her, "and learning how to make each day seem as if it were.

"Cheese?" Justin asked.

"Oh, but I—"

"I brought some," he said, reaching into the duffel bag again and pulling out a package of Brie and a small cutting board and knife.

Ann leaned forward, trying to get a glimpse into the bag. She wouldn't be at all surprised to discover he had an inflatable mattress with him or a golden carriage with six white horses. She smiled, intrigued. "Are we working at cross purposes here?" she asked. "Didn't I invite you to dinner?"

"You did," he confirmed, offering her some cheese. "But I never like my hostess to do all the work. I'm even handy in the kitchen when it comes dish-washing time."

Ann bit into the cheese to keep her mouth from gaping. How could he be so romantic and have a practical streak as well? She lifted her feet off the floor and curled her legs beneath herself on the chair and she nibbled at the cheese.

"I'm enchanted," she admitted, feeling like a little girl who was being treated to the circus for the first time in her life.

"You're supposed to be," he said, smiling wider and then laughing.

"Does this mean if something disastrous happens, like if I should burn dinner," she said, pausing to sniff in case that was already happening, "which, by the way, I should check on . . . if I burn the main course you won't hold it against me, will you?"

"There are things besides dinner I'd rather hold against you," he said.

Ann blushed. Before she could think of a funny reply Justin leaned across the space between them, took her face between his two hands, and gently kissed her mouth.

Ann arched toward him, letting her lips immerse themselves in his kiss. Their lips formed the only contact between them, yet the firm, expressive nibbling and gentle biting and exploratory taste of his tongue against hers was like an electric charge running from the tip of her nose to the bottom of her toes. He didn't have to touch her elsewhere to let her know how explosive more intimate contact would be between them.

He kissed around her mouth, bringing her lower lip into his mouth, then running his tongue between her teeth and upper lip. He could speak so eloquently to her with nothing more than his lips.

He moved away from her slightly and smiled, taking her wineglass out of her hands and putting his hands on her shoulders. "Come here," he whispered, gently guiding her out of her chair and into his lap. The pressure of his hands on her shoulders told Ann she could trust him. He wanted her closer to him, yet he was not forcing her to do anything she didn't want to do.

She let him lead her across the space to the couch, wrapping her arms around his neck as he settled her onto his lap, where he continued kissing her, his lips playing against her own.

"Relax," he whispered. "I'm not going to hurt you."

Ann smiled against his lips. She believed him. Already he had shown her how different he was from most men. No one had ever kissed her so tenderly before. He had barely touched her anywhere but on the lips, and what he was doing to her mouth made her heart flutter with anticipation of what he would do once he got past the kissing stage.

She sighed and tried imitating the movements of his tongue against her own.

"You like kissing, don't you?" Justin asked.

"Uhm," Ann murmured. "I never knew how much until I met you."

He chuckled at the way she kept his mouth too busy to say much. "I could do this all night," he said, his hands gently kneading the muscles of her shoulders.

All night, Ann thought. Where was this leading? She sat back, putting her hands against his chest to keep him from coming too close to her. "I'd better check on dinner. Something's starting to burn."

He laughed, knowing she wasn't alluding to food. "Can I help?"

She shook her head and slid off of his lap, pleased that, unlike other men she had dated, he let her go. Whatever happened tonight, she knew it would not end in a struggle. And Bess had thought he needed oysters!

When Ann came back from the kitchen a slim box wrapped with a gold bow was sitting on the sofa beside Justin. He had picked up the book *Gods, Graves and Scholars*, which she left on the coffee table. So engrossed was he in one of the stories of great archeological discoveries that he didn't hear her approach.

Ann looked from him to the present beside him and couldn't decide which she wanted to ask him about first. Could it be possible that he was as interested in ancient history as she was? What was in that box?

"Hi," he said, noticing her presence and closing the book as he looked up at her. "This is interesting reading. Didn't you say you were going to Cancún soon to research some ruins?"

"I'm leaving Wednesday," she said, wondering if she should tell him about her serious book, *The Golden Arrow.* Few people knew about that book, especially since it was out of print, but it was one she had most enjoyed writing because of the amount of research she had poured into it. "What were you reading just now?"

"About Chichén Itzá and the sacred well of sacrificial virgins. Didn't you mention that to me?"

She nodded, pleased that he had remembered their conversation. "It's a fascinating place."

"You've been there before, then?"

She shook her head. "I was on a cruise that had a Mexican fiesta theme for all the ports, and Cancún, Tulúm, and Chichén Itzá were some of the options. The story of the Mayan pyramids made me want to go back."

"What stories?"

"Oh, well . . ." She searched her brain for one she could explain to him. "At Chichén Itzá the El Castillo temple is dedicated to the serpent god. The steps including the top level number three hundred sixty-five—the days of the year. And on the equinox the serpent god walks down them."

"How?"

"I've seen postcards of it," she explained. "The sunlight hits the steps in such a way that the light and shadow snake down to the ground."

"I'd like to see that," he said. Although she knew he was genuinely interested, ancient history wasn't uppermost in his mind at the moment.

"They have a sound-and-light show to create the same effect at other times of the year," she said, looking again at the box beside him. "What's this, more surprises?"

"Naturally," he said, picking up the box so that she could sit next to him. "Open it."

She smiled, looking from him to the box and back again. The ribbon slipped easily off the top and the two pieces of tape separated from the lid. Ann pushed the tissue paper aside to reveal an elaborate, and she guessed expensive, feather mask. "What is this for?" she asked, smiling. "It's beautiful."

Justin picked up his wineglass, studying her reaction to his gift. "I was walking through the French Quarter early this afternoon and saw this in the window of a shop that happened to be open. It reminded me of you so much I decided I had to buy it."

"Why did it remind you of me?"

"Because the person behind this mask would have to be mysterious."

"I'm not a mysterious woman behind a mask," she protested. "Am I?"

He laughed. "Every time I see you I see someone different. It won't be easy figuring you out, my lady."

"If it would be it wouldn't be any fun." She giggled, holding the mask up to her face and peering through the eye holes. "It is simply gorgeous. I've always admired these. They're used in the Mardi Gras balls, you know, right before Mardi Gras day."

"No, I didn't know. I've never been to Mardi Gras before. But I imagine you've always been involved with that celebration."

Ann smiled. "I've been to parades and I've been to a lot of parties leading up to the great day. King Cake is served at all the parties."

"What's that?"

"Just a regular cake, but party favors are baked into it, like a thimble and ring and tiny doll. They're symbols. The person who got the thimble in her piece of cake was the one who would always end up the old maid." She wouldn't tell him how many times she had gotten that and watched with envy while her prettier friends always got the rings. They were the same girls who always caught bouquets at weddings. "And the ring symbolized approaching marriage."

"I can't believe you haven't succumbed to that long before now. You must have collected quite a few rings. What did the doll mean?"

"Oh, that was the person who had to give the next party. They used to bake a bean into the cake in earlier days. If a man got the bean he had to pay for the party. If a woman got it she had to hold the party at her house. It could get quite expensive, and people started swallowing the bean. I guess that's why they started baking a small doll into the cake."

"Thumbtacks would have been more effective."

Ann giggled, stroking the silky feathers of the mask he had given her. It was an assortment of peacock blues and greens skillfully arranged to swirl away from the eyes. "I'm not sure what I should do with this," Ann said, looking at it in her lap. "But I love it. Mardi Gras is one big party. People dance in the streets and dress in elaborate costumes. It's trying to get in all the last revelry before repenting begins on Ash Wednesday, just the next day."

"I guess I've never really understood what it is."

Ann sighed and thought and sighed again. "There is no way to describe it to you. It's a mad rush to try to catch things the Krewes throw from the floats."

"Krewes?"

"The group who produces all the different parades around the city. They all have names like the Krewe of Rex, which is the king of Carnival; Endymion; Proteus, who's God of the sea; Mystery. They throw doubloon coins that become collectors' items because they're designed differently each year. And unless you've stood in a parade crowd and gotten caught in the scramble over a pair of plastic beads— or, worse, stepped on someone's knuckles deliberately to get them—I just can't describe it to you," she said, laughing.

"People take these things seriously, don't they?"

"It's part of the fun. You get swept up into the spirit. A friend of mine who has seven kids is a Mardi Gras expert. She invented the Tinkle Strategy for getting doubloons."

"The Tinkle Strategy?" He laughed, reaching for the bottle of wine and refilling both their glasses.

"You go out to your carport and record the sound of coins hitting the concrete. When the floats come by you turn your recorder on to full blast. While everyone is making a mad dash for nonexistent doubloons, you just stand there and wait for them."

Justin laughed. "This sounds more and more interesting. I think I will come back for some of this year's excitement. Do you have to wear a costume?"

"No. But those who come to Mardi Gras year after year generally do on Mardi Gras day. The best costume I ever heard of wasn't a costume at all." She wiggled into a more comfortable position on the sofa, tucking her feet under her as she explained how most people dressed in costumes to catch more of the "throws" from the floats. "It was a man dressed in an ordinary business suit right down to his little bowtie. But he also had a button in his lapel. It read, "Official Judge," so naturally everyone on the floats pelted him with trinkets."

Justin laughed, stretching his hand along the back of the couch to make it more natural for Ann to relax into the curve of his shoulder. "If I come back to New Orleans, would you take me to Mardi Gras?"

Ann laughed at his quaint terminology about Mardi Gras. It was the type of celebration that needed no invitation. It simply happened around you. "I don't think you'd want to make a special trip for Mardi Gras."

"True, that's just beside the point. I'd like to make a special trip here to see you."

She blushed, flattered, but of course he wouldn't

do it. He was just saying that because it was something she had always wanted to hear from one special man. After these pleasant hours with Justin, she was beginning to think he was more special than he had a right to realize. "Well, maybe if your business coincides with the trip," she said, hoping she sounded businesslike enough to overcome the fluttery feeling his seductive words evoked. "Like this trip. That way you won't be disappointed if you decide Mardi Gras isn't your cup of tea."

"My only business in New Orleans this trip was to see you."

Ann blinked. His eyes had darkened into that intense, deep gray. His words had not been designed to flatter her. "But I thought you said—"

"I didn't want to scare you away by letting you know how badly I wanted to see you again. A day and a half last week, especially after the fool I made of myself, wasn't nearly enough time to get to know you."

"Last night wasn't, either," she said, "and don't start thinking tonight could end up any better." She leaned slightly away from him.

"You see," he said, smiling, reaching up and touching her cheek, "you're getting worried already. I'm not a big bad hungry wolf who's going to devour you."

He had flown in from Miami just to see her? No wonder he was flying back in the morning. He could spare only a weekend from his business. She thought of how expensive this trip must be for him, flight and hotel and meals, just to spend a few hours with her.

And all of this programming this evening—the wine, cheese, and Mardi Gras mask were all designed to impress her. Okay, she was impressed, but not enough to pick up his hand and lead him into bed.

"Something's burning," he said. This time it was dinner.

Chapter Eight

Justin reached the kitchen before Ann did and he took control. Smoke had just started to collect in the room but Ann couldn't see any flames.

"My jambalaya!" she wailed while Justin rushed to the stove and turned it off. He scooped a towel off the countertop and slid the vat of bubbling ingredients off the burner and onto the metallic surface of the stove, fanned the smoke, and opened a window to vent the room.

Ann stood in the doorway thinking it was nice to have a man around the house who could take charge when the situation demanded quick action. But it wasn't too pleasant when those actions emphasized her own ineptitude.

Justin picked up a spoon and was poking through the bubbling mass. "Smells terrific," he complimented, "now that the smoke is clearing."

"Ohhh!" she wailed.

"Hey!" he said, smiling and putting his arm around her shoulder. "It's all right. It could have been serious, but as it is the house is okay, nobody's hurt, and I think the bottom of this—jambalaya, did you say?—is all that's burned. There's plenty we can skim off the top for a meal. It's only one little dinner."

"It wasn't one little meal," she protested, hoping she wouldn't start crying. "It was my one big meal and it wasn't my only cooking failure."

He laughed at her expression. "You remind me of June."

"The month?"

"No, the character. June—what was her name? The girl in your book who had a knack for burning soup. It stood out in my mind because in all of the other books your heroines are gourmets."

Ann frowned. She had written so many books it was sometimes difficult to remember characters' names and isolated incidents, especially when she was in the heat of writing another book. But, yes, she did remember that scene from *Bite from the Apple*. She had written it on one of those days when her imagination was on the blink, and the pot of soup on the stove really had caught fire. Writing that true-life incident pushed the story along and the next day she had resumed writing, using her imagination.

He kissed her downturned mouth. "You're acting as if it's the end of the world." He stroked her hair and smiled.

"It's just that . . . well"—she took a deep breath —"I wanted to impress you," she finally blurted out.

He laughed. "You did, with your brand of excitement. Never a dull moment in your company."

"That wasn't what I meant. Anyone can burn a house down. But cooking's not so easy." His laughter wasn't making it easier for her to take this failure with grace.

"You don't have to impress me with your cooking. I already know you're a great cook."

"How can you know that?" she demanded. "I've never cooked anything for you until now, and, and—" She looked at the disorder in the kitchen. The smoke was still swirling near the ceiling.

"You don't have to cook a meal for me to know that," he said, still trying to coax her into a better humor. "I've read about it in all your books."

"Well, you've read the wrong books, then," she said, frowning, "because I'm only an expert on yogurt and Granola."

He leaned back against the counter, still smiling, still unconvinced. "I find that hard to believe. All those recipes you subtly insert into your plots. Only someone who cooks would know how to create some of those dishes."

Ann sighed, then picked up a spoon to taste the remains of her jambalaya. "When I need some authenticity for details I read a book on whatever subject it is I'm dealing with. When I need some exotic food details I pick up back issues of *Gourmet* and fill in the blanks. And sometimes I just make stuff up. Unfortunately, that sense of creativity never extended to pork loins with Brussels sprouts."

He was silent and she turned to look at him. The smile was replaced with a frown and narrowed eyes as he watched her licking the spoon. "I thought you told me your books were reflections of yourself."

"They are. I've never denied that," she said. She embellished her hopes and dreams in her books. Through her writing she became everything she could ever imagine being—a great cook, a sensuous lover, a mysterious woman worthy of a lovingly faithful man. She had become a ballerina, a television executive, a concert pianist, and once a housewife. And she had married the rich and the famous and had affairs with the most influential men of the community—all between the pages of her books. Her feelings, desires, and emotions filled the books she wrote. And sometimes, like the burned-pot incident, she did include true-to-life incidents in her plots.

Ann cupped her hand beneath the spoon she dipped out of the pot for Justin to taste. "What do you think?"

He opened his mouth to taste the jambalaya. "I think I jumped ahead to the end of the book before I read the beginning."

Once the smoke had cleared and Ann and Justin moved out of the scorched scene of the dinner disaster, the evening ran smoothly. Justin raved about her cooking so much she had to smile. He was trying to be nice. The jambalaya was okay, but it wasn't worthy of any awards. She tried to convince him he didn't have to ask for seconds, but he insisted. She sat back and sipped wine, watching him eat as if he really liked it. She had left the oysters in the refrigerator, convinced that one mistake was enough for the evening.

Afterward, despite her protests, Justin helped her clear the table and took charge in the kitchen again. He rolled up his sleeves and plunged his hands into dish water, tackling the scorched pot and sticky remains with a wad of steel wool. Ann watched in amazement, not at all surprised to see the pot cleaner than it had been when she brought it home from the store. She had never met such a macho man who not only admitted he washed dishes, but did a better job than she ever could.

"Are you willing to trust me with dessert?" she asked after he had dried the last dish, had put it away, and had wiped down the countertops, making her conscious of how dusty the kitchen was. She wondered if he hired himself out as a maid.

"I'd trust you with anything," he said, catching her by the waist and pulling her close to him. He smiled into her face, deliberately not kissing her, but bringing his face close to hers, daring her to make the first move.

She shook her head and pushed him away. "Why don't you go back into the living room and let me make one last attempt at redeeming my culinary accomplishments? If I fail this time, you can take me to the French market for *beignets* and *café au lait*."

When she appeared in the doorway of the living room with the parfait glasses of ice cream and Kahlua, she had a moment to look at him before he noticed her presence. He was sprawled against the pillows of her couch, his long legs crossed comfortably in front of him, his hand touching his nearly empty wineglass. His eyes were closed, with his thick lashes fanned against his rugged cheeks, and he was listening to one of her favorite Beethoven symphonies.

A surge of desire pierced her heart. What would it be like to have this man waiting for her just this way every night? How wonderful it would be to know that no matter how long and hard the day might be, whether she was stuck in traffic or stuck in the middle of a book plot, he would be waiting for her every evening. He would wrap his arms around her and hold her and make her know that everything would be all right as long as he was there. Ann had never had the comfort of depending on anyone. She had always had her own resources to rely on without a helping hand from a man. That forced independence had given her a tough exterior. It disguised her vulnerability.

Ann seldom let down her guard in public. Even tonight with Justin she had been pretending to be a great hostess the way her public image demanded. Her defenses had cracked with the burned meal, and Justin had gotten her to admit how much she wanted to impress him. It wasn't like her to admit her feelings so easily to another person, especially a man like Justin.

He must have sensed her presence because his eyes opened and he smiled at her. The look was a lazy one that drew her to his side.

He sat a little straighter on the couch, making room for her to cuddle against his shoulder after she had set the parfait glasses on the coffee table. She kicked off her shoes and curled her legs beneath her. "How did you know that was my favorite record?" she asked.

"It was on the stereo."

"Oh," she said. There was no reason he should have mysterious powers of perception. She must keep telling herself that he was just a man. But with a man like Justin, it was difficult to include him in the same category with everyone else.

"Now that I think of it, don't you allude to Beethoven in your books?"

She shrugged. "Probably. Along with Chopin and Elton John. It depends on what's on the radio when I'm writing."

Over the ice cream they talked about music. Justin told her of his love for the classics, how on particularly hectic days he would lock the doors and clamp on a headset to let the music carry him away. He often fell asleep while connected to the stereo.

Ann smiled, comforted by the information. She had imagined him to be out with a different girl every evening. This view of the silent person within him pleased her. He had already admitted he liked to read a lot, and now she knew he listened to classical music. She couldn't picture him spending too many evenings in front of a TV set. The images excited her because they were so close to her own quiet ways of ending the day. She couldn't imagine anything cozier than curling up next to him on the couch, each engrossed in the latest novel, with Beethoven music on the stereo.

She turned and looked at him. He seemed as contented as a bull in a field of clover. She relaxed just knowing she didn't have to perform tap dances to entertain him. He seemed pleased simply to have her beside him, touching, not even kissing.

"Has anyone ever told you you're a comfortable person to have around?" Justin asked.

Ann shook her head, pleased by his comment. "Thank you. I was thinking the same about you."

"When am I going to see you again?" he asked.

"Do you want to?"

"Of course I do," he said, laughing. "Do you think I would have traveled all this way just to see New Orleans?"

"Most people do."

"Then they don't know about the best-kept secret of the city," he said, cupping the back of her head and stroking her hair. He touched his lips to hers, flicking his tongue around her mouth as if she were as sweet as the ice cream he had just eaten.

"When will you be in New Orleans again?" she asked, blushing, smiling, her heart fluttering in confusion when his lips left hers.

"When will you invite me?"

"Oh, I—" Ann stuttered. It was one thing to have a man turn up on her front porch. It was another to blatantly invite him. If she did that, what would he expect? Accommodations in her spare room, or the spare side of her bed?

"I could come back for Mardi Gras," he offered.

"I'm not sure if I'll be here then," she answered. "Maybe I could stop in Miami for a few days between trips and see you." Now that she had said it, Ann wondered what she was doing. She did want to see him again, but somehow having him in her territory made her uneasy. It would be simpler to stay a few days in his city. That would give her the option to pack her suitcases and leave if she decided on the spur of the moment she didn't like what she was seeing.

"When?" he asked, pinning her down.

"I'm not sure," she hedged. "It will all depend on how my trips go, if I see where I'll have a day's leeway or not. I can't tell you anything definite."

"If I know ahead of time I'll take a few days off to show you the real Miami. My kids are coming to stay with me this week, so I'll be busy with them."

"I'll be in Cancún," she reminded him.

"Right," he said. "I won't rule out Mardi Gras, either."

She smiled, then frowned as he stood up, and, reaching down for her hands, pulled her up beside him.

"Give me a kiss that will make it hard for me to walk away from you."

"You're leaving?"

"Uh-huh," he said, his hands cradling her close against his chest. "Have to. I have an early flight in the morning and an important meeting at ten o'clock that I can't miss."

"Oh," she said, depression overwhelming her when moments before she had been inventing excuses to commit herself to seeing him again.

"Unless you'd like me to stay," he said, his lower lip catching hers.

"Uhm!" She moaned at the excitement charging through her. She pushed her hands against his chest to allow herself to talk. "I do and I don't."

He smiled. "I thought it would be like that. Until you're sure I won't pressure you."

"Oh," said Ann, wishing he would pressure her and take the decision-making process out of her hands. She wanted this man, but she didn't want to admit it. Sometimes she regretted her Southern upbringing that curbed her aggressive desires. It kept her out of a lot of trouble, but it probably left her out of a lot of adventures, too.

As long as he's leaving, she thought, *how can it hurt to give him the kind of kiss he deserves?* "I'll miss you," she said, knowing that would be true. She wound her hands around his neck, her fingers inching into his hair as she rubbed her breasts against his chest and stood thigh to thigh against him.

Her lips parted and he accepted the invitation, his tongue swirling inside, thrusting and darting to explore the roof of her mouth and the tip of her tongue, while his hands brought her hips in tightly against him.

His hands, she thought, *haven't even begun to seduce me, but his mouth has me halfway there.* She abandoned herself to his kiss, letting his mouth take the lead and imitating and following his delicate, teasing, and tempestuous movements.

"I really will miss you," she whispered when his lips finally left hers and they were both breathing heavily.

His hand trailed down her cheek and he kissed the corner of her eyelid. "You're a hard woman for a man to turn his back on," he said, smiling.

Stay, she wanted to say, but she couldn't bring her lips to form the words. She had never invited a man to spend the night with her before. Why did she want this man so badly? It couldn't be love. She hadn't known him long enough.

Ann was still asking herself that question long after Justin had driven away. The memory of his warmth and the clinging scent of his cologne stayed with her. What was different about the man to make him linger in her mind? It was more than his towering height and good looks.

On Monday night Justin called, just to see how she was and to tell her how his day had gone. *How nice of him to share his day with me,* she thought and realized she was telling him in minute detail how she had spent her day, as well.

He phoned again the next night, knowing it would be his last chance to talk with her before she flew to Mexico. When she got off the phone she realized they had talked for an hour, and yet she couldn't recall any major purpose to the conversation. He was spoiling her with this daily attention.

Her flight to Cancún the next morning passed quickly, as it always did for Ann. She had learned to work during the hours she spent in airports and on planes, which made the flight seem as if it took only minutes instead of hours.

She took a taxi to her hotel at El Camino Real, the architecture reminding her of the pryamid ruins she would be visiting during the next two days. El Camino Real had one of the largest swimming pools Ann had ever seen, and it was attached to a lagoon. The frothy surf of the Caribbean splashed right up to the shore on the other side of the hotel, where there was a wide stretch of beach.

She pulled on her bathing suit and settled into a lounge chair with the last pages of her manuscript. When she returned home she would be ready to send this book to her publisher in New York. Then she could start another one.

It was late in the afternoon when she finally went inside. After a shower and a change of clothes, Ann didn't feel like facing the hotel's restaurant alone. She called room service instead and ordered a hamburger, which arrived on an elegantly arranged tray. Maybe she would tackle a book tonight— someone else's after the long day she had had with her own prose.

When the phone rang she thought it must be the wrong number, or perhaps it was the guide she had hired to take her to the ruins of Chichén Itzá in the morning.

"Justin!" she cried, laughing, recognizing his voice. "What are you doing calling me here?"

"I missed you," he said, "and thought, what the heck, it's only a phone call. I can afford that."

She laughed, delighted. "But I didn't tell you where I was staying."

"I knew it was Cancún," he answered, "so I got the operator to help me."

"But there are a lot of places down here. How did you find this one?"

"The operator was getting annoyed when she realized I was making her call every hotel on her list, so I went down to the library and found a map and some information on Cancún. You told me you would be staying at the end of the peninsula."

"I did?" She was impressed. This man remembered details about her that she didn't even recall giving him.

"And so it was simply a matter of deduction, and about five wrong numbers."

Ann laughed. "But this is outrageous. I would have told you where I was staying, but I never dreamed you would try to reach me."

"Dream again, dream girl. I'm getting addicted to you, just like somebody who's on drugs. In my case I have a heroine addiction."

She laughed, wishing more than ever that she hadn't let him leave her house so early that night. But his leaving had taught her that what he saw in her was more than sexual interest. Just hearing his voice reminded her how much she wanted to see him again.

I'll stop by in Miami on my way home, she decided, *even if it is out of the way. He's gone out of his way to see me. I can at least return the interest.*

"Tell me what you did today and talk fast," she commanded, "because this has to be costing you a fortune."

"Don't rush me," he protested. "I haven't heard your voice all day. Don't deprive me of the little pleasures."

"You are so sweet," she told him, tears coming to her eyes. "You have just made my entire day complete."

"I'd like to make your nights complete," he answered.

"Don't start on that," she said, laughing. "I was just beginning to be convinced you're not the big bad wolf I thought you were. You're negating your image."

"But I am a big bad wolf. I've never denied that I was."

"Maybe," she said. "But I like to think of you otherwise."

He changed the subject and told her about the kind of business he had conducted that day and she told him that she had finished her manuscript.

"Tomorrow's going to be a long day for you," he said, showing his concern. "Don't get eaten alive by jungle insects. Save something for me."

She laughed. "Things are much more civilized here than when Edward Herbert Thompson rediscovered the ruins. It will be a long, hot, dusty day, though. Thank you for your concern."

"I have a business meeting tomorrow night," he told her, "so I may not be able to call. When are you going home?"

"I'm not sure," she answered, thinking she would go to Miami on her way home, but she wanted to surprise him with her visit.

"Take care, and I'll talk to you before you leave."

I love you, she wanted to tell him. *I love you for caring about me when I'm traveling and am out of your sight.* With most of the others she had dated, "out of sight" had been "out of mind."

Ann was awake early the next morning. The guide she had hired to drive her to the ruins of Chichén Itzá met her in the lobby after breakfast. They started driving on the long narrow highway through the rocky terrain. They arrived early enough at the site so Ann and her guide had it practically to themselves. A few other tourists who had driven in private cars were exploring the Mayan remains of the Ball Court and Castillo, but it wasn't until after they had eaten their box lunch that the tour buses with their crowds of sightseers arrived. By that time Ann had acquired weakened Chichén Itzá knees from the number of steps she had climbed inside and outside the temples and from hiking from one side of the highway to the other, making notes and jotting down impressions for background material in her next book.

She dozed fitfully on the return drive to the hotel and made arrangements to meet the guide a little later for the trip to Tulúm the next morning. She was hot and tired and curious about the business partner Justin was having dinner with this evening. She showered, changed, and crawled into bed too tired to eat, but awake enough to wonder if he might still call.

The next morning she awoke stiff from her climbing and exploring the day before, wondering if Justin would call her tonight when she got back to the hotel. Just in case he should, she hurried through her exploration of the seaside ruins so that she could rush back to El Camino Real and be in her room by early evening.

It was a shame, she thought as she waited by the phone, to come so far and not take longer to appreciate the images of the Diving God and the Temple of the Frescoes. The Tulúm setting of temples tumbling beside the sea was dramatic, but all Ann could think of during her hours in the hot Mexican sun was getting back to the cool hotel room in case Justin should call.

It was late when the phone finally rang and she heard his voice. "You're always calling me," Ann told him. "But I have no idea of how to get in touch with you. What if I want to call you sometime?"

"Now you're beginning to sound like one of those aggressive ladies in your books." He chuckled and recited the various numbers where he could be reached at different times of the day.

"I thought you men liked forward ladies," she replied, wondering if she had deeper aggressive tendencies than she realized.

"Sometimes, but not all the time," he admitted. "This women's-lib movement has men all stirred up. We're not sure what our roles are supposed to be anymore."

"I never considered myself part of the movement." Ann bristled. "As far as I'm concerned a gentleman should always act like a gentleman around a lady."

"Oh, I agree." His voice traveled smoothly over the long distance line. "The problem is that not all women are ladies."

"A matter of semantics," she complained.

"Don't start bickering with me when I can't properly take you in my arms and silence you, woman."

"It's 'woman' now?" she questioned. "Whatever happened to the lady?"

"The lady is out of town and I want to know when she'll be back so that I can make plans accordingly."

"Do you have more business in New Orleans?"

"My business is here," he replied. "My pleasure is in New Orleans, although at the moment slightly removed to the Yucatán."

Ann smiled, laughing at his flattery. Just the sound of his voice could make her want him. His persistence in wanting to see her again added to the fluttery feeling pumping through her chest. "I plan to be back in New Orleans sometime Monday," she answered, keeping the surprise to herself that she was flying from here to Miami the next morning to see him.

She checked into the Fontainebleau Hilton again and took her time unpacking her clothes, her heart pounding each moment she delayed phoning Justin. What if her surprise backfired? He might have plans for the remainder of the weekend. He might have been leading her on about his interest in her over the phone, not dreaming she would show up in town expecting to be entertained.

Even if he had plans, she reasoned, now that she was here, surely he would make some kind of effort to see her. Ann unpacked the remainder of her notebooks and writing materials. One good thing about being a writer—she could work anywhere. If he was busy, she'd turn the remainder of the weekend into a working vacation—the way she always did.

It was early afternoon when she picked up the phone, no longer able to think of excuses to delay calling him. All he could do was say no. She worried as the phone rang twice, then four times. Her racing heart slowed its pace and disappointment sank in. *He's not at home,* she decided, as she continued to hold the phone and let it ring.

"Hello," a young feminine voice said.

Ann's heart jolted. She hadn't considered the possibility of there being another woman with Justin. Maybe she had the wrong number, she thought, somewhat less encouraged by the thought than she wanted to be. "Is Justin Frye there?" she asked haltingly.

"Just a minute," the girl said, and the phone receiver dropped with a clunk.

Terrific! Ann thought, he had a POSSLQ living with him. Now what should she say? "Justin? I'm sorry, did I interrupt anything?"

"Ann?" He recognized the sound of her voice but didn't pick up on the reservation in her tone. "How's the weather in Mexico?"

Ann sighed. Had they digressed to chitchat about the weather now that there was another woman involved? "Fine when I left it."

"Are you home already? I thought you weren't leaving until Monday."

"I'm going to New Orleans Monday," she reconfirmed. "I'm in Miami now."

"Here! Well why didn't you tell me? I would have met your plane."

"I wanted to surprise you," she admitted, then bit her tongue, thinking she should have concocted some sort of excuse for being here so that he wouldn't get the idea she had made this detour for his sake. "I . . . uh . . . had some writing I wanted to do here before going back to the cold weather in Louisiana. I've decided I'm a warm-natured person."

"I already knew that," he chuckled.

"But . . . uh . . . you have company."

"I do? Oh! The girls."

More than one? Her eyebrows shot up.

"I told you I was going to have them here for a couple of days."

"Oh! *The* girls," Ann said, realizing that he was referring to his daughters. It *had* sounded like a youthful voice, now that she thought about it. "You did tell me about them."

"What are your plans?"

"I don't really have any," she said, hoping he would fill in her schedule of free time as easily as he had booked her autographing engagements.

"The girls are leaving this afternoon, so let's have dinner together. I have to do some research on a presentation I need to organize for a client, so I won't be able to make it a late evening."

"I hope your girls aren't leaving on my account. I know you don't get to see them every day."

"It has nothing to do with your arrival," he answered her. "They've been invited to a weekend pool party, and they've decided they can't resist it. I guess that's more exciting than being with their father, so you won't be interrupting the schedule. I just wish I didn't have all this work to do tonight."

"If you're sure."

Ann sighed in relief and started thinking about what she would wear.

"Would seven o'clock give you enough time?" Justin asked.

Too much time, she thought, then hung up. Now that she was here and knew that she would be seeing him again she didn't want to wait.

He took her to Wong Kai, at the bottom of the Omni, where they dined on wonton soup, egg roll, and a combination of mixed Oriental vegetables and seafood, finishing the dinner with wine and Chinese tea. The decor of the restaurant, with its bamboo accents and paper parasols suspended from the ceiling, made Ann feel at home. She accused Justin of bringing her there to relax. Then he had added wine for the correct effect of helpless, hopeless adoration he had achieved.

"Are you helpless, hopelessly in love? Already?" he asked.

"Oh, yes!" she sighed. Then she quickly added, "With this place."

"That's what I thought," he said, his voice holding a hint of disappointment. "What I have planned for tomorrow night should change the emphasis of your . . . uh . . . affection."

She looked expectantly at him, wanting him to continue.

"I can't tell you anything about it now, mainly because I haven't managed to arrange it, but if a friend of a friend of a friend comes through with a favor he owes me, I think you'll be more than in love with the . . . uh . . . place I have in mind."

As long as the place included him, she probably would be. She leaned forward, intending to tell him how much she would enjoy a walk on the beach tonight, somewhere along the strip near the Fontainebleau.

He leaned forward and kissed her, smiling. "Unfortunately, I have that promotional package I need to finish preparing for my Monday presentation. And if I'm going to treat you to a special evening tomorrow, I need to burn some midnight oil this evening. I have to drop you back at the hotel now."

Ann hoped her disappointment didn't show. "I was just thinking about going for a walk on the beach," she said, undeterred, somewhat defiantly. "Maybe I'll do that anyway."

"Not alone," he stated.

"Why not?" she protested.

"After hours is not a good time for anyone as gorgeous as you to be out alone, beach or no beach, city or no city. Anything could happen. Some deep-sea diver could rise up out of the sea and kidnap you. Don't you read any of your books?"

She shook her head. "I just write them. They're only fantasies anyway. Why should I believe them?"

"Well, you're not walking on the beach alone tonight. If you want to walk on any beach it'll be the beach of my choosing tomorrow night. I'll throw it into the itinerary if you're so set on it."

"But I want to walk on the beach tonight," she said in defiance of him.

"Then I'll get a security guard at the hotel to go with you, because I can't, and you're not going alone."

Ann pouted, secretly pleased that he was so concerned about her safety, knowing walking the beach alone at night wouldn't be nearly the same as walking anywhere with Justin's arm around her.

"Promise me you won't go out alone after I drop you off," he said, his hand on her arm as if she would dash out of the restaurant right then if not for his restraint.

She nodded reluctantly. Attempts to entice him to stay with her tonight wouldn't work when they were weighed against his responsibilities as an independent businessman. She admired that even though it annoyed her that she couldn't be with him longer.

"I'll drive you back to the hotel then," he said, paying the bill and escorting her over the little footbridge at the entrance of the Wong Kai. The distance to the hotel seemed shorter than usual tonight, knowing he wouldn't be staying with her and that the evening was ending so soon. She smiled and kissed him when they arrived back at the hotel, insisting that he stay in the car instead of walking her the long distance to her room.

"It's nearly ten," she reminded him. "You have a lot of work ahead of you."

"I know," he mumbled, trying to get a steady aim on her lips. "Shut up and let me kiss you properly."

"How can you possibly kiss me properly if you can't finish what you begin?" She provoked him, knowing it was safe to be suggestive when he had to drive away in two seconds.

He drew away from her and his eyes darkened to a coal black. "If you'd quit squirming I would finish this properly."

"Masterful, aren't you?" She giggled, snuggling closer to him as she wrapped her arms around his neck and offered her lips for a kiss. She felt his lips hot against her own.

His tongue invaded her mouth as his thumbs probed the sensitive area of her neck. His hands slid increasingly unsteadily across her shoulders to grasp her upper arms, pressing her ever closer against him. He knew how to set her awash with sensations as a weak submission invaded her bones. A delicious sigh of satisfaction broke the silence around them.

"Don't start purring," he whispered against her lips, "or I might not leave you."

"No, you'd better go," she said, pushing away from him. "It was a lovely evening, however short."

"Tomorrow will be different," he promised, stroking her cheek with the back of his hand. "You know what?"

"What?"

"I missed you."

Ann laughed. "But it's only been a few days since we last saw each other, and you've called me nearly every day since then."

"Having you in my arms like this reminds me how little that was and how much more I want."

"You'd better go," she reminded him, her heart racing at the ardent look she saw in his eyes.

"I know," he said, straightening his tie and moving out of close proximity to her. "I'll pick you up early tomorrow evening, around six."

After Justin had driven away and Ann had walked to her hotel room, the thought of him lingered with her. It was such a beautiful moonlit night that it was a shame to spend it alone in a hotel room. The sandy strip of beach looked inviting from her room, but she had promised Justin she wouldn't go out alone and so she would have to content herself with TV and a magazine.

She stepped out onto her balcony, where the stiff breeze from the ocean tossed her hair back and caused her to shiver. After walking back into the room, she pulled the curtains open so that she could sit in front of the window and watch the ocean. But it wasn't the same because the closed doors blocked out the ocean's sounds.

The night ahead seemed interminable and she was bored already. She would have done just as well to have flown home to New Orleans, she thought, wondering what plans Justin was making for tomorrow.

It was sometime later when Ann heard a knock at her door. She glanced at the clock. It was after eleven and she hadn't ordered room service. Maybe it was Justin having more flowers delivered the way he had done the first morning after meeting her. But then, it could also be someone knocking on the wrong door. She tiptoed to her door to look through the peephole and saw Justin standing in the hallway. He had changed into blue jeans and a knobby sweater and was carrying a brown grocery bag. She thought of the night he had arrived at her house with his bag full of wine and cheese and wondered what he had in his bag of tricks tonight.

She unlatched the door and opened it. "Justin!"

"Don't just stand there, woman! Get your sandals on."

She laughed. "What are you doing back here? I thought you had to get some work done."

"I did, and I did," he said, smiling. "But the thought of you walking along that moonlit beach, without me, drove me batty. The whole time I was driving home I was wracking my brain trying to think how I could get through the pile of research I had to do."

"And?" she quipped, opening the door wider as she invited him into the room.

"I thought of my secretary. Actually, I had to bribe her, and it's really costing me this time," he answered, then smiled. "But I have a feeling it's going to be worth it."

Ann sat down in the wicker chair near the couch, pleased that the thought of her had brought him back sooner than either of them had planned. "What's in the bag?" she asked.

"Provisions," he answered, withdrawing a wine bottle for her inspection. "I thought we could steal a blanket from the hotel. Well, are you just going to sit there, or are you going to find your sandals? I only have all night, you know."

She laughed, looking down at her dress and up at his jeans. "I should change clothes, too."

"Wonderful," he said, grinning, "but I should warn you that sexy negligées are not allowed on beaches. In fact, in certain situations they aren't even allowed in hotel rooms."

"I was thinking of dungarees," she stated.

"Oh," he said, nodding. "I just thought I'd better mention that. Jeans will be fine this time."

Ann blushed and stepped past him to enter the

closet and find a pair of slacks and a shirt. She wondered if she had brought anything warm enough for the evening chill. A jacket might do, just until she could talk Justin into sharing some of his body heat. In his mood that might not be too hard to do. She grinned to herself as she walked into the bathroom to change out of her dress. He certainly had a knack for surprising her.

"Where are the spare blankets in this room?" he asked through the door.

"I'm not sure," she said. "Try the closet shelf, or maybe one of the bureau drawers."

She heard him as he slid drawers open and walked into her closet. "Found one."

Great! she thought, hurrying with the zipper of her jeans, anxious to be with him, wondering what he had in mind for tomorrow night when he was creating such magic tonight.

Ann showed Justin the back way out of the hotel, thinking it would be better to leave that way since they were borrowing the hotel's blanket on their moonlit mission. "Why won't you tell me what's in the bag?" she asked, clinging to his arm as they went through the picket-fence gate of the hotel grounds onto the solidly packed sand.

"All in good time," he said, humming, taking her closer to the water's edge, where the sand was softer. His hand went around her waist, encouraging her to hug her arms around him.

Ann sighed deeply, thinking how she had thought she was going to have to spend the rest of the evening alone.

"Are you cold?" he asked.

"Not at all. It's warmer than I thought it would be."

"Here," he said, stopping, "hold on to me while you take your shoes off."

The way he said it made Ann blush. The words sounded intimate, as if he were asking her to undress in front of him. In her present state of euphoria, and with the moonlight and the seductive sound of the waves, she wouldn't be at all surprised if that had been what he had asked her to do, and even less shocked to find herself responding unreservedly to his suggestion.

She balanced on one foot, leaning against his arm as she unbuckled her sandal strap and her bare foot met the cool, damp sand. She handed him her shoe while she removed the shoe from the other foot.

"How about you?" Ann lifted her face to him. "Want to hold on to me while you take your shoes off?"

"Nope." He smiled back. "I just want to hold, period."

She laughed and snuggled against him, loving the way her soft breasts felt when they encountered the firmness of his rib cage. She could see in the semi-light from the moon that a few other people shared their lust for walking the beach at this hour. It wasn't the same deserted atmosphere they would have found on an island like Antigua, where there were as many beaches as there were individual days in the year. But any beach was romantic when there was a man like Justin Frye beside her.

He rearranged the bag in his arms so that he could get a closer hold around her shoulders as they walked slowly away from the Fontainebleau. There were no words between them, and Ann didn't feel like talking. She lifted her face, content to feel the warmth of the man beside her, hear the sensuous splash of the ocean against the shore, and feel the sand beneath her bare toes.

"Let's spread out the blanket here," Justin suggested after they had walked at least a mile.

"Right here?" Ann asked, looking at the site he had chosen. It was the driest edge of the shore where the tides retreated, on an incline that would make them less conspicuous to other midnight beachcombers. It was too bad there was a wall of hotels behind them, instead of a wall of secluded palm trees on a private beach. Ann had always wondered what it would be like to be made love to with the surf splashing at her toes.

"That's what I brought the blanket for," he said.

"For what?" she asked, wondering if he had read her thoughts.

"So we can sit down, watch the ocean, and investigate my provisions."

"Oh," she said, watching him shake out the blanket. Justin smoothed it out as if he were making a bed and sat down, holding a hand to invite her down beside him.

Ann sat next to him with her legs crossed beneath her, Indian style. She turned and smiled at him, nervously wondering what was expected of her. "What's in the bag?" she asked, deciding now that they had stopped walking that she should say something.

He laughed and opened the bag, digging around in

it to pull out a box of crackers. "Open that," he said, "while I get everything else ready."

Ann tried to hold the box up to the moonlight. This was no ordinary box of Saltines, but something with a Melba round. She flipped open the lid and opened the plastic wrapping inside, then glanced back at Justin to see what he was doing.

He was fiddling with the lid of a small jar, holding a plastic spoon in his hand while he tried to free the stubborn lid.

"Need any help?" she asked.

He glared at her. Even in the moonlight she could tell it was a definite, mind-your-own-feminine-helplessness stare. Ann lifted her shoulders and smiled, content to let him demonstrate his macho strength with the jar. "The crackers are ready when you are," she said.

The jar opened with a pop the way a Champagne bottle would, and Justin reached for the box of crackers, spooning some of the contents of the jar onto a cracker. "Open your mouth," he said.

Ann followed his directions and closed her teeth around the salty-fishy-filled cracker. "Uhm." She grunted, grimacing, trying to chew the odd tidbits and swallow quickly before she got too much of a taste of whatever it was. She reached back for the box and stuck her hand inside for a fistful of plain crackers to help make the fish taste disappear. "What was that?" she asked when she could speak again and the taste was nearly gone from a few hurriedly eaten crackers.

"Caviar," he said, ready to hand her another portion of the delicacy.

"Is that what it tastes like?"

"Open up," he urged, pushing the cracker her way.

"No, thanks," she said, smiling. "I don't think I like it and I think that's good since it must have cost a fortune."

"I thought you loved caviar," he said, the cracker wavering in front of her.

"I've never had it before. Why would you think I was crazy about it?"

She watched his shoulders slump in the moonlight.

"In your books," he said, "the heroines are always ordering caviar."

"Sometimes it's necessary for the plot," she said. "It has a romantic sound to it, caviar—exotic, expensive, romantic. But heck, if it tastes like . . . like . . . like fish, I think I'll leave it out in the future. Sorry. Why don't you just save the caviar for yourself and I'll enjoy the crackers, plain."

Justin screwed the lid back on the caviar jar. "Does this mean you don't like Dom Perignon either?"

"Is that the other thing you have in the bag?" Ann asked, leaning forward to take a peek. "Do you know how much a bottle of that Champagne costs?" She looked at him, her mouth agape. "Oh. You do."

"Do you like it or not?" he asked, taking the bottle out of the bag and no longer treating it as an actor would an award-winning Oscar.

"Dom Perignon is delicious," she said.

He didn't look convinced.

"Honestly," she said, "I love it. But you don't have to open that bottle for me. I like all kinds of domestic champagne—pink, white, you name it. But a two-dollar bottle of Ripple would have the same effect. I'm no connoisseur."

"Now you tell me," he said, opening the bottle and pulling two glasses out of the grocery bag.

"I never pretended I was," she said. "Did you ask me?"

He shook his head, muttering, and handed her a glass of Champagne. "I just figured since caviar and Dom Perignon kept cropping up in all your books you liked both."

"Do they keep cropping up a lot?"

He nodded.

"Gee," she said, taking the glass from him. "Thank you." She sipped the Champagne. "Very good. Excellent choice. Actually, if I'm getting in a rut with this Champagne-and-caviar bit, I'd better switch to something else before the rest of my readers pick up on it and get bored with what I'm writing. Thanks for telling me," she said. "I hope I remember to make a note of that when I get back to the room." She looked at Justin, frowning at her, and thought: *it'll be just as hard to forget Champagne and caviar as it'll be that I've turned his romantic gesture into a disaster.* "Delicious Champagne," she said, quickly finishing her glass and holding it out for a refill.

"You don't have to drink it if you don't like it," he said, his face stony.

"I love it. But if you'd rather save it for a special occasion, I'll understand." She set the glass down on the blanket between them.

He picked it up and began refilling it. "This *was* the special occasion."

"It can still be," Ann said, moving closer to sit beside him. She still had enough pride not to throw her arms around him in total submission, but she would at least position herself within his reach if he should decide to make the next move.

Justin handed the second glass of Champagne to her and didn't say anything.

"I'm sorry," Ann said again, "but I didn't grow up with expensive tastes and I guess that's why I keep adding those expensive little touches to what I write. You mustn't always take me at my word."

"If I don't do that," he mused, his eyes in the moonlight cast in shadows as he gazed in her direction, "how am I to know who you are?"

"By being with me," she said, "like now."

He had tried so hard to please her with his Champagne and caviar that she wanted to do something to cheer him up. She took his glass out of his hand and with her own glass stuck them upright in the sand. Rising on her knees beside him, she circled her arms around his neck. Her heart raced at her shamelessness as she hoped she made the correct moves to please him and didn't scare him with her attempts at seduction.

She kissed him softly at the edge of his lips and felt no answering response. She leaned closer, laying her cheek against his, softly kissing his cheek, working her way toward his ear. Gently she took his ear lobe between her teeth and nibbled ever so lightly, then thrust her tongue slowly into his ear, smiling as his hands caught her ribs and his head nuzzled pleasurably against her. "Uhm," he mumbled.

Ann tried to move away from him, smiling.

"Don't go away," he whispered, his hands sliding up her back to pull her against him as he lay back on the sand, his lips enticing hers.

Ann laughed deep in her throat, falling onto his chest. She opened her mouth to his, loving the plundering exploration of his tongue and the wandering lust of his hands slipping from her back to tease along the sides of her body, up and down, skirting the softness of her breasts as his hands lifted her blouse to feel the warm contact of her bare skin. "I love the Dom Perignon," she whispered against his lips, laughter still lurking in her voice. "I love the beach and the moonlight. I may even love you."

"Uhm," he mumbled again. "I knew the Dom Perignon would be worth its price. But you're not close enough."

She laughed, her lips still touching, kissing, teasing his as she moved off her knees to lie entirely on top of him. Every pulse in her body was aware of his awakening desire.

Damn the hotel windows! she thought. If he wanted to make love to her, she'd just close her eyes and love every sensuous minute of it. But somehow, she thought, closing her eyes, like making love in a pitch-black room, would be depriving the senses of total love.

His hands continued to trace every inch of her back and sides. She felt him loosen the snap of her bra, but his hands continued to tease her breasts without touching them, the sensation all the more sensuous because his hands enticed her skin by deliberately approaching the fullness of her breasts but never fully grasping them.

Ann was breathless with longing for Justin. She began tugging at the edge of his sweater, tugging it up off his stomach to feel the bare contact of his chest against her breasts.

"You're driving me crazy," he said, regret and longing filling his voice as he rolled her over and lay on his elbows, looking down at her. His hands fumbled to unbutton her blouse, exposing the full swelling of her breasts to the moonlight and his view. "But I can't make love to you here," he said, his tongue flicking over her skin.

"I know," Ann said, her hands still linked behind his neck, not wanting him to stop, but knowing for propriety's sake he had to.

He cradled her face in his hands, kissing her lips, drugging her senses with his sexy touches. She slid down to stretch more completely against the full length of his body. Ann had never begged a man to love her before, but tonight that was what she wanted from Justin. She wanted to please him as well as experience the full sensation of his pleasure.

She pulled him down to her so that she could feel his bare chest against her breasts again; her toes curled in delight with the sensations racing through her body caused by his arousal. His mouth opened on hers, his tongue thrusting as his hips rocked against her, thigh against thigh, the barrier of their clothes seemingly nonexistent in the heat of their desire.

Ann arched against him, unmindful now of where

they were, conscious only of Justin, wanting him to take all of her. She was vaguely aware of the surf pounding against the shore until one surging wave splashed ice-cold against her foot. Ann shrieked and skittered from Justin's hold. Realizing what had happened, and embarrassed about what had distracted her, she laughed nervously and sat up, buttoning her blouse. "Justin, you have to stop this," she said, knowing she was blushing as she kept her eyes on the buttons, which didn't seem to fit the holes anymore.

"It's kind of hard to do," he said, watching her and clenching his hands. "Might I add that you haven't been helping me in the least?"

She glanced at him and smiled, then looked back at her half-buttoned blouse. "I know. It's not like me."

He laughed, pushing her hands aside and unbuttoning her blouse again.

"No, stop that," she said, "we can't—not here on the beach."

"I'm not trying to undress you again," he said, resisting her hands. "I'm only undressing you to dress you properly. You have the buttons in all the wrong holes. Stop wiggling or I'll forget I'm supposed to button these things up again." She sat still beneath his hands, afraid that if she made the slightest movement he would resume the lovemaking where he had left off. "I wouldn't have made love to you on the beach," he assured her, "as tempting as you make it. I respect you too much for public displays like that, even here at night. We're fairly sheltered by the sloping of the beach."

"But too close to the water," she reminded him.

He finished the buttoning and she straightened her blouse and tucked it in. "I will admit," he continued, "that you were making it very difficult for me to remember where we were. But I'd already guessed you were a temptress."

"Oh," she said, flattered. "Thank you. I never think of myself that way."

"But you don't have to," he told her, "as long as the man you're with thinks so, right?"

She shrugged. She had never been with a man like Justin Frye before. She had never considered herself the sexy siren who probably best appealed to a man like him. "I never thought about it."

He laughed, picking up the wine bottle and the two glasses. "You must have thought about it. Your books are laced with your sexiness."

"But that's just my imagination," she admitted. "I hope it comes across as real to the readers."

He looked at her, swallowing some Champagne. Leaning forward, he kissed her. They laughed together, the expensive Dom Perignon on their lips.

"I'd better take you back to the hotel before some film crew stumbles over us and wants to use us in their next B-grade flick." He put all the provisions he had brought with them into the bag and watched her strap her sandals on her feet before helping her up. It took a lot of shaking to get most of the sand off the blanket, and Ann knew no matter what they did, there would still be a considerable amount left in its folds.

She watched Justin without speaking, even more curious than ever about what making love with

Justin would be like. Now that she had time to think about the situation reasonably, she felt shy, afraid to continue from where they had just left off. What if she disappointed him? What if he discovered how inexperienced she was? What if she let him love her because she loved him, and then discovered in the morning that to him it was just another affair?

She walked hand in hand with him back to her hotel room, not speaking, too nervous to know what to say. In situations like these it was always best not to say anything. Silence could always be interpreted as deep intelligence or mutual consent or assurance in what one was doing, instead of what it really meant in this case—fear of being inadequate.

When they arrived at her room, Justin didn't enter it with her. He stood in the hallway, looking toward the bed, and smiled. "You know I want to make love to you."

She nodded. It wasn't a question as much as a statement.

"But not the way it would have been on the beach, and not here in a hotel room. That's too impersonal."

Half of her relaxed. Half of her wondered what he was going to suggest.

"I want our first time together to be something memorable. I don't want to leave you right after I make love to you."

Ann nodded, yet now that she had had a taste of a passion, she didn't want to let him go at all.

"Unfortunately, my bribe with my secretary extended my curfew only a few hours tonight. But tomorrow night I won't have to be in until well after dawn."

Tomorrow, she thought, when she wanted him now—now before she had time tomorrow to talk herself out of letting him fulfill her as only Justin Frye knew how.

"Besides," he said, kissing her, stroking her cheek as he spoke, "anticipation is half of the excitement."

She had had anticipation all her life. She wanted to know what the other half was all about.

Chapter Nine

*J*ustin's romantic evening the next night was worth waiting for, Ann thought as she watched him unload a full wicker basket from his car after they had parked at the marina.

Because she had anticipated this evening, and had worried about it all day, she nervously followed him along the wooden docks, past the gently rocking vessels to the sailboat he had borrowed for the evening. She had to admit it was a different sort of date, especially since Justin had already admitted he didn't know how to sail. His friend was usually along to tell him what to do and when. She didn't have to ask what would happen after the picnic basket was empty. The proper ending to last evening's beginning on the beach lay heavily unspoken between them.

The boat rocked on the water as Justin stepped on

board and, turning, held out a hand to help Ann across the narrow gap of water. "Watch your head," he warned, as he stepped along the bow and indicated that she should follow him around the cabin to the stern.

"Lovely boat," Ann said, taking her time walking behind him. She couldn't even ask him questions about the boat to dispel her nervousness because he had forewarned her that he knew practically nothing about it.

"My friend, Hal, spends every available moment on the weekend sailing her. The girls love it, too. Actually, they know more about it than I do."

How often did he use this place for a rendezvous? she wondered.

"Hal lets them sail it once we're out in open water." Justin continued talking, his voice now muffled since he had gone below. "It's embarrassing to have Beth and Sue giving me orders to loosen that line or tighten this one.

"Hal has considered chucking everything and just sailing her around the world for a couple of years, just following the wind and flowing with the tides."

"Sounds nice," Ann said, coming to the entrance of the cabin and looking in. "But I don't know if I'd want to live in such a confined space for such a long time, even knowing you'd have the world at your oar tips."

Justin turned from unpacking the wicker basket at the galley and smiled. "You don't use oars on a boat like this."

"Sorry," she said, sitting on the cushion beside the door where she could still feel in control of the situation. "It's a beautiful night. Can we eat on deck?"

"Exactly what I had in mind." He had brought china plates and crystal stemware, linen napkins and silverware.

"You don't believe in paper plates and plastic spoons, do you?" she teased.

"Can't stand paper napkins, and plastic forks always seem to break on me. Maybe it's the advertising side of me, but I've been spoiled by genuine articles. Things that have texture and strength to them serve my purposes better."

"I should have known about your individuality by this invitation to the boat this evening. I have to admit this is original, at least in my experience," she added, wondering again how often he invited women aboard his friend's boat. Did he rent out the cabin space on hourly rates?

"The boat was an accidental stroke of genius," he admitted, beginning now to uncork the Champagne bottle, Dom Perignon again, she noticed. "Although, ideally, I would have loved to show you the kinds of meals I can cook. Another time I'll invite you to my house."

"I'm glad you didn't, then," she said. "You probably would have ended up making me feel inadequate with my can opener and Pop Tart packages."

"The jambalaya was delicious," he said. "Even the best cooks have food stick to the bottom of pots from time to time." He climbed up the ladder steps to hand her a glass of Champagne, tipping his glass to hers. "No special toasts tonight," he said, his eyes dark in the disappearing light as the sun began to set.

"To you, the most beautiful woman I've seen sitting on Hal's boat."

Ann smiled and sipped the Champagne. "You're probably just saying that because everyone else gets up and works when they're aboard."

"In Beth's and Sue's case, yes, but, come to think of it, they're the only other women I've brought aboard. Now, Hal usually comes prepared, but I always have my girls for a date."

Ann glowed, and it wasn't from the Champagne. "I'm not certain I believe that," she said, afraid to look at him and see the truth of his statement reflected in his eyes. "This is such a natural romantic date. You mean you don't do this sort of thing every weekend?"

"Bringing a woman here, like you?"

She nodded, looking around again at all the other boats berthed next to them and behind them in the marina.

He was silent a long while. When she looked back at him he said, "This is a first for me, too. I might not have even thought of it if Hal hadn't phoned right before you did yesterday to tell me about his own plans for the weekend. I wanted to bring you somewhere special. And you know from last night how I feel about hotel rooms, even plush ones like the Fontainebleau. Hotel rooms, especially in the same town where you live, should be reserved for the times after you're married when you need a wicked escape from the daily routine."

Ann laughed, then sipped more Champagne. "There seem to be a lot of other people spending their evening on board. Is Sunday evening the night for it?" She could see lights on several other ships, including the one berthed next to Hal's boat.

"They probably live aboard," Justin said, coming out on deck to sit next to her. "For a lot of people this is their life."

"What do they do for a living?"

Justin laughed. "For a romance writer, you should know all about this. It's part of the great life, living aboard ship. They charter their boats, for a day or week or longer, and drop anchor whenever the mood suits them."

"Oh."

"Some of these boats have more comforts than regular homes do, from color television sets to microwave ovens."

"Now that you mention it," Ann said, "I recall seeing some of the larger ones in St. Thomas with helicopters on special launch pads on board."

"Those are for the ultra rich. People who have sailing in their blood put their entire life into the ship. Docking fees are a lot cheaper than rent in some of the resorts they frequent, and they're a lot like a turtle—they take their home with them when they decide to move."

Ann leaned back on her arms, relaxing with the Champagne, grateful that Justin wasn't trying to rush her into anything. It was a pleasant evening, an ideal location, and she had the most perfect man she had met in years beside her. She sighed, thinking about the kind of life he was describing. "I have to envy them. I don't think I could do it. I've become too accustomed to having my car and my answering machine and my typewriter and my word processor with me, not to mention my king-sized bed and the few antiques I've picked up over the years. I've been spoiled by possessions."

"But don't you give up a lot with the kind of life you lead traveling as much as you do?" he asked, his voice deadly serious.

"Like what?" she asked, tensed for his answer. He may be wildly guessing, but it was as if he saw the loneliness she inflicted upon herself with the intensity of her career.

He looked at her with eyes narrowing and answered, "Little things, like time to sit and do nothing, or take the dog for a walk around the block."

"I don't have a dog."

He shrugged. "Or spending an entire day trying to figure out how to bake the perfect loaf of bread."

Ann blushed because she did envision herself with an apron tied around her waist and her arms up to her elbows in flour with a child tugging at the hem of her skirt.

"Or time," he said, reaching up and touching her cheek with the back of his hand, "to enjoy the kind of pleasure only a man and woman can bring to each other."

Ann's lower lip quivered. Lucky guess or not, he had pinned her down to exactly what she had been running from with her writing as an excuse. She touched his wrist, circling it with her hand. She always kept telling herself that someday she'd take time: someday she'd take time to play the piano; someday she'd take time to learn how to fly an airplane; someday she'd take time to go for riding lessons; someday she'd take time to fall in love.

Now she knew clearly that Justin had taken the decision out of her hands. He hadn't given her time to think or act, only to react to him, in love.

He picked up her hand and brought it to his lips, kissing the back of it and then the palm, sliding his tongue between the juncture of each finger, deliciously exploring her hand as thoroughly as he would an Eskimo Pie on a stick. Ann melted at his touch, quivering from his sensuality.

He kissed her next, pulling her lower lip into his mouth, tracing the form of her teeth with his tongue, teaching her with his tongue what tenderness could mean. His hands slid from her cheeks to the back of her neck, massaging the tight muscles, while his tongue slipped inside her mouth.

Ann sighed against him, giving in to the sensations racing through her body. She leaned her head back and imitated his kisses, catching both of his wrists with her hands to slide and massage the soft skin at his wrists in a sensuous movement that she hoped could halfway compare to the gentleness of his kisses.

A soft moan escaped his lips as he felt her answering response and pulled her closer to him toward his lap. Ann laughed as she fell against him.

"Come here," he whispered, his lips barely leaving hers.

She sat across his knees and let him situate her so that she was comfortably cradled in his arms, his mouth locked even more intimately against her own, his hands moving up and down her back.

"You drive a man crazy," he whispered, kissing her ears and her eyelids. "Do you know that?"

"Not if you don't tell me," she returned, amazed that he could make her entire body feel so sexy by touching so little of her. It was the way he did it, with soft, unexpected kisses around her mouth and at her neck and on her ears, his hands bringing alive every nerve ending in her back.

It would be so easy for him to undress her here and now. She wanted to help him; at the same time she wanted to find some way to bottle the quivering sensations he was causing in the pit of her body. His hands taught her anticipation; his lips promised fulfillment.

"Love me," whispered Ann, *the way I love you,* she added to herself.

Justin cradled her face in his hands and looked at her in the dimming light. "I do love you," he said, causing her heart to pump harder at the words she had dared not ask to hear.

It's what I want to hear, she thought, her heart overjoyed at the statement. She put her arms around his neck, hugging him tightly. He seemed to sense exactly what she wanted and needed.

Ann nuzzled her head against his neck, content to lie in his arms and follow his lead. She loved Justin and it was only in love that she would give herself to any man.

"Let's go below," Justin said, letting Ann slide off his lap, but not letting her hand slip out of his grasp. He steadied her as she climbed down the narrow steps, her legs more wobbly from contact with Justin than from the boat's rocking in the unsteady water.

Justin had carried their Champagne glasses with him. As he stood close behind Ann, he handed one of the glasses to her and set the other down. He wrapped his arms around her from behind and pulled her against his chest, kissing the back of her neck, blowing softly against the nape. "You do drive this man crazy," Justin said. He whispered, "I can't get enough of you."

"I love having your arms around me," Ann told him, reaching up to grab his arm and clasp herself more tightly in his hold.

He squeezed her tightly, then rocked her gently in his arms. After a while he picked up his Champagne glass and took a swallow from it before returning it to the galley's countertop.

Ann sipped her Champagne, knowing it couldn't make her half as delirious as Justin's kisses did. Her heart was racing and she was growing more heated with desire, grateful that he wasn't the kind of man who took off a woman's clothes as if they were a single unit, making her feel like a paper doll. Justin knew how to sustain the moment, to create the highest form of anticipation from a look, a word, a touch. He was kissing her neck again. She nuzzled closer against him.

Then his hands began unbuttoning her blouse from where he stood behind her. He took his time, one button by one button, kissing her neck and blowing softly in her ear as he undressed her.

Ann trembled in his arms, hoping that when it came time for her to turn her loving on him she would not disappoint him in her lack of experience.

The blouse came off her shoulders and he slid his hands along her silky skin to grasp and tenderly hold the swells of her breasts through the sheer material of her bra. Justin turned her gently in his arms. Ann set her glass down on the counter beside his and placed her hands against the firm angles of his shoulders, standing on tiptoes to kiss him.

As he unhooked her bra and peeled it off her, her unsteady hands began undoing the buttons of his shirt. She was grateful he wasn't wearing a tie tonight because, as nervous as she felt doing this simple task, she didn't think she would be able to figure out the mystery woven into the knot of a tie.

His hands were on her shoulder blades, his fingers walking up and down her spine. His lips clasped hers as his hands moved down to her hips, crushing her against him. Then his hands were on her waist, and on the front closure of her jeans, unsnapping and unzipping them, slipping them down while she helped him take them off.

Ann pulsed with awareness of Justin, her own hands shyly unsnapping his pants, but leaving it to him to take his pants off and stand naked against her.

"I could touch you all night," he said, his hands on every inch of her silky skin.

"Sounds good to me," she answered, her own hands smoothing over the muscles of his back, afraid to touch him too intimately, yet knowing by the end of the night there would not be an inch of him her body would not know.

She pulled his head down to hers, needing his lips against hers. With a soft moan she opened her mouth to him, letting all of her senses revel in the heat of his kiss, his tongue roaming sensuously against her lips, teasing her tongue, firing her desire with an aching need. Ann put her arms around him, digging her nails into his back. She could feel her heart racing against his bared chest as he deftly picked her up and carried her to the narrow bed. His lips never left hers as he lay down beside her, stroking her skin as they touched.

His mouth was on hers again, telling her how much she excited him, yet showing her with tenderness how much he respected her. His kisses revealed his desire, and invited her response, taking her step by step toward fulfillment, teaching her that it would be only half as good for him if she didn't feel part of the experience, too.

Ann arched closer to him, wanting all of him now, yet wishing this time together could linger for days and weeks as they hovered on the brink of expectancy.

He nibbled on her ear, burying his face in her hair, running his fingers down her side, along her thighs, as he began blowing on her neck. Ann moaned against him, melting further at his tenderness and ability to put her pleasure before his, delaying his own need for fulfillment as he brought her body to a fever pitch beside him.

He took his time, heightening Ann's desire to pull him to her and make him one with her. His hands warmed her hips and caressed her curves, while his mouth traveled from her chin to her throat, across her shoulders and back to her collarbone. Tenderly he stroked her cheeks and her breasts, then took her hand again, kissing her fingers, one by one until she wanted him to devour the rest of her in as great an intimacy.

Ann put her hands against his chest, unable to kiss his lips while he seduced her hand, but wanting to stroke him as thoroughly as he was teaching her. She kissed his shoulder, loving the feel of the sparse hair on his chest against the softness of her breasts. She let her hands follow the muscled line of his thighs, across the breadth of his legs, and up past the firmness of his stomach and chest. His body was as tight as it looked, as smooth and unmarred as a statue, yet alive with nerve endings that answered her touch with pleasure.

His tongue traveled first to one breast and then to the other, teasing the hard tips of her nipples as his hand spread across her abdomen and continued to slide up and down her back. He seemed to know instinctively how tender and sensitive the area between her shoulder blades was, as he gently stroked her back with his hand while his mouth met hers in another soul-drenching kiss.

Justin scooped Ann into his arms and pulled her onto his chest while he lay beneath her. His hands stayed at her shoulder blades, but his mouth spoke to her in exploring thrusts of his tongue, nibbles with his lips, and nuzzling cheek to cheek. Ann felt overwhelmed with love from his tenderness.

He kissed her chest, glowing in the dim light with a sheen of perspiration, the soft breasts above him inviting his touch. He pulled her down, down against him and then became part of her.

Ann moaned at the sensations she felt rocking gently against him, beside him, with him, as the creaks of the boat's wood echoed their motions. She was locked together with Justin, riding out the storm of passion he created with his touch and his mouth blazing new sensuous paths around her breasts and along the inside of her arm. She wanted to cry from the feelings of love and happiness that filled her.

He carried her with him in wave after wave of feeling that seemed to swell and swell with love, but not quite peak. "Oh, baby," he whispered, his voice fevered and frantic. Ann clung to him as desire engulfed both of them, cresting in a pool of sensation that swirled and eddied and then swept them away again.

Justin's voice was full of laughter at the release they had both deliciously shared. He blew at the damp hair of her neck and hugged her possessively beside him, their bodies still together in the miracle of motion and love they had just shared. "Ann, you are a love," he whispered as he continued to blow softly at the flushed skin of her neck.

Ann lay in his arms deliciously tasting the feel of his smooth skin against hers as she listened to the gentle lapping sounds of the water as the boat rocked at its moorings. She wouldn't mind sailing into never-never land with Justin.

She ran her hands along his skin, enjoying the moment, enjoying the images that flooded her thinking. For such an independent man, what kind of a wife would he need? Someone to take care of the kids, stand in the background stirring a pot of stew, letting the limelight shine on him and his accomplishments? If she had to play that role, could she?

Ann lifted herself up on her elbow to look down at

his face through the musky darkness. He felt her looking at him and opened his eyes, smiling up at her. Ann smiled back, then lay down on her outstretched arm.

For the right man she could play any role he asked. Hadn't she already done that countless times in her books? But if the role were not one naturally suited to her personality, it wouldn't work for long. It would do no good to play games with this man. He, as would any man who wanted to keep her in his life, would have to accept her as she was without plans for changing her—the same way she would have to do with him. While she would be capable of sharing the limelight with someone, she wouldn't be happy if it were taken totally away from her. She needed her career and the satisfaction it gave her. And it had taken her so long to build up her success, she couldn't easily give it up.

What was he looking for, she wondered, in a woman, in a wife, for his life? What was it about her that had appealed to him in the first place?

Would a house in the country appeal to this man? Could he live with horses and dogs running through the fields and come home to a woman burning the keys on a word processor with nothing on the stove? Would they need to hire a housekeeper?

No, that wouldn't work. Ann amended her thinking. There would be times when she wouldn't want anyone else in her house. Justin's children could spend the night with a friend once in a while, and she would have the house dark and mysterious when he drove home. It would be just dark enough and out of the ordinary to make him wonder if they might have accidentally forgotten to pay the electric bill that month.

But he'd only wonder about that long enough to find her in the bedroom, where she would have dinner set for two by candlelight. It would be a dinner she would have fixed herself, without the help of the frozen foods or Bess's explicit instructions. And although he might not say a word about the food, she would know by his grin there wouldn't be anything better he'd rather have that evening.

Ann sighed against him. His arms tightened around her. She smiled. She couldn't remember the last time she had felt this happy.

"Uhm," she mumbled, busy kissing the damp skin of his shoulder as she lay in his arms beside him. "Do you want to try for an epilogue?"

He chuckled and gently nipped her ear. "You don't give a man a long shelf life, do you?"

"Not when I enjoy the ending as much as the one you just helped me write."

He continued laughing, his finger trailing down her nose to her chin, along her neck to her breasts. "Put your notebook away for the rest of the night, okay?"

"Why?" she teased. "Are you afraid of what I might write about you in my next book?"

"I certainly don't want to end up being another Ron Carrington," he said, blowing at the dampness between her breasts.

Ann drew away from him, catching his hand with hers. "What do you know about him?" she asked, frowning.

"Nothing," he answered, unaware of her agitation, continuing to kiss her shoulder, "other than that I've met him and don't want to end up like him."

"Which is?" She caught his hand and made him look at her, her eyes riveted on his face.

"Knowing that you live up to the passion you suggest in your books, I don't want to be discarded once my usefulness as a character is finished." He tried to pull her back into his arms, but she resisted. "I'd like to become a more permanent fixture, maybe the subject of an ongoing saga."

Ann scrambled away from him, dragging the sheets with her as a sarong to hide her nakedness from his eyes. "Is that what you think of me?" she accused.

All this time while she had been luxuriating in his arms he had been comparing her to the characters she had imagined in her books. It was as if he had used her fiction as a maintenance manual to retain her heart. What made it especially irritating was that he'd been good at it!

"Hey!" he said, reaching up to touch her cheek, but she backed away. "What is wrong with you? A minute ago—"

"That's what I'd like to know!" she blazed. "A minute ago you were finally getting the culmination of the last few weeks of attention you paid to me. And for what? Just to say that you've taken the romance novelist to bed and she takes her notebook with her. Is that all it meant to you?"

"Hey!" he said, trying to calm her.

Ann continued, ignoring his single uttered word.

"Just what do you think I am—one of those sensationalist writers who doesn't care where her information comes from or how much she makes up about prominent people as long as they can find some kind of way to make money off it? Is that how little you think of me?"

"Ann—" He tried to interrupt her tirade.

"I don't want to hear it!" She cut him off. "You've just been reading me like some kind of article in a *Playboy* magazine, haven't you?"

"I have read your books to gain an understanding of you," he admitted. "What's wrong with that?"

"Nothing—*if* you're taking a course in Ann Straus Literature One. If you're trying to understand me as a person, you should treat me as a person and not a figment of my own imagination."

"What we just shared together didn't feel too imaginary to me," Justin pointed out.

"That's beside the point," Ann said, blushing. His lovemaking had felt genuine to her until she realized how contrived it had really been. "Obviously you studied the books very well."

"I resent that," Justin said.

"We-e-ll." Ann drew out the word. "At least we agree there. I resent the way you've treated me."

"Funny, I thought you were enjoying that about two minutes ago."

Ann tucked the bedsheets closer around her. "I guess I have to give you credit. You swept me right into your plan."

"Listen," he said, staring her down, "I'll admit it did cross my mind to try to make love to you the way

Marcus did to Jane, and Samuel did with Angelique, but no one's ever had to tell me how to make love to a woman before. And if I had tried to follow your blueprint for bed, I would probably be interrupting the spontaneity of what was happening between us when I turned pages in your damned books to see what I was supposed to do next—where I was supposed to put my hands and where my feet went and how I was supposed to kiss you. There are certain things I don't take instructions for."

"You could have fooled me," Ann pouted.

"Obviously I did," he said sarcastically, "until you got this cockeyed idea in your head about my trying to read you like I read your books."

"You must think that," she argued, "to believe I used Ron just so I could create a real-life character for one of my books."

He didn't answer her right away, and when he did speak it made her even angrier than ever. "Maybe I don't resent the idea that you used him as a character in your books so much as the thought of him in bed with you."

"I never let that man in my bed!" she said.

"His bed, then. A hotel room. What difference does it make where the event took place?"

"The event *never* took place with him!" Ann denied vehemently. "You have some wild imagination yourself if you think that. That's why I quit seeing him. I don't have to go to bed with a man to imagine what it would be like. There are enough sex manuals on the market today for me to do all the research I need for that in the library."

"But the Lear jet and the jet-setting life-style . . . damn, even the description of the man! I can't be mistaken that it was him."

"It was only him as I imagined him to be," Ann explained. "Outwardly, he looked like, and lived the life of, the perfect hero. But when you get to know him as a person, he's not. Far from it. And I didn't want to get to know him any better as a person than I had already experienced on a superficial basis. I thought that you and I were going beyond the superficial level. But if all you're interested in is staring at one of my novels—"

"You're twisting everything I've said," Justin said in a calm voice. "Of course I don't think you're trying to use me. Even if you were, I'd be a willing victim."

"Even if I were—" she sputtered.

"Listen," he said, his voice as smooth as honey in a hive, "if anything, I would take it as a compliment if you decided to use me as the basis for one of the characters in a book of yours."

"Oh," she said, crossing her arms over her chest and glaring at him in the near darkness of the cabin, "was that an audition just now? Is this boat the new version of a casting couch? Will you settle for a bit part?"

"I'll settle for you to settle down and tell me what's upsetting you so much. Two minutes ago we were making love together. Now it's as if we're fencing with fully loaded umbrellas about to pop open with a barrage of sharpened pencils."

"There, you see," she said, still pouting. "You're doing it again."

His eyebrows went up, but his silence caused her to finish the sentence with, "You're making fun of my writing."

Justin started laughing, which caused Ann to retreat farther into the corner. "I am hardly the man to make fun of a woman's career when that woman makes a hell of a lot more money than I do and has a damned reputation for her art that can set people talking around the world. I happen to like your writing. Have I ever complained about it to you?"

"I just don't know what you expect," she complained. "You're always making references to the books I've written, dredging up details I don't remember writing because the books you're reading were written so long ago. How can you know what's in my head now?"

"By reading your books," he insisted. "You once told me so much of what you write comes through your life."

"Partly," she admitted. "But I do not take my male heroes from my bed partners."

"Not even Ron Carrington?"

"There! You see! You're accusing me again of using him."

"I still can't take this in. What you wrote about him was so real—I mean, so real that I recognized him as the rake in *Cast My Shadow* when I actually met him. The part fit him better than an alligator T-shirt."

Ann rearranged the folds of the sheet around her body as if it were a satin ball gown and she were holding court as the queen. "His life-style appealed to me so I fictionalized it. Give me a little credit for creative imagination. On second thought, better give me a lot of credit where that excuse of a man is concerned. It took a lot of effort to make him sound good as a hero. You'll just have to take my word for it."

Justin looked blankly at her. He raised himself onto one hip, his elbow propped onto his raised knee. "I guess it's a good thing for me that I didn't rent that Lear jet I was thinking of chartering to fly you to Atlanta for dinner this evening."

"You were going to do what?" She brought her knees up against her chin, tucking the sheets tighter around her.

"I wanted you to have a memorable evening and I assumed from your book that picking up on the spur of the minute and flying to some other city for a meal or a cup of coffee appealed to you. It's hard to top some of the events you describe in your books."

Ann looked incredulously at him for a long moment and then started laughing. "You were actually going to charter a plane for a date this evening?"

"And probably have to take out a bank loan to pay for it."

She hugged her sides, still laughing. "But that's ridiculous. Why did you think you had to go to such lengths to take me on a date?"

"Look at you. You're a world traveler. You've been places and done things most people only dream of doing all their lives. Meeting kings and queens is part of a steady diet for you."

"I've never met a king or a queen, except the burger variety. And once aboard the *QE Two*."

"Exactly," he said, running a hand through his

hair. "How many people get the opportunity to take a cruise in their life? How many people jet from one city to the next as if they were running down to the local convenience store for a loaf of bread?"

Ann lifted her shoulders. She knew exactly what he was saying and how true it was. But he was overlooking the fact that there was a person behind all of that outward flamboyance, a person who was locked in a lonely shell because of her life-style, a person whom very few people took time or effort to try to get to know better. "It just sounds like a good life," she said. "That doesn't necessarily mean that it is. People like to read about that kind of fantasy existence. It happens to be easy for me to write because I can base the spark of creation on fact. But there's a lot about that dream world that I leave out."

"I think I'm beginning to realize that," he said. "But give me an example so that I know for certain I'm not misinterpreting you again."

"I leave out the lonely hotel rooms. The anxiety of going into another strange restaurant to eat a meal alone. I leave out the twelve-dollar hamburgers ordered from room service just because I don't feel like dressing up in a facade of self-confidence to dine out alone. I've left out the ache for another person, the longing for another life in which I can count on where the next hug is coming from in the morning."

"But you put a lot of love in your books," he said, swinging his legs off the bed and stepping across the confined space to pull on his jeans.

She watched him, aware of his nakedness and how unselfconsciously he moved. "I put a lot of sex in the books because the readers enjoy that. But just because you read it in my books doesn't mean I orchestrate every move to make certain it works before I write it. Is that what you think about me—that I'm this experienced woman who flits from man to man, taking the best parts of each one and sucking them dry like some kind of black-widow spider? Just for the sake of my books? If I use anyone in my novels, it's a compliment to the fact they made an impression on me—usually favorably. I use only the best qualities for my hero."

He had his back to her, zipping up his slacks, pulling on his shirt.

Ann slid out of bed, dragging the sheet with her, looking for her clothes. "That is what you thought, isn't it? That I'm some sort of hedonist who has no room for feelings or emotions. Because if you've looked at my books at all—and I'm beginning to see that you've not only looked at them, but studied them like some kind of lesson plan—I think you'll see my women characters reveal very little emotion."

"I do find them reacting purely out of bodily need," he admitted, turning to her and watching her clutch her clothes against the sheet she was struggling to keep around her.

"Have you ever asked yourself why?" She paused, staring him down. "Have you ever asked me why?"

He didn't answer her. She continued to stare at him, willing the tears not to fall—at least not in front of him. He didn't deserve a display of emotion from her. He, like all the rest, cared to treat her only superficially. There was no reason she could see to explain to him why she kept emotion out of her books, because she left it out of her life, because no man she had ever met had taken the time to touch her heart. They all expected her to be the best-selling author. None ever wanted to know the heart and soul of Ann Straus. It was enough that she was a prize to show other men, nothing more than bits and pieces of anatomy, nicely enough packaged like one of her sexy, best-selling book covers.

She pulled the sheet over her head, not wanting to look at him anymore, not caring how ridiculously childish her actions appeared to him as she struggled into her clothes beneath the sheet.

"I will admit," she said when she was semi-decently dressed, "that you did go to a lot of trouble to get me into bed with you. I don't think anyone else has ever researched me quite the way you have."

He leaned back against the galley counter.

Ann looked at him, wishing he would reach across the space and pull her to him. She wanted him to tell her everything would be all right, that he could love her for the person she really was. But obviously he couldn't. Maybe nobody could.

"You're a busy woman," he said matter-of-factly. "I'm a market researcher. It seemed logical to study everything I could about you to find out who you were. The books were the natural material. Not everyone has such a ready medium for open review in the public domain. And I knew that because you travel so much, I had a limited amount of time to make an impression on you."

"You definitely succeeded there."

He shrugged. "I see now I went about it the wrong way."

"I'm kind of sorry you failed," she admitted, taking a deep breath, hoping that would steady her rocky emotions. "You certainly put more effort into the seduction than anyone else has ever done. But you've drawn all the wrong conclusions from what you've read. In fact," she said, anger still filling her voice, "I'll let you in on a secret."

He waited.

"I hide behind my words. Don't believe everything you read. Don't try to second-guess me. Don't make me into one of my out-for-sex-only heroines.

He did reach for her then, putting his hands on her upper arms, but she shrugged away from him. "If you don't mind," she said, squaring her chin, "I'd like to take my notebook and go home. And I don't mean to the hotel, either. I'm ready for a flight out of Miami." *Out of your life,* she added to herself.

"I'll take you to your hotel," he said, "and I'll take you to the airport, and I'll agree you have every justification for feeling the way you do. But I won't let you go feeling cold-hearted toward me. No, wait," he said, catching her shoulders as she turned her back on him. "Listen to me."

Justin turned her around to face him. "You're an exciting woman. I felt that the first time I met you, before I'd read a word you'd written. All I knew was I wanted to get to know you better and this seemed the easiest way to fit into your schedule. I failed, miserably, but that doesn't mean I won't try to see you again."

"Then do me a favor," she said, her chin lifting

even higher in defiance. "Don't play any games with me. I don't know which part of you is real now or which part of you is fake. I don't know if I can trust you."

He nodded. "I've made it tougher on myself, haven't I?"

Ann didn't answer him. Part of her didn't want to leave him. Part of her was still pulsing from the gentleness of his lovemaking. But most of her was outraged. She should have guessed sooner what it was he was doing. She shouldn't have thought it was so flattering that he was reading her books because he liked what he read. She should have guessed he had used her books only to make fun of her.

She had to get away from him, to retreat into her books, where she understood the characters she was dealing with, where she could manipulate the men she created in her mind. This man made her uneasy because she didn't know how to handle him.

A real man wouldn't even try to copy the love scenes she had written in her books. He would create a genuine love of his own. It didn't even make her feel better to accept as flattery how realistically she had written her love stories to make him believe they were based on fact.

Chapter Ten

Ann arrived back in New Orleans in the chill of early morning, trying to put the warmth of Justin's touch out of her mind. It was difficult to maintain her clipped, angry tone when he phoned her shortly after she got to her house, just checking to see that she had arrived safely.

Maybe she was being unreasonable in her anger toward him, but she couldn't help feeling used. He had not, as she had thought during their initial meetings, been treating her as an ordinary person. He had stacked all of her books between them, read between the lines to decide who she was, and had filled in all the wrong blanks.

But had he interpreted her personality more accurately than she wanted to admit? Was she writing more of herself into the books than she thought she was? Maybe he knew her by reading her books better than she knew herself.

Ann stomped off to bed, not even bothering to unpack her suitcases as she usually did after a trip. She didn't want to deal with that clutter tonight. She didn't want to deal with anything. She would just content herself with her sheltered existence at the word processor. It was so much easier than confronting reality in the shape of someone like Justin Frye.

She looked at the mask he had given her on the last evening she had shared with him here at her home. How accurately had that gift described her? How much did she hide behind the mask of her books? How much did she want to believe her own image that the books had created, of the glamorous globe-trotting single woman who could make it in this man's world? And what points would she be proving to herself or anyone else if she did manage to make a success of her career alone? If there was no one there to share the success with her, how valuable could it be?

"To heck with it," Ann said to the walls, throwing off her clothes and climbing into bed. "Why can't someone just accept me for myself? Why do they have to expect me to live up to certain roles?"

Maybe what really frightened her, she decided as she lay sleeplessly in the big empty bed, was that she wasn't sure what role she wanted to play for the rest of her life.

Ann threw herself back into her work the next day. But as she worked on each page she asked herself if this was really her. She wondered how much of herself was real, and how much was invented. If she took away the imagination, what would be left? A very dull person, Ann realized, and someone who had a boring routine.

She didn't like Justin's assuming she was more exciting and glamorous and jet-setting than she really was. But if she removed that activity from her life, what was left? She didn't want him to think she was as much of a stick in the mud as she thought herself to be, either.

She found herself wondering what Justin would think of various passages she wrote, particularly the newest seduction scene, which, as she read over it, she realized did incorporate his own gentle brand of lovemaking. At least she could see how he could begin thinking her writing was self-revealing.

But how could he have thought Ron Carrington would make a great lover after meeting that jerk?

She slaved over the word processor, turning out more pages in a single day than she had produced in total the past week. But when she read over the manuscript to make minor changes and correct her grammatical errors, she realized she had written Justin Frye's name in place of the current hero's.

Two days after she was home a bouquet of flowers turned up on her doorstep. Ann had been to the grocery store and had an armful of bags while she was trying to maneuver the key in the lock. Once she had turned the knob and kicked the door open she could peer down at the bouquet for a better look.

It was a mixed collection of freshly cut flowers. She put the groceries on the kitchen counter and went back to the door to bring the flowers inside, pulling the card from the prongs where the florist had stuck it.

I wasn't sure if you liked the orchids, or violets, or roses best, so I decided to order something that wouldn't involve second-guessing your tastes to let you know I'm thinking about you and want to see you again.

Ann smiled. A variety of flowers was a safe choice. He didn't have to know what her favorite flower was. The flowers themselves carried all the necessary messages.

Maybe I'll give him a second chance, she thought. How many women ever got a second chance loving a man?

She sat down at the table and thought about love. Blast it all, but as much as she might like to deny it, that was the feeling she got whenever she thought of Justin Frye, anger or no anger.

But maybe she just felt that love toward him because she wanted so desperately to feel it from any man. She really wasn't certain she could trust him, no matter how good his intentions had been. He had play-acted to produce the kind of man he thought would appeal to her. What if she discovered beneath that façade that she didn't like the man who really lived there?

What if he bored her?

She'd think about it while she was in Curaçao,

visiting her friend next week, she told herself. Right now she had work to do.

She did more than think about Justin while she was in the Dutch Caribbean city, walking past the fish-market stalls beside the docks, watching the cruise ships come through the wooden pontoon bridge. She talked about Justin every day and took long walks through the narrow lanes thinking about him, missing him more as she watched couples walking hand in hand around her.

She *had* written too many romance novels. She had come to expect that the perfect man was out there somewhere for her. But he wasn't. He didn't exist, not without some help. The perfect man, like the perfect relationships she wrote about, took work and a lot of effort, from both people. Justin had already put forth a lot of effort. The least she could do was help steer him in the right direction.

Ann talked with her friend Angelique for long hours during her stay on the sugar-sand beaches of Curaçao. Idly they passed their days watching the waves roll in while Angelique listened. When Ann asked her for advice, she was told, "You already know what you want and what you're going to do about this mysterious man. You just needed to hear yourself out on the subject."

"But what do you think about it?" Ann asked. "What should I do?"

"Exactly what you have in mind to do," her friend said, smiling. "Go after him."

Ann smiled. Yes, she did want to see Justin. But she wouldn't fly into Miami again. She would wait for him to come to her. If he wanted to see her again with a new beginning, she shouldn't have too long to wait.

Besides, for once she wanted to be the helpless female in need of a strong male. What did handling all her burdens herself prove except that she had a strong back?

"Look at it this way," Angelique told Ann one afternoon as the hot December sun toasted their bodies a warm bronze. "He took the time and effort to try to figure out what you're all about. How many men have you run into these days who even give a damn about a woman's pleasure?"

"I haven't met any," Ann answered, squeezing a cool dollop of sunscreen onto her heated shoulders.

"Exactly. Most men care about nothing but their own creature comforts. If a woman works into that—and generally they manage to have one or more around them—fine. Otherwise, they go through life, relationships, and marriages assuming."

"Assuming what?" Ann asked, snapping the lid down on the tube and readjusting her sunglasses.

"Assuming we don't need any of the affection we give them," Angelique answered, holding out her hand. "Let me have some of that lotion. Thanks. Assuming"—she resumed her speech—"we will stay home and mind the kids, hold down the household, and never complain while they go out and have a wild-party time. Assuming we know they love us even though they never tell us and even more rarely show us once the courtship's over."

"And sometimes not even then," Ann answered.

Angelique nodded. "They expect us to be bloody mind readers and complain to high heaven when we're not. And still—" Angelique shook her head and grew silent.

Ann waited, respecting her friend's observations, having learned from her in a short time how much wisdom and philosophy she had acquired in her years of living and loving.

Angelique turned to Ann and smiled helplessly. "And damn every single one of them, but there's nothing to compare with having a man in your life."

Ann silently agreed. There was something warm and exciting in just the thought of Justin. And part of her burned when he touched her.

"That's why I'm telling you," Angelique continued, "if he means anything to you, do everything you can for him. But just get in the habit of not expecting anything in return. That way you'll be pleasantly surprised if he's affectionate back to you."

Ann didn't think she'd have to worry about that. If she gave him half a chance, she already knew Justin could be the most affectionate man she'd ever met. But part of her still resented the image he had built of her from her books, and she would just let him make the first move.

Ann stayed with Angelique through Christmas in the Caribbean. She didn't want to face the holidays alone in the States and knew that even if Justin contacted her, he would want to be with his girls for Christmas, instead of with Ann. The sunshine and the warmth of the islands made her forget that it was

Christmas and how lonely she always felt on that day, even when she was invited by friends to share Christmas dinner. One of these years, she promised herself, she would have an old-fashioned Christmas and become totally wrapped up in the spirit. But Christmas was for children and for families and she had neither.

She did, however, send Justin a present from Curaçao, a crystal paperweight sailboat, along with a brief note of holiday greetings. But she listed her home address on the return for the package. She didn't want him to know how to find her in Curaçao until she made up her mind she wanted to see him again. Instinctively she seemed to realize all that would take was hearing his voice, or seeing his handwriting scrawled across a letter.

In January when she could no longer avoid getting back to her writing routine, Ann went home and found stacks of mail and packages that had arrived in her absence. All the packages had Justin's return address on them, each postmarked one day after the other. There were twelve boxes, timed to arrive in her possession twelve days prior to and including Christmas Eve. A present a day to celebrate the twelve days of Christmas.

Ann couldn't resist him any longer. She phoned him to thank him for the presents and to hear how he had spent his holidays. Mainly she phoned him just to hear his voice.

He wanted her to fly to Miami, but she refused. It would have been easy enough for her to hop onto a plane and fly into his arms, but she still wasn't ready to trust herself near him. He wanted to fly to New Orleans to see her, but she told him she was too busy to spend time with him now and she would be leaving the country in a week. Maybe, when she got back, she told him, he could fly up then. She wanted to know him as a person, aside from their physical attraction for one another, and the phone, she decided, was the best way for her to accomplish that.

She left the States again without telling him where she was going or when she was leaving. It was becoming increasingly difficult for her to pretend she didn't want to see him. During her stay in Bermuda, she knew she couldn't keep away from him much longer.

Sometime soon she was going to have to see him. She was going to have to gamble that she would be able to judge his genuine caring from whatever images he might be creating about her from her books. She wanted to be treated like a real human being and not a carbon copy of her characters.

Ann flew back to New Orleans the weekend before Mardi Gras, remembering as she joined the tourists jamming the airport that Justin had talked about coming back for the festivities. Why not invite him for the celebration?

Ann phoned Justin the day after she returned home. She could tell from the delight in his voice that he hadn't expected her to be calling him. She blushed at the sound of his voice, thinking how much just hearing him could make her want him here beside her, kissing knee to nose.

"I was wondering if you weren't speaking to me again," Justin said, "or if you were just out of town again."

"I was out of town," Ann answered. "Why did you think that? I talked to you last week."

"Didn't you get my messages?"

"What messages?"

"On your answering machine. I called two or three times."

"Oh!" Ann said, remembering she had forgotten to check her phone messages upon her return home. Her mind must have been elsewhere. "I'm sorry. I didn't get around to that yet. Did you need something?"

"Just to hear your voice, to know that you're okay, to find out if you're talking to me again."

"I'm calling, aren't I?" she asked, smiling, thinking she liked keeping him in a little suspense as to whether she wanted to hear from him.

"That's right, and obviously it isn't as a result of responding to my own phone calls to you."

"Uhm," she said, smiling, thinking she liked his voice. That was one aspect of himself that was true. He couldn't alter that to suit her based on anything he might read in her books. And she liked his persistence. Anyone else would have written her off after the way she talked down to him last time they were together.

"Is there anything I can do for you?" he asked.

She took a deep breath and replied, "I'm not sure. I think it's something I can do for you, if you're still interested."

"I'm definitely interested," he said.

"Wait a minute," she answered, laughing. "I haven't told you what the subject is yet."

"Does it have anything to do with you?"

"Could," she said, smiling. He was genuinely interested in seeing her again. That much she could tell for certain.

"You have my curiosity aroused," he said, laughter filtering through his voice, "among other things."

She smiled, remembering how sexy he had been their last evening together. That wasn't something he could fake, not as thoroughly as he had made her aware of him and of herself. She would admit to herself, if not to him, that he could very easily become her weakness.

"Are you going to let me in on the secret reason for this call?" he teased.

"It's no secret. Remember Mardi Gras?"

"Vaguely," he said, "since I've never really been to Mardi Gras, and only learned some of the traditions from what you've told me."

"You've never been to Mardi Gras," she said. "But you said you might be coming back to New Orleans for the festivities."

"Do these festivities coincide with your own residence in the big city, or are you flying off to Mozambique or some other such place?"

"I thought I'd stick around this year," she answered, running her finger around the Mardi Gras mask he had given her. She had propped it up on the table when she decided to make her phone call to remind herself of the pleasure she had received by being in his company the evening he had given it to her. She remembered him saying he'd like to make a special trip to New Orleans during Mardi Gras time, but that the purpose of the trip would really be to see her. "Are you interested in seeing the real Mardi Gras, not just being on the fringes of the event?"

"Depends," he answered, and her heart pounded at the reservation in his tone.

"What are the conditions?" she asked, holding her breath.

"Do you think on such short notice I could get a personal tour guide? Sort of a one-on-one situation?"

"Very probably," she answered, her heart beating rapidly again. "Anyone in particular?"

"I know it may be too much to ask, but I sort of had my heart set on Ann Straus, the best-selling romance novelist, as my guide. Any chance of that?"

"None whatsoever," Ann answered, picking up the mask and holding it in front of her eyes. Maybe if she stopped acting like the best-selling romance novelist he'd stop thinking of her that way. "She's not available. However, if you'd settle for Ann Straus the person, I might be able to arrange things."

"Sorry," Justin said, realizing that was still a sore point with her. "I shouldn't have mentioned that. I think Ann Straus the person is who I really wanted all along."

Ann's heart pounded. They were playing word games, making references to wanting her and needing her and having his heart set on her.

"Mardi Gras's on Tuesday," she reminded him.

"Fat Tuesday," he translated. "I think I could take

a few days off from my projects at the office. Let me check on getting a hotel reservation."

Ann took another deep breath. "That might be a problem. You see, hotel space during Mardi Gras is at a premium. The best rooms, which are on Canal Street overlooking the parade route, have been booked over a year in advance."

"You get that many out-of-towners?"

"Plenty," she answered. "But a lot of those rooms are booked by the local people. They pool together for the ideal view. So, I've been checking around, just in case you did decide you could fly in for the celebration, and I think I've located a room for you in a private home."

"How private?" he asked.

She laughed. "Not too private considering one of the parades passes within viewing distance of the attic window of my house."

"This does sound interesting," he said. "A garret."

"Hardly," she answered, "but we wouldn't really have to leave the house and could sleep late instead of hassling with staking a claim to a patch of standing space on the parade route, which starts before the crack of dawn."

"Does it start building up that early?"

"Oh, yes," she said, swiveling around in her chair and propping her feet on the seat of the chair across the table. "You see, no matter how early you might decide to show up with your lawn chair and ice chest and ladder seats—"

"What's a ladder seat?"

"A seat on top of a ladder for whatever kids you might have. Anyway, no matter how early you try to get a good place, somebody's beaten you to it. And there are strategies to staking a claim to your space."

"Such as?" He encouraged her to continue with the explanation.

"Never bring a blanket and lay it out on the ground. People will step on it, and you, and totally block your view. You have to stake out your space with your body."

"I could see where that could get interesting."

"Not when you have to stand there for hours just so you don't lose your space. You see what you'd be missing by having this upper-attic-window view of a patch of parade passing on St. Charles Avenue?"

"If this attic window is in your house, I don't think I'd be missing anything I wanted to see."

Ann smiled. He did say the nicest, most flattering things. "How soon can you come?" she asked, wanting more than ever to see him again.

"I'd like to say tomorrow," he answered, "but I have some things I need to get squared away first. Can I call you back?"

"All right," she answered. "I'll consider these accommodations in this private home reserved for you." And then she added, because she wasn't ready to accept him totally, "I do have a guest room, you know."

"Oh," he said, considering that statement. Then he replied, "I suppose that's all I deserve since the best suite in this private home is already occupied."

She laughed, happy that he was willing to see her

again after the way things had gone between them the last time they were together. She was eager to be with him and make a new start.

"Since this is your first official Mardi Gras," she said, "I'll see what I can do about arranging a welcoming committee." And then she added, "One on one."

Justin couldn't arrange to arrive any earlier than the day before Mardi Gras. Ann had worried about her decision all through the weekend. She had never invited a man to her home before, especially one who had been her lover and who she hoped would be again. She had never taken this initiative with any man. And yet her books reflected the attitude of a modern woman able to bed any man on a whim and find lasting and sustained happiness. She wondered if she could take a lesson from her books and learn something about them. Obviously something about the books had appealed to Justin to make him want to pursue her from the pages she had written.

So concerned was she about pleasing him and appealing to him in all the ways a woman should appeal to a man, she took her own books and reread them, studying the heroines and memorizing the love scenes. She wanted to try to learn what Justin had seen by reading her paperbacks.

She had offered to pick him up at the airport, but he had told her he would manage to get to her house on his own. He knew the address and he could hire a cab to take him there rather than have her fight the traffic.

Ann tried to tell him she wanted to pick him up, but he insisted she not go out of her way for his sake. She decided to spend her time fixing the dinner she planned to serve him, and this time she could concentrate her full attention on the meal and be somewhat certain the same burning disaster as last time wouldn't occur.

She couldn't help listening for the sound of the cab, the sound of the doorbell, her heart in a constant state of agitation as she waited for his arrival.

Then suddenly she heard him at the door and hurried to answer his knock.

He stood in front of her, towering above her, his eyes smiling at the sight of her. She could tell he wanted to take her into his arms, but she could also tell he wasn't certain if she would get upset with him for doing that. She took the uncertainty out of his look by standing on tiptoes to place her arms around his neck and hug and kiss him.

"I brought something for you," he said, once he slid his suitcase through the door and shut the heavy beveled-glass door behind them.

"Oh, a present!" she squealed.

"No, your mail," he answered, handing her a wad of envelopes and circulars. "It was practically growing out of your mailbox."

Ann blushed. She had been so wrapped up in planning for Justin's visit she hadn't checked the mail in a couple of days, and hadn't even realized it. It was unlike her when her career, and everything connected with it, especially the mail, was something she had devoted her full attention to, until she had met Justin Frye.

"Thank you," she said, putting the stack on the table in the wide hallway and taking his hand to lead him into the living room.

"Here I was thinking you were bearing gifts like Sabrina in *Steal My Heart* when Adrian arrived home from his long tour of duty in Europe."

"Sorry," he said, sitting on the couch where she led him and slipping his arm around her shoulder as she sat next to him. "I suppose I should have brought something—flowers at least, like the Europeans do when they are house guests."

She shook her head, snuggling against his shoulder. "All you needed to bring was yourself. I'm happy to be with you again, in case you didn't know that."

He looked down at her, his eyes narrowing as he smiled and kissed her gently on the cheek. "I feel lucky to be here. I'm glad you decided to invite me."

"I'll show you the guest room in a little while," she said, smiling, remembering that she wanted to keep a degree of distance between them before she decided who Justin Frye was and if she liked him as much as Sabrina liked Adrian in her book.

Justin sighed, giving her an intense hug against his side, stretching his long legs out in front of the coffee table as he let her snuggle more comfortably against him. "Is something burning?" he asked.

She shook her head against his shoulder. "I cooked everything before you got here and nothing is on the stove that could burn. I never make the same mistakes twice, at least not in the same way. I will admit that I'm an expert at variations on a theme, so it could happen again, just not tonight."

"You smell good," he said, burying his head in her hair. "I could just sit like this all night as long as you're next to me."

"Rachel to James in *Take Me, Take Me,* right?" Ann queried, thinking she'd better not let his flattery get too serious too quickly. And that was just the kind of flowery sentiments her two characters would have said to one another in that book.

"Wrong, Justin Frye to Ann Straus in her living room," he corrected, and kissed her forehead. He picked up her hand and brought it to her lips, kissing the back of her hand and turning it over to run his tongue in circles in the palm.

That all-too-familiar charge of arousal that always seemed to happen when she was near him or thinking of him ignited within her. Her heart fluttered and she looked briefly at him. She didn't want him to stop because the sensations felt so enticing, but she didn't want him to continue either because she still wasn't ready to trust him. "Don't get too comfortable," she told him. "We're not staying in tonight."

"You mean you don't have evil designs on my body?" he teased, smiling. "I'm disappointed."

"I invited you to Mardi Gras," she said. "Remember?"

He nodded.

"I intend to do the best job I can of showing you what the celebration is all about."

"Fine," he answered. "What time does it begin?" He kept kissing her hand, tenderly, finger by finger, his mouth smooth and sultry against her skin.

She laughed, trying to take her hand away from him while she still could. "Mardi Gras doesn't begin or end. It just *is*."

"Oh," he said, no further enlightened, kissing the top of her head now. "What happens tonight?"

"I've arranged with a friend to get invitations to one of the society balls given by the Krewes who organize the parades. I hope you brought a suit."

"I did," he answered, "but I'd rather lie and say I didn't if it means we could stay here."

She cupped his cheek in her hand. "Thank you for the thought, but no, thanks. I'm going to show you Mardi Gras the best way I know how. Besides, I'm curious myself to really experience all the festivities. I'm usually out of town. In a way we'll be seeing it all for the first time together." She had carefully planned the evening. She was afraid to be alone with him because she knew how easily he could make her want to make love with him. And she wasn't ready. She had to know more about who he was since he had played all the different roles of her characters in the few weeks they had known one another.

He kissed her neck and the hollow of her throat. No matter how exciting the Mardi Gras ball might be, Ann thought, it probably wouldn't match the tremors of excitement coursing through her.

"I think something is burning," Ann said, reluctantly skittering away from him and putting the distance of the coffee table between them.

"I don't smell anything," he said, smiling at her retreat.

"Nevertheless," she said, knowing it wasn't food

that was on fire, "I'd better check on dinner. We don't want to be late for the ball."

He grinned, knowing that his touch could still arouse her.

The ball was held in the municipal auditorium. The invitations Ann had gotten placed them in seats on the floor level. Ann didn't want to tell Justin she had called Ron Carrington in order to get the invitations. Ron was the only one she knew who could get anyone in anywhere. He was a good friend to have for events like that, but as far as being the lover Justin had assumed he was, she was less than receptive to that idea.

Ann wore a dress designed with gold lamé leaves that were layered upward from the nipped-in waist of the dress, low-necked at the bodice and flowing in swirls at the skirt. The look Justin had given her when she stepped into the living room after dressing was still vivid in her mind. It was a look of awe and pride, almost as if he were afraid to touch her, yet pleased that by being his date he had more right to be near her than any other envious man would that evening.

Justin was dressed in a very distinguished suit that made him look as formal as Ann.

"That's the dress from *Carry Me Home,* isn't it?" Justin asked as he escorted her to her car.

"Yes, it is," she said, pleased that he had noted details like the dresses she had outfitted her heroines in. "How did you remember?"

"I recall your description of the leaves. It stuck in

my mind because I couldn't quite figure out what the dress would look like. You didn't mention how sexy it was."

She smiled, handing him the keys to her car, intent on giving him directions to let him drive to the auditorium. "No one ever told me it was." She wouldn't tell him that she had never worn the dress before. But when she had seen it in the You boutique about two years ago, she had known she was going to buy it, even though it had cost as much as the entire advance for her first novel. She had never paid so much for any one dress before. At the time she had received satisfaction in knowing she could afford such a dress. Someday, she had told herself, she'd find the appropriate event to wear the dress to.

Justin had to park quite a distance from the entrance to the auditorium. Ann clung to his arm as they walked to the door, feeling delicate next to his towering height.

"Are we going to run into a lot of people you know here tonight, the way we did last time I took you out to dinner?" he asked as they found their places on the floor.

"I don't know," Ann said, looking around for familiar faces. "This isn't my normal crowd so I have no idea who we'll see. I'm just here, like you, as an observer."

For the next hour they watched the pageantry of the Mardi Gras Krewe in the presentation of the court. The king and queen were elaborately dressed in gowns with flowing trains trailing from bejeweled capes caught at the neck. The introduction of the maids held all the glitter and splendor of a wedding cake with living figures. Every detail of the ladies' ball gowns and men's costumes made Ann feel as if they were viewing something from a medieval court in Europe.

After the presentation of the court, dancing began with the king leading his queen in the first song. "You can dance only if you've been invited on to the floor," Ann said, leaning across to whisper the rules of protocol to Justin. "Isn't it exciting with the men wearing masks so that you're not really sure who you'll be dancing with?"

"It does add a touch of mystery to it," he admitted.

"Mystery is the name of one of the Krewes," she explained. Then she pointed out another detail she had learned: "After a girl has been invited to dance she is given a favor."

"What kind of favor?" Justin's eyebrows rose.

"Oh, like a silver compact or a small goblet. And it will be engraved with an emblem of the particular Krewe so that you can tell which party it was you attended. They've become much more valuable as a collector's item than the doubloons because they're generally made of real silver."

"I think you're being paged," Justin said, casting his eyes to an area behind Ann's shoulder.

Ann turned in her seat to see one of the Krewe members bending forward, extending a hand as he asked, "May I have the pleasure of this dance?"

"Oh," Ann said, nervously looking from Justin to the masked figure beside her. The idea excited her because this was her first ball, and to be invited to dance was an honor, but she didn't want Justin to feel slighted. "Would you mind?" she asked him.

"By all means," he said, indicating she should accept the invitation. He did mind, but he wouldn't put it in such clear terms.

Ann looked from one to the other and put her hand in the extended palm in front of her. "Thank you," she said to Justin and to her mysterious escort as she allowed him to lead her to the dance floor.

She held her skirt slightly as she walked to avoid tripping over the hem while her other hand was formally linked in the arm of her masked man. She felt nervous, wondering what it was one talked about to a stranger when one was dancing in front of an auditorium filled with people.

"Thank you very much for asking me to dance," she said formally to her masked figure as he swept her into his arms and swirled her around the dance floor.

"Entirely my pleasure, Ann," he replied.

Ann laughed and tried to peer through the mask to guess who she was dancing with. It had to be someone who knew her well enough to call her by her first name. She wouldn't let him know that she hadn't guessed who it was. She would ask him some other questions to get him to talk so that she could pick out his personality from the timbre of his voice.

"Doesn't all that costume weigh heavily on your shoulders?" she asked.

"I'll admit it isn't the type of thing I'd like to get caught walking down Canal Street in," he answered, "not even for Mardi Gras, but for one night out of the year I can live with it."

She'd placed him now. It was Ron Carrington. "I didn't expect you to be here," she said, relaxing now that she knew who she danced with. "It was so good of you to get the invitations for me."

He smiled. "I'm happy you asked me to do a favor for you. It's been a while since we've had any time together, and I've missed you."

You've missed having the romance authoress on your arm, she thought. *You haven't missed me.*

"Isn't that the same man I saw you with a few weeks ago in the Quarter?"

"Yes, it is," she admitted, wondering if she should reinforce Justin's position in her life to keep Ron from thinking he could re-invade her world. She decided not to offer any further explanations until they were called upon. It would put him at a disadvantage if she could manage to answer his questions with "yes" and "no."

"Well," Ron said, drawing out the word as he swirled her around, "if I had known that was who the other ticket was for I might not have gone to such trouble to get it for you."

"Was it a lot of trouble?" Ann asked.

He laughed. "Not really, but I did envision you spending the evening dancing with me again."

"I am dancing with you," she said and looked down at the floor, "or trying to if I wouldn't keep stumbling over your feet." She knew she should have asked someone else to help her get the invitations, but Ron had been the first person she had thought of. She hadn't realized he would have given her request a second thought once he had gotten the invitations. Usually it was enough of a boost to his ego to know he could perform social miracles where others couldn't.

"Sorry," he said, tightening his grip on her waist and pulling her closer against him so that she could smell the liquor on his breath. "I was hoping the second invitation was for one of your visiting girl friends and this might be an attempt on your part to get back together with me."

"Why would you think that?" she demanded, losing step with the beat as they continued to loop and turn with the music. "I'm not fresh out of high school, you know. If I had wanted to get in touch with you again I know how to use a telephone. Didn't I prove that with the request for the invitations here tonight?"

He shrugged, hugging her tighter against him. Ann tried to look over his shoulder as the music kept her locked in his arms. What must everyone be thinking from the intimacy of his grasp? Most of all, what would Justin be thinking, especially when he already assumed she had made love with this man with a notebook beside the bed?

"I still never figured out why you stopped seeing me," he whispered in her ear, making certain she felt every hard and less-than-subtle movement of his body.

"I was busy," she told him. "I do work nights, at home, and during the day, at home, and travel a lot, away from home. You probably caught me in the middle of some of that."

"It would be hard not to catch you in the middle of anything," he said, his hands tightening on her waist as his feet stumbled over her toes again. "Sometimes I think you do it deliberately."

Oh dear, Ann thought, *he's smarter than I'm giving him credit for.*

"If you don't mind," Ann said, turning up her nose at the whiff of liquor she got as Ron attempted to kiss her moving neck, "I think my feet are crying 'uncle.' How much against the social graces would it be if I left you in the middle of the dance floor?"

"Not too nice," he said, tightening his hold.

"That's what I thought." Ann sighed. "It wouldn't look too good for your image, would it? I can see the headline now in the society pages of the *Times-Picayune-States-Item:* Carrington Crowned by Angry Fiancé of Romance Novelist. And I don't mean 'crowned' as in making you king of the Krewe."

Ron laughed. "Does he know who I am?"

"Uh-huh," Ann said. "Enough to know he doesn't like you holding me this close. I'm not a piece of fly paper, you know. Give me some breathing room." How, she wondered, did she manage to get herself in these situations? It was just like the time Judy had the blind date with Henry Warlord in *Set Me Afire.* It seemed to follow naturally. Like raisins in corn flakes.

"Hey!" he said, holding her away, but not, she soon realized, because she had asked him to. "What did you just call him?" Something she had said had caught his attention.

"What? Who? When?"

"Him. Just now. Did I hear you right? Fiancé?"

Ann laughed. Had she called Justin that without realizing it? Had she been hoping that so much lately she had unconsciously absorbed the idea into her speech? Or had she used the word only like a dart, trying to wound Ron? "Yes," she said, "that's right. I did say fiancé." She wondered if that could be the proper term when a woman proposed to a man. Between whirls around the dance floor, Ann tried to look toward the table where she had left Justin. What would he think of her if he weren't the marrying kind of man?

All he could do was say no, she reasoned. And if he said no, she wondered if he would be the kind of man who would enjoy being kept. She could probably keep him in a style more luxurious than the one he was accustomed to. Plus, she could let him keep the home fires burning whenever she would have to travel. Men were better with woodpiles than women were anyway.

The problem with that scenario was she probably wouldn't want to travel, or not nearly as much, if she did marry him. She would rather be kept barefoot and pregnant. But that didn't fit her image.

Why should it? she suddenly asked herself. She was only partially the person revealed in her books. There were aspects of herself she hadn't even test-driven yet—like the role of wife and mother. No wonder Justin had been so confused by her when he had tried studying her books. What other man, she asked herself, had ever taken the time to do more than just superficially read her words, out of politeness? Justin Frye had been intrigued by her to the point of taking her books and using them as a strategic battle plan. He didn't realize it yet, she decided, but he was going to have to be prepared to follow through with the consequences.

Ron was still staring at her, his feet having lost the beat of the music from Ann's shocking words. "I can't believe this," he said, his mouth falling open.

Ann smiled. She remembered that aspect of his facial features perfectly, like the time she had told him she didn't think she wanted to go to bed with him, because she had something more important to do—like picking the dead leaves off her plants. Even with the mask over the upper portion of his face, she would have recognized that disbelieving expression on his face. "Why can't you believe it?"

"I never figured you as the marrying type. I mean, look at you," he said. He was holding her a bit farther away now as they danced and Ann realized it was making it easier on her feet. "You have everything."

"Do I?" She smiled. "Tell me what I have."

"You have the four M's."

She frowned. "Which are?"

"Money, Money, and More Money."

Ann laughed. He had such an unclear picture of who she was and what she wanted out of life. No wonder Justin had taken wrong turns from her books. But getting to know Justin these past few weeks had pointed out how little she did have and how much more she wanted. And the things she wanted didn't involve money. In fact, no amount of money in the world could buy her happiness, any more than they could buy Ron prestige.

"I've had nothing until now," Ann said to Ron. She hoped those words would be prophetic.

The music finally ended and Ann gratefully turned to leave the dance floor. Coming to this ball hadn't been the great idea she had intended it to be. But it had given her another insight into what she did want with Justin Frye—and that was to be alone with him.

Ron caught her hand, trying to pull her back into his arms to begin the next dance. "You owe me another dance," he told her. "I did get two invitations for you."

Ann shook her head. "No, thanks, Ron. It's been enlightening and you're really a good man in a pinch—mainly where you manage to step on my feet, but I don't think I owe you anything. How much did the invitations cost you? If you want to put a monetary value on them like you do everything else, I'll be happy to write out a check."

They were standing on the edge of the dance floor now as other couples milled around them in the exchange of partners on the dance floor. Ron still had a hand on her arm, but Ann wasn't allowing him to lead her back into the flow of dancers.

"Don't you want to earn the favor that you're entitled to as my partner?" Ron asked, turning on what was, to his way of thinking, his persuasive charm.

"If there are going to be any favors to give out," a voice spoke behind them, "I'll do it."

Ann turned to see Justin standing tall and distinguished beside them, a scowl across his face. She smiled, pulling her hand from Ron's and putting it in Justin's. "Thank you for the tickets and the dance," she said, curtseying slightly to his costumed figure, "but Justin and I are quite content to be spectators."

She nudged Justin, letting him know she was ready to go back to their table, but when they got there she asked him, "Have you had enough? Could we go now?"

"I've had more than enough for one night," he answered, his voice clipped.

Inwardly, Ann cringed. Dancing hadn't been such a good move. If he knew it was Ron Carrington it would be an even worse move. "I don't think this is a world I was cut out for anyway," she said, picking up her purse from where she had left it at the table, then following him through the auditorium to the parking lot.

"I would have thought all this glitter and glamor was exactly where you belong," he commented once they were outside.

"Not you, too!" Ann sighed, allowing him to assist her with her long skirt as she got into the passenger's side of her car.

He got in on the driver's side before he spoke again. "Who else has been expressing that opinion?"

Ann bit her tongue. It wouldn't help to mention Ron Carrington's name. Later, when he understood, and perhaps trusted her love for him better, she could tell him how little Ron Carrington meant to her. But tonight it would be best to keep him out of the conversation. "Ella to Fenster Sims in *Ravishes For Lunch*."

"I haven't read that one."

"Oh. It's not published yet," Ann said, knowing it hadn't even been written yet. She had just invented the book and the names and the excuse. "It's not important anyway. What is important is that you know the way back to my house."

He looked across at her in the dim light of the car. "It's still early. Are you sure that's where you want to go?"

She nodded.

"You looked like you were having a ball of a time," he commented, turning the key in the ignition and steering the car out of the parking lot.

She shook her head. "I realized all I really wanted was to be with you. Do you mind?"

He glanced across at her briefly as he drove. Wordlessly he reached for her hand and squeezed it. "Did I ever tell you I like the way you think?"

She smiled. "No. I'm kind of surprised to hear you say that because I think my books are sometimes rather frivolous."

"I wouldn't call *The Golden Arrow* frivolous."

Ann turned in her seat. "You read *The Golden Arrow?* Where did you find it?"

"A secondhand bookshop. You pack a powerful amount of research into a book when you set your mind to it, don't you?"

Ann smiled. She was proud of that book. It hadn't earned much in sales and even less in publicity. But it revealed an intellectual side of her that her romance novels didn't even touch.

"Justin?" she asked as they reached the drive at her house and he walked her up to the front door. "Why did you go to so much trouble to try to get to know me? No one else has ever taken half as much time as you did trying to figure me out."

"You're an exciting woman," he said, taking the house keys from her hand and opening the door for her. "I wanted to be around and part of that excitement. Researching you through the books seemed to be the best way. That's why I planned the indoor picnic with the wine and cheese and the Mardi Gras mask. I wanted to copy what Harold did for Beatrice in *Shadow of My Love*."

"I didn't even guess the similarity," she said, entering the house with him and leading him toward the living room, although she lingered, talking with him in the wide hallway. "What about the night on the beach?"

"You didn't give me a chance to plan that," he said. "Remember? You were determined to go for a walk and all I knew was I wanted to be with you. That was sort of an improvisation on my part."

She stood on tiptoes to kiss him. "I think it was the best part," she said, smiling. "I was wondering if you'd mind participating in an experiment," she asked him, sliding her hand down from his shoulder, along his arm to his hand.

His eyes darkened and his eyebrows twitched upward, but he didn't speak.

"I have a new story in mind," she explained. "Sort of a cross between *The Golden Arrow* and an as yet untitled love story."

"Where do I fit into this story?" he asked, his mouth lifting in a hint of a smile.

"Oh," she said, smiling, cocking her head to one side, "I'd say somewhere right about now." She turned and tugged at his hand, leading him past the living room, down the main entrance hall, up the stairs to the second floor. At the top of the stairs she paused and, looking over her shoulder, asked, "Do you think you might be interested?"

"In what?"

"A little research," she said, the grin on her face spreading. "Do you like books with happy endings?"

His hand came up, touching her cheek with the back of his hand, then turning to cup the curve of her neck and move across the smooth angles of her shoulder. "Haven't I told you I like the way you write books, lady?"

She nodded. "I really am sorry I overreacted to your analysis of me when we were in Miami. I think I was afraid of what you would do to me."

He frowned. "What did you think I was trying to do?"

She put her trust in him as she said, "I think you were trying to make me fall in love with you. No, don't say anything," she said, smiling, putting her finger over his lips. "Maybe you only wanted to take me to bed with you, and I can't condemn you for that. You make love beautifully and I enjoy being with you. But you did make me fall in love with you, you know."

Still she didn't take her fingers off his lips as she continued to tell him, "Maybe that was why I was so angry with you the night we were on the yacht. I didn't want to admit that I was falling in love with you. It's never happened to me before, not in real life. I wasn't sure how to handle it."

He kissed her fingers against his lips. Taking her wrist with his hand, he moved it aside to his neck, where he turned his head to nuzzle against her hand.

"Do you think I have all the answers? Why do you think I was so determined to try to impress you by reading your books? Why do you think I was so confused when I made all the wrong mistakes?"

"When did you make mistakes?" she asked, remembering only the good times, conscious mainly of his standing before her this minute, warm and loving.

"The morning after I met you. I'd lost sleep that night over your rape scene in *Flames Of Desire* and figured that was the kind of passion you expected from a man."

"Oh," Ann said, remembering his commando tactics after the arrival of the orchids that morning and his suggestions of promising her how to wake up on the right side of the bed in the morning. She laughed, holding her sides from the realization of what he had tried to copy.

"What's so funny?"

Flames Of Desire," she said, giggling. "That book was a cliché. It was a parody of all my romances—it wasn't even meant to be taken seriously. And you thought—"

He shook his head, looking at her, smiling as he realized the humor of the situation was at his expense. "Okay, so I'll admit you're a good writer. You can handle different writing challenges. I think I began to realize the seriousness of your skill from reading *The Golden Arrow*." Have you ever considered writing true-to-life romances?"

She shook her head now, smiling. "But I have considered writing up a new kind of contract." She took his hand again and pulled him toward the bedroom—hers, not the guest room. "This one takes a partner," she explained. "And I was thinking of giving you the right of first rejection. Are you interested in taking up the options?"

"What kind of contract?" he asked, following her.

"No, don't turn on the light," she said as they came through the bedroom doorway. "Just undress me."

"Uhm," he said, his hands on her, his mouth seeking hers in the reflected light from the street below that filtered through the trees into the room. "Only if you let me take your notebook and pen away from you as well."

"I promise never to bring my word processor to bed," she said, slipping out of her shoes and twining her hands around his neck, then loosening his tie and beginning to unbutton his shirt.

His hands had found the zipper of her dress and his hand was on the cool, bare skin of her back now, letting the gold lamé dress fall to the floor like leaves falling from an autumn tree.

Ann tugged his shirt out of his pants and let him finish undressing her. "I hate to admit this," she whispered, "but I don't know how cuff links work."

She could hear his low chuckle. "I think your imagination has served you well in the past, but maybe it's time you had some instruction in certain areas." He pulled her toward the bed, folding back the covers as he invited her to lie down beside him. "What is this contract you are trying to interest me in?"

Ann's hands were running over his body now,

loving the feel of his soft skin pressed warmly against her. If she mentioned marriage now it might put an end to this lovely sensation. She wanted him and he wanted her. She loved him and she wanted him to love her, but he had only once uttered those words to her. Would she frighten him out of her arms if she mentioned love and marriage in the same sentence? And yet, could she let him make love to her without giving him a hint of how committed she felt toward him? Didn't he have the right to know how involved she felt with him?

He was kissing her shoulder now, his hands following the contours of her body from the top of her knees to her ear lobes. "Tell me," he whispered, his mouth at her ear, his tongue gently tracing the delicate structure.

"I don't want to talk now," she said, her mouth against his neck, swirling her tongue down to the hard-muscled breadth of his chest. "I just want to feel you."

"Then feel loved," he said, whispering, his breath cool against the area he had just been kissing, "the way you deserve to be."

He cradled her body with his hands, his lips gently bringing her skin alive with tenderly reverent kisses.

Ann followed his example, kissing the inside of his wrist, down to the inside of his elbow as his lips and tongue explored the firmness of her abdomen. "Is it permissible," she asked, changing places with him so that she could run her tongue across his chest, teasing his nipples as he had done for her, "to tell you I love you?"

"It's permissible to do or say anything you want," he said, letting her love him with the aggression she had long held back from him. "Why shouldn't it be?"

She cradled his face in her hands. "I don't want to scare you away."

"Why do you think you could do that?"

"Because," she answered, frowning, totally aware of his hardened desire for her, "I've never met anyone I wanted to love as much as I do you. I don't want to lose you after finding you so soon."

His tongue was traveling from her neck to her navel, his breath coolly replacing the path. "Oh," he said, "now I see. That's the reason for the contract. If you have me in some sort of written agreement you think you won't lose me as easily?"

She nodded, her hair brushing against his skin. "I really don't have a right to tie you down."

"Only if I want to be tied down," he agreed. "But it's possible depending on the terms of the contract."

She continued running her hands along his skin, memorizing the lines of his body, just in case she never saw him again after tonight. If he should leave her his memory would live for a long time with her. "The one I had in mind would be rather binding," she admitted.

"Uhm," he said, his tongue flicking against her shoulder, exciting her in his tender passion. "I'm beginning to think I know what kind of contract you're talking about."

"Oh," she said, her heart pounding. This was probably not the best time in the world to try to get a man to make lifetime decisions. She should have known better than to expect a real-life situation to end as happily as her books usually did. "Well, maybe we'd better not discuss it."

"No," he said. "I think we need to get this out in the open and settled before anything else interrupts us, like the phone for one thing, or someone knocking on your door to ask for directions to the nearest Mardi Gras parade."

She shook her head. "I don't want to spoil the mood."

"I think," he whispered, "it would only add to the mood."

Still she wouldn't voice her desires and longings.

"Shall I," he asked, "propose this contract to you?"

Ann held her breath, holding him tightly in the near darkness of the bedroom, wishing she had never brought it up. Not now anyway, later, in the morning, when it would be easier to face if he decided he wanted to leave her.

"Although the contract I'm thinking of may not be the same one you have in mind."

"True," she said, "so let's not even discuss it."

"No," he answered. "I want to discuss this. And if what I suggest isn't the same thing you had in mind, you'll just have to live with the contract I propose."

She tried to see his eyes in the half light. They never gave his true feelings away, but she couldn't see the sincerity in them right now.

"Agreed?"

She bit her lip. She shook her head. Let him say

what he wanted to say. She would just listen and agree and pretend she had never had any ideas of actually asking a man like Justin Frye to marry her.

"I'd like to propose a marriage contract," he said, his fingers massaging against her spine, "binding in its exclusivity."

"Justin!" Ann cried, laughing, while tears welled in her eyes. "You can't mean it!" And then she pounced on him. "If you're joking, I'm not. I accept, and you can draw up all the terms." She kissed his mouth, his eyes, his ears, his neck, hugging him tightly in her happiness. "We'll do everything exactly the way you like it, right by the book."

He caught her hands behind her back, holding her away from him, smiling at her above him. "Nope. We've tried that and it all backfired. This time I think we need to write our own story, starting with a love scene. I might, however, need a little collaboration on that. Are you interested?"

"Only," she said, kissing him again, as she snuggled against his chest, "if you promise once we hit the page that says The End, we start right away on book two of this continuing family saga. I figure we should have several generations to create."

"Uhm," he agreed, his lips seeking the soft swells of her breasts. "How does this sound? Chapter one, page one." He stopped speaking long enough to trail kisses along her skin. "His lips invited her to lie down beside him. . . ."

MORE ROMANCE FOR
A SPECIAL WAY TO RELAX
$1.95 each

2 ☐ Hastings	23 ☐ Charles	45 ☐ Charles	66 ☐ Mikels
3 ☐ Dixon	24 ☐ Dixon	46 ☐ Howard	67 ☐ Shaw
4 ☐ Vitek	25 ☐ Hardy	47 ☐ Stephens	68 ☐ Sinclair
5 ☐ Converse	26 ☐ Scott	48 ☐ Ferrell	69 ☐ Dalton
6 ☐ Douglass	27 ☐ Wisdom	49 ☐ Hastings	70 ☐ Clare
7 ☐ Stanford	28 ☐ Ripy	50 ☐ Browning	71 ☐ Skillern
8 ☐ Halston	29 ☐ Bergen	51 ☐ Trent	72 ☐ Belmont
9 ☐ Baxter	30 ☐ Stephens	52 ☐ Sinclair	73 ☐ Taylor
10 ☐ Thiels	31 ☐ Baxter	53 ☐ Thomas	74 ☐ Wisdom
11 ☐ Thornton	32 ☐ Douglass	54 ☐ Hohl	75 ☐ John
12 ☐ Sinclair	33 ☐ Palmer	55 ☐ Stanford	76 ☐ Ripy
13 ☐ Beckman	35 ☐ James	56 ☐ Wallace	77 ☐ Bergen
14 ☐ Keene	36 ☐ Dailey	57 ☐ Thornton	78 ☐ Gladstone
15 ☐ James	37 ☐ Stanford	58 ☐ Douglass	79 ☐ Hastings
16 ☐ Carr	38 ☐ John	59 ☐ Roberts	80 ☐ Douglass
17 ☐ John	39 ☐ Milan	60 ☐ Thorne	81 ☐ Thornton
18 ☐ Hamilton	40 ☐ Converse	61 ☐ Beckman	82 ☐ McKenna
19 ☐ Shaw	41 ☐ Halston	62 ☐ Bright	83 ☐ Major
20 ☐ Musgrave	42 ☐ Drummond	63 ☐ Wallace	84 ☐ Stephens
21 ☐ Hastings	43 ☐ Shaw	64 ☐ Converse	85 ☐ Beckman
22 ☐ Howard	44 ☐ Eden	65 ☐ Cates	86 ☐ Halston

Silhouette Special Edition

87 ☐ Dixon	103 ☐ Taylor	119 ☐ Langan	135 ☐ Seger
88 ☐ Saxon	104 ☐ Wallace	120 ☐ Dixon	136 ☐ Scott
89 ☐ Meriwether	105 ☐ Sinclair	121 ☐ Shaw	137 ☐ Parker
90 ☐ Justin	106 ☐ John	122 ☐ Walker	138 ☐ Thornton
91 ☐ Stanford	107 ☐ Ross	123 ☐ Douglass	139 ☐ Halston
92 ☐ Hamilton	108 ☐ Stephens	124 ☐ Mikels	140 ☐ Sinclair
93 ☐ Lacey	109 ☐ Beckman	125 ☐ Cates	141 ☐ Saxon
94 ☐ Barrie	110 ☐ Browning	126 ☐ Wildman	142 ☐ Bergen
95 ☐ Doyle	111 ☐ Thorne	127 ☐ Taylor	143 ☐ Bright
96 ☐ Baxter	112 ☐ Belmont	128 ☐ Macomber	144 ☐ Meriwether
97 ☐ Shaw	113 ☐ Camp	129 ☐ Rowe	145 ☐ Wallace
98 ☐ Hurley	114 ☐ Ripy	130 ☐ Carr	146 ☐ Thornton
99 ☐ Dixon	115 ☐ Halston	131 ☐ Lee	147 ☐ Dalton
100 ☐ Roberts	116 ☐ Roberts	132 ☐ Dailey	148 ☐ Gordon
101 ☐ Bergen	117 ☐ Converse	133 ☐ Douglass	149 ☐ Claire
102 ☐ Wallace	118 ☐ Jackson	134 ☐ Ripy	150 ☐ Dailey

SILHOUETTE SPECIAL EDITION, Department SE/2
1230 Avenue of the Americas
New York, NY 10020

Please send me the books I have checked above. I am enclosing $_____
(please add 75¢ to cover postage and handling. NYS and NYC residents please
add appropriate sales tax). Send check or money order—no cash or C.O.D.'s
please. Allow six weeks for delivery.

NAME _____

ADDRESS _____

CITY _____ STATE/ZIP _____

Silhouette Special Edition

Coming Next Month

A Love Song And You by Linda Shaw

By all rights Laura Remington and country and western star Dallas Jones should have been enemies. But nothing seemed to matter but the magnetic energy that charged the atmosphere when they were together.

Gentle Possession by Melodie Adams

Caleb Stone and Randi Warner had a contract: he needed a son and she needed to pay her father's debt. Randi fulfilled her part of the bargain, but how could she leave Caleb when through their child they found the promise of forever?

The Tangled Web by Tracy Sinclair

Trapped in a deception, Nicole never thought she'd find herself drawn to the man she'd schemed to deceive. But falling in love with Flint Lockridge could put her at his mercy—and completely destroy her plans.

A Ruling Passion by Doreen Owens Malek

Try as she might, journalist Megan Fielding couldn't keep her objectivity when she was around Mike Henley. He touched her as no man ever had, but could she do her job and keep Michael as well?

Softly At Sunset by Anne Lacey

Tragedy had touched Cade Thornton's family, and Jill had the task of healing his daughter's pain. Soon her tenderness extended to the father as well, and her job of healing was complicated by new feelings of love.

Tell Me No Lies by Brooke Hastings

Maggie got a kick out of masquerading as an eighteen year old student to get an audition with director Carson McDermitt. But the joke was on her, for how could her growing passion for him be indulged when he was fighting his feelings for the woman he thought of as a young girl?